LIVING THE STORY

LIVING THE STORY

*Biblical Spirituality
for Everyday Christians*

R. Paul Stevens & Michael Green

William B. Eerdmans Publishing Company • Grand Rapids | Cambridge
Lime Grove House Publishing Ltd • Sydney | Auckland
Regent College Publishing • Vancouver

Published jointly 2003 by
Wm. B. Eerdmans Publishing Co.
255 Jefferson Ave. S.E., Grand Rapids, Michigan 49503 /
P.O. Box 163, Cambridge CB3 9PU U.K.
www.eerdmans.com
and by
Lime Grove House Publishing Ltd
PO Box 37-955, Parnell, Auckland, NZ
www.limegrovehouse.co.nz
and by
Regent College Publishing
an imprint of Regent College Bookstore
5800 University Boulevard, Vancouver, B.C. V6T 2E4
www.regentpublishing.com

Printed in the United States of America

08 07 06 05 04 03   7 6 5 4 3 2 1

Library of Congress Cataloging-in-Publication Data

Stevens, R. Paul, 1937-
Living the story: biblical spirituality for everyday Christians /
R. Paul Stevens & Michael Green.
p.   cm.
Includes bibliographical references and index.
ISBN 0-8028-6074-5
1. Spirituality — Biblical teaching. I. Green, Michael, 1930- II. Title.
BS680.S7S83   2003

248 — dc21

2003049069

Eerdmans ISBN 0-8028-6074-5
Lime Grove House Publishing ISBN 1 876798 01 7
Regent College Publishing ISBN 1-57383-255-3

Contents

CONTENTS

Foreword

C hristians have a great gift to offer the world in all matters of spirituality. It is the Holy Scripture. There is nothing quite like it. It is the greatest gift we can provide for people who are fed up with the hand-to-mouth existence of mere appetite. It is the perfect gift for people who are bored with the head-trip existence of mere intellect. It is the exactly right gift for people who have gone stale on second-hand religion.

Spirituality. The word promises something. Sometimes it seems to promise everything. In a world like ours, where there is much disappointment and much unhappiness, it is understandable that the word is much used. For the word "spirituality" suggests that there is more here than meets the eye, and that this "more" might be just the ticket to a life that has some zest and beauty and worth to it. But the word in itself is hardly more than a hint, a "hint followed by guesses." And the guesses proliferate exponentially.

Meanwhile Christians have this document, the Holy Scripture, that has all the marks of the real thing. They have been reading and meditating on it for nearly two thousand years. Every kind and sort of Christian has tested it against every kind and sort of circumstance and condition of living and stood up to give witness to its validity. Tested against the reality of actual lives, it turns out to be not another of many "guesses" about spirituality, but spirituality itself. Instead of reading *about* spirituality, getting careful definitions or elaborate descriptions of it, we come upon spirituality in action. Reading the Bible, we are immersed in the intricate tangle of human life as it is entered, addressed, confronted, saved, healed, and blessed by the living God — God's Spirit breathed into human lives. Spirituality.

It is the great responsibility and privilege of Christians today to place this proven and essential source document on spirituality in the hands of those who are bewilderingly searching through a welter of spiritualities for something authentic, something true.

This present book is the lively product of two professors who teamed up to teach Christian spirituality to classrooms of graduate students from all over the world, using the Bible as their text. The international character of the students in the classroom — Africans, Asians, Europeans, North and South Americans — keeps this teaching from being unconsciously reduced to the cultural predispositions of the affluent middle-class. And the activist character of the professors prevents this teaching from drifting off into anything remotely resembling self-indulgence or narcissism. Michael Green and Paul Stevens are nothing if not *involved* — committed both personally and vocationally to an evangelical integration of church and world, prayer and discipleship, learning and marketplace. It is quite wonderful to be taught by professors who not only pray what they read in Holy Scripture but also live what they teach from it.

EUGENE H. PETERSON
Professor Emeritus of Spiritual Theology
Regent College, Vancouver

Introduction

What Is Biblical Spirituality?

R. PAUL STEVENS AND MICHAEL GREEN

The Bible is a story, and it contains within its grand metanarrative many stories, some of which we will explore in this book. But essentially it is one story, the story of God's romance with the world — God's unquenchable and gratuitous love for humankind. As a story it has a beginning, a middle, and an end. It is going somewhere. But it is also taking us with it. Because the biblical story is the grand story of who we are, who is the God that we are dealing with, and what it all means — it is a story that enfolds our own stories in a grander narrative. And by including us it changes our way of thinking and behavior.

Inevitably we are in the middle of our own stories (not knowing fully the beginning and the end of our own lives). David Jeffrey speaks of this as "inextricably middled" and thence muddled.[1] But the Grand Story of God's beautiful purpose for creation and all humankind, gives us the beginning and the end of our own stories, as well as making sense of the muddled middle. Biblical spirituality is simply living that story.

---

1. Quoted in Loren Wilkinson, "Stories, Your Story and God's Story," *Crux* 33, no. 3 (September 1997): 30.

Spiritualities and Biblical Spirituality

Spirituality, as we are defining it here, is our lived experience of God in the multiple contexts of life in which the seeking Father finds us. This experience of God enables us to discover the transcendent meaning of everyday life including our work, relationships, life in the church and world. But today, "spirituality" is a buzz word and almost any scheme for self-realization can pass for "spirituality." There is "business spirituality," "native spirituality," "ascetic spirituality," and "environmental spirituality." These are all authentic in the sense that they lead to genuine experiences. But do they lead to communion with the living God and wholistic living in the world?

It is here that the Bible plays a critical role. The Bible reveals the God who is the subject, the object, and the means of true spirituality. As Eugene Peterson says in his Foreword, the Bible "turns out not to be another of many 'guesses' about spirituality, but spirituality itself. Instead of reading *about* spirituality, getting careful definitions or elaborate descriptions of it, we come upon spirituality in action." Peterson continues, "We are immersed in the intricate tangle of human life as it is entered, addressed, confronted, saved, healed and blessed by the living God — God's Spirit breathed into human lives." Spirituality is Spirit-uality.

Being Mastered by the Text

Not that it is easy for us to let the Story get into us! In *Shaped by the Word* Robert Mulholland explains that "we have a deeply engrained way of reading in which we are the masters of the material we read. . . . The text [is] an object 'out there' over which we have control."[2] Much more than merely informing us (through our mastering the material), supremely Scripture forms and transforms us. It nurtures us in our primal

---

2. M. Robert Mulholland, *Shaped by the Word: The Power of Scripture in Spiritual Formation* (Nashville: The Upper Room, 1985), p. 21. Mulholland draws heavily on Wesley's pattern of Bible reading, emphasizing listening with the heart and obedience with a firm intent to do the will of God, not yielding to a mere functionalist orientation that uses Scripture instrumentally.

relationships: with God, with self, with others, and with the world.[3] But getting to a biblical spirituality is not as simple as collecting a few Scripture texts and mouthing them, like a schoolboy learning his multiplication tables. Speaking to this misunderstanding Eugene Peterson says: "Biblical . . . does not mean cobbling texts together to prove or substantiate a dogma or practice."[4]

The Bible is not a manual of how-to's. It doesn't say as so many spiritual directors say today, if you pray this way, or give up this or that, or sit in a certain posture and look at your navel, you will achieve enlightenment. Not so. Rather, it engages us with God pure and simple. We get a God-sized view of life — our life. And also a God-sized view of the world — God's world. We get into the story and the story gets into us. God, who is the true author of Scripture, wants us to have firsthand direct contact with him, and not to have a hand-me-down faith and a rule-based approach to life.

So we will begin with the incredibly good news that we are invited to worship and even to join the Triune God — worshiping Abba, being disciples of Jesus, and being temples of the Spirit. We will look at some of the great themes of biblical spirituality in the Old and New Testaments: the patriarchs as pilgrims of faith, prophetic spirituality, the way of wisdom, experiencing fellowship, being people of prayer, the sacraments, engaging the struggle, healing and deliverance, being children of hope, and finally being ambassadors of love. But to start with we must ask: What is a biblical experience of God and life? Is there an orthodoxy of experience? As we explore the Story we will discover that there are many "spiritualities" in both the Old and New Testaments which together contribute to a rich, life-giving relationship with God.[5]

A Heart after God's Heart

Surely there are as many experiences as there are people, and our loving and creative God shapes his engagement with each of us according to

3. Mulholland, *Shaped by the Word*, p. 33.

4. Eugene Peterson, "Biblical Spirituality" (unpublished lecture, Regent College, Vancouver, B.C.).

5. Steven Harper, "Old Testament Spirituality," in Kenneth Collins, ed., *Exploring Christian Spirituality: An Ecumenical Reader* (Grand Rapids: Baker Books, 2000), p. 312.

our unique personality. There is not "one size fits all." At the same time we can find a common thread: each of the persons who was engaged by God discovered the heart of God himself and, in return, gained some of the heart of God for herself or himself. There is an orthopathy. This lovely word was coined by Richard Mouw and is based on the writings of Abraham Heschel. "Ortho" means straight (as in orthodontics). And "pathy" means passion. Heschel maintained that the prophets were gripped by the pathos of God — not God's pity (as unfortunately the English word sometimes suggests), but God's deep emotion and concern. They had God's heart and passion for justice and mercy. So orthodoxy of experience is simply real experience of God that livens our hearts and lines up with the heart of God, a heart of mercy and justice, a heart given in unconditional love and blinding holiness. And this is attested in its full range by saints and sinners in Scripture. But to gain this perspective we need the whole Scripture, not just one part.

Conformed to the Whole Word of God

"All Scripture is God-breathed and is useful for teaching, rebuking, correcting and training in righteousness, so that the [person] of God may be thoroughly equipped for every good work" (2 Tim. 3:16-17). As we open up Genesis we discover, with Adam and Eve, that we are *priests of creation* — representing God's interest and purpose for the whole of creation as sub-creators. Further, we offer up our work and relational life to God as a sacrifice of praise. To be a human being is to be *homo adorans,* essentially a priest. Alexander Schmemann says that humankind "stands in the center of the world and unifies it in his act of blessing God, of both receiving the world from God and offering it to God — and by filling the world with this eucharist, he transforms his life, the one he receives from the world, into life in God, into communion with him."[6]

Then there is the *Exodus* — liberation from internal and external bondage. Jürgen Moltmann has noted that there are two great motifs in the Old Testament for justification by faith and not by works. One is the exodus — that great liberation from slavery in Egypt by the mighty hand of God. The other is the Sabbath. How, he asks, can one see a whole na-

---

6. Alexander Schmemann, *For the Life of the World: Sacraments and Orthodoxy* (Crestwood, N.Y.: St. Vladimir's Seminary Press, 1988), p. 15.

tion ceasing from work for a day and claim they are working their way to acceptance with God by their performance? Sabbath expresses resting in God's work and God's accomplishments, being justified by faith. This theme gets extended in the Jubilee — "Exodus spelled out in terms of social salvation."[7] In the New Testament this is the gospel of the kingdom.

The Wilderness, the Kingdom, and Justice

God deliberately leads people into the desert, either physically, emotionally, or relationally. He does this to strengthen our faith. "In a desert land [the Lord] found him, in a barren and howling waste. He shielded him [encircled him] and cared for him as the apple of his eye" (Deut. 32:9-10). Being in a desert means being removed from habitual attachments and addictions in order to attend to God. Removing people from the siren appeal of civilization is a consistent theme from Abraham to Hosea, John the Baptist to Jesus, and even to the apostle Paul for many years after his conversion.

Biblical *history* shows the progressive rule of the sovereign God in this world.[8] The *law and covenant* — that unconditional belonging to God — form the foundation and motivation for service and life. Ministry is covenant service.[9] *The prophets* not only foretell but "tell forth." They demonstrate the pathos/passion of God for righteousness and justice in the world.

The Psalms and the Writings

The *Psalms* occupy a unique place in Scripture. The Psalter is the Word of God, and with only a few exceptions, the prayer of men as well.[10] The

---

7. Kenneth Leech, *Experiencing God: Theology as Spirituality* (San Francisco: Harper & Row, 1985), p. 54.

8. See Carl Armerding, "When the Spirit Came Mightily: The Spirituality of Israel's Charismatic Leaders," in James Packer and Loren Wilkinson, eds., *Alive to God: Studies in Spirituality* (Downers Grove, Ill.: InterVarsity Press, 1985), p. 17.

9. See David Baker, "Piety in the Pentateuch," in Packer/Wilkinson, eds., *Alive to God*, pp. 34ff.

10. Dietrich Bonhoeffer, *Life Together,* trans. John W. Doberstein (New York: Harper & Row, 1954), p. 44.

Psalms show us that the full range of our experience can be brought to God in prayer: innocency (17:3-5); the absence of God (22); seeing everything collapsing (11:1-5); depression (43:5); joy (126); dignity (8); and, yes, even feeling like a worm (22). In one sense the Psalter is the Word of God because it demonstrates that we have a God who wants us to come to him just as we are. There are no bad prayers. To this John Calvin offers an insightful comment:

> Not without reason, is it my custom to call this book [Psalms] An Anatomy of All Parts of the Soul since there is no emotion anyone will experience whose image is not reflected in this mirror. . . . The heart, purged of hypocrisy . . . is brought into the light of day. . . . The Psalms are a series of shouts: shouts of love and hatred; shouts of suffering and rejoicing; shouts of faith and hope. . . . they force us to that meeting with the God without whom we cannot live and who transforms our whole life.[11]

The writings, such as Job, Song of Songs, Proverbs, and Ecclesiastes, show us spirituality "in process" as people question, explore, and interact with God and life. These books are particularly messy (as we will see in a later chapter) partly because they do not offer neat and tidy answers to the big questions of life.

The Gospels, Letters, and Apocalypse

In the New Testament the *Gospels* invite people to become disciples of Jesus. "The really good news for humanity," says Dallas Willard, "is that Jesus is now taking students in the master class of life."[12] The *letters* not only teach us how to live as the people of God. They have a theological framework that moves from the indicative (who we are) to the imperative (what we are to do). This is the shape of Christian spirituality. And finally there is the *Apocalypse* (Revelation), which is an inspired appeal

---

11. John Calvin, in Ford Lewis Battles, *The Piety of John Calvin* (Grand Rapids: Baker Books, 1978), pp. 27-28, quoted in Don Postema, *Space for God: The Study and Practice of Prayer and Spirituality* (Grand Rapids: Bible Way, 1983), pp. 114-15.

12. Dallas Willard, *The Divine Conspiracy: Rediscovering Our Hidden Life in God* (San Francisco: HarperSanFrancisco, 1998), p. xvii.

to the imagination concerning the glorious end to which the travail of history will lead and to which God is determined to consummate his rule on earth. What God is doing in the Story is to bring everything under the unified headship of Jesus Christ (Eph. 1:22). And he will surely do it.

Trinitarian Spirituality

Through the Story we discover that we cannot relate to an abstract God. The God who is lover, beloved, and love itself invites us into God's own love-life. In the New Testament this is expressed in the awesome words of John: "our fellowship is with the father and with his son, Jesus Christ" (1 John 1:3). We are included in the Triune God — Father, Son, and Spirit. Speaking to this with great eloquence, Thomas Torrance says this:

> The doctrine of the Holy Trinity [is] . . . the fundamental grammar of our knowledge of God. Why is that? Because the doctrine of the Trinity gives expression to the fact that through his self-revelation in the incarnation God has opened himself to us in such a way that we may know him in the inner relations of his divine Being and have communion with him in his divine life as Father, Son and Holy Spirit.[13]

This is the gospel. God draws us into relationship with himself within the circle of God's own loving communion. The God who is "us" is not solitary, is not abstractly "one" but a unified communion of personal relationships. And this God gives us access to God's own personal life.[14] What could be better than this?

To explore this we turn first to our relationship with the three per-

13. Thomas F. Torrance, *Trinitarian Perspective: Toward Doctrinal Agreement* (Edinburgh: T. & T. Clark, 1994), p. 1.

14. Waltke speaks of what Jacob's encounter teaches us about knowing God: (1) it may be marked by ambiguity; (2) it does not mean ease of conflict; (3) it defies human understanding; (4) God in humility makes himself available to humanity; (5) "When they stop wrestling with God and start clinging to him, they discover that he has been there for their good, to bless them." Bruce K. Waltke, *Genesis* (Grand Rapids: Zondervan, 2001), p. 448.

sons of the Trinity, then to the witness of the Old Testament, and finally to the New Testament. In all this Michael Green and I, who first taught much of this book as a spiritual theology course at Regent College, are praying that you the reader will join us in living this wonderful Story. We will start as we should with worship, since it is only through worship that we come to know God as God is, and get the Story (and our own stories) right. We will end with love because love is the life of God and also the life of fully human people.

Part One

Knowing and Loving the Triune God

Abba Worshipers

MICHAEL GREEN

The Meaning of "Worship"

The heart of spirituality, for the first Christians, lay in worship. For many of us in Western lands today, rediscovery of spirituality lies in a trip into our interior consciousness, attaining affinity with the earth goddess Gaia, or an attempt to maximize our human potential. But not for them. Spirituality meant worship, ascribing ultimate worth not to some fashionable idol, but to the Creator of the universe. He was the God of Abraham, Isaac, and Jacob, the God who had invaded time and space and come to seek them in the person of Jesus the Messiah. He alone was worthy of worship.

But we must begin by looking more closely at this word that slips so glibly off the tongue. Christians today talk about holding a "service of worship." By that we mean either a liturgy, written by specialists and re-cited by the congregation — with or without hymns, sermon, or the full attention of the participants. Or else we mean a freewheeling event, with an opening invitation to "worship," a few hymns or choruses, a choir item, and an address. In either case, and on both sides of the Atlan-tic, it must be over within the hour.

I am indebted in this chapter to insights from my friend and erstwhile colleague Canon David Prior.

That is a travesty of worship. It has nothing to bring us low before God, nothing to take us out of ourselves. When in such a service were you last "lost in wonder, love and praise"?

The Letter to Hebrews gives us a glimpse of what true worship means. "Let us offer to God acceptable worship, with reverence and awe; for our God is a consuming fire. . . . Through him (i.e., Jesus) then let us continually offer up a sacrifice of praise to God, that is, the fruit of lips that acknowledge his name. Do not neglect to do good and to share what you have, for such sacrifices are pleasing to God" (Heb. 12:28; 13:15-16). Here we are given five marks of "acceptable worship." It is offered in deep *awe and adoration,* a quality scarce today. It is *radiant with praise.* It is *the fruit of a life* and lips that consistently shine for God throughout the week: otherwise Sunday worship is a sham. It *does good,* in practical ways. We are to "be content with what we have" (13:5) and to "share what we have" (13:16) — in strong contrast to the greed and selfishness that are two of the main characteristics of modern, as of ancient, society. Real worship changes all that. It leads to *a simple and a generous lifestyle.* Open to God, it is open to others. This may find its most obvious expression on Sundays, but it springs from seven-days-a-week living. Therein lies the truth of the old adage *laborare est orare* "to work is to pray." Worship and life cannot be divorced. They belong together. Worship without work is hollow. Work without worship is barren.

A good deal of light is shed on the nature of authentic worship by the two main words used for it in the Old Testament, which certainly influenced the outlook of the first Christians.

One is a word that means *bowing down in awe.* Both the Hebrew and the Greek word mean literally "to prostrate yourself" before the Lord, to kiss his feet. That is what the Persians did in the presence of their "divine" kings: it is a picture of total surrender and devotion, such as we find taken over into a Christian context in Revelation 5:9. That is what we are called to, as we come to worship. Contrast it with the casualness of our approach to worship: no preparation, no recognition of whom we are meeting, but a casual, hands-in-pockets attitude that treats God with familiarity, if not with contempt. But when real worship is carried out, when there is deep awe before the mystery and the majesty of God, men and women are drawn, as if by an unseen magnet, to join in that worship. It is profoundly attractive. It is, after all, what humankind was made for. "O God you have made us for yourself. And our hearts are restless until they find their rest in you." So spoke Augustine a millennium and a half ago. He was right.

There is another word for worship both in Hebrew and in Greek. It means *service.* The Hebrew *abodah* comes from the same root as *ebed,* meaning "servant," supremely displayed by Jesus, the Servant of the Lord. It is worth noting that the Hebrew view of servanthood is very different from the Greek. It denoted privilege and honor, not abasement and bondage. To be a servant of God was seen to be a high privilege. When the seer gives us a picture of heaven, he can rise no higher than to say "his servants will serve him" (Rev. 22:3 NIV).

These two characteristics are vital in worship. If there is no sense of awe and wonder before God, allied to practical, joyful service of God, worship will fail to thrill, and worshipers will either continue to shop around, unsatisfied, among our earthbound, uncommitted congregations; or else they will drop out. Protestant and Evangelical Christians do themselves a disservice when they despise the emphasis, characteristic of the Orthodox and Roman Catholic communions, on beauty in buildings, reverence in gesture, and ornateness in ritual. They are equally far off the mark when they dismiss as "liberal" any emphasis on social concern and striving for justice among their fellow churchpeople. Both are profoundly biblical strands in true worship of God; and the early Christians knew it.

The God We Worship

It is perhaps significant that the most common secular Greek word for worship is conspicuously absent from Christian terminology in the New Testament. It is *therapeuein,* which means literally "to heal." But its only occurrence meaning "worship" is in Acts 17:25, where Paul *repudiates* it! The sublime Creator requires no "therapy" from human hands. No, Christian worship springs from awe and glad surrender before the God who is utterly different from all idols, and whose worship must, accordingly, reflect that.

There are at least five characteristics of the God Christians worship that define the nature of that worship. They display what God has revealed of himself through the scriptures of the Old Testament.

First, *he is alive.* He is the living God, the Creator and Sustainer of heaven and earth, from whom all life derives, and to whom all life must come. He is the absolute contrast to the dead and dumb idols against whom the Old Testament prophets so constantly inveighed. And that has a great message for our congregations. True worship will have expectancy, silence, waiting on God. We shall expect to meet with him each time we go to worship. The service should both embody his vitality and leave room for his intervention.

Second, *he is holy.* "Holy, holy, holy is the Lord of hosts." That holiness drove Abraham to confess he was just dust (Gen. 18:27). It drove Job from self-justification to awe in the light of God's holy presence (Job 42:5-6). It drove Isaiah to a recognition of his utter unworthiness (Isa. 6:5). And we find the same with Peter (Luke 5:8), Paul (Acts 9:3-4), and John (Rev. 1:17). God is indeed, as Rudolf Otto saw, the *mysterium tremendum et fascinans.* He is utterly "other" and transcendent. And this induces awe in us, but at the same time intrigues us and invites us to draw near.

Our services need to embody this element in worship, so that none are "pally with the deity," but that all are brought low, and all are lifted up. The Eastern Orthodox Church is strong in this respect, with its *epiclesis,* inviting the awesome Spirit of God to come; and with its *anaphora,* lifting the whole congregation up to share in the worship of heaven.

Third, *he is unique.* He is to be worshiped to the exclusion of all else. He is a "jealous God" (Exod. 20:5; Isa. 42:8). His glory he will not share with another. That would be *lèse-majesté.* Not that he is selfish; simply that he is true. Any divided worship, any split loyalty, contradicts reality. It is against the nature of things. He alone is Creator and Redeemer. He alone, therefore, merits the wholehearted worship of his people. Idolatry is both an insult and a lie.

We would be gravely mistaken to imagine that the day of idolatry had passed. The building in which we worship can become an idol. The minister can. Tradition can. So can denominational rules. But the God we worship cannot brook any rival to his sovereignty over his people's loyalties.

Fourth, *he is grace.* God is not just gracious, but grace itself: total self-giving for the utterly unworthy. He is "the God of all grace" (1 Peter 5:10). He is the one who made us and all the world. He sustains it, and breathes life into it. He is the one who came to seek us out, when we would never have sought him. He is the one who died for us, rose for us, and comes to enter our hearts and direct our way. He is the one who will, at the end of the road, receive us into his glory. Amazing grace!

So our worship needs to declare his grace, admit our unworthiness, and yet have a deep confidence of access in the name of Jesus — which naturally leads to praise. The New Testament abounds in praise and adoration. *Eucharistein, eulogein,* and *ainein* are constantly in use; and the book of Revelation gives a marvelous insight into the praises of the people of God, here as well as hereafter (cf. Rev. 4:11; 5:9-10; 12–14). Praise and adoration are the only fitting response to grace. That is the answer to people who wonder why God wants to be praised!

In the Bible men and women praise God for a welter of things in their lives. He daily loads us with benefits (Ps. 68:19). He gives us the fruits of the earth (Acts 14:17). He is the source of every good and perfect gift (James 1:17), including the money that so often becomes an idol (1 Tim. 6:17). Yes, he "gives us all things richly to enjoy." But supremely Christians give praise to God for Christ, who brings us into God's family and makes new people of us (1 Peter 1:3; Eph. 2:19). Jesus, therefore, needs to be central in our praises; and this the best hymn writers have perceived. Jesus incarnate, Jesus crucified, Jesus risen and exalted — these are the three themes of that "new song" to be sung in heaven (Rev. 5:9-14). One of the worst forms of ingratitude is to be so busy thanking God for his many minor mercies that we do not thank him for his supreme gift.

Fifth, *he is challenge.* Grace means "all of him for me." Faith means "all of me for him." That grace-faith reciprocal dominates worship from the time of Abraham until today. Grace is costly. So is faith. It calls for total surrender in practical, life-changing ways. It did for Abraham. It did for Jesus. It did for Paul. And so it does for us. Spiritual worship means not an hour on Sunday, but the responsive surrender of our bodies as a living sacrifice (Rom. 12:1). It means the continual offering of a "sacrifice of praise" in our daily lives, whatever the circumstances. That may mean hard times. It may mean prison. It did for Paul. But his response? "Imprisonment and afflictions await me. But I do not account my life of any value, nor as precious to myself, if only I may accomplish my course and the ministry which I received from the Lord Jesus, to testify to the gospel of the grace of God" (Acts 20:24). That is worship. It offers every side of me as a love gift to the great Lover who has sought and redeemed my soul. Duty and privilege coalesce. It becomes not only our reasonable service but our highest joy to go up to the house of the Lord and to mingle in the courts of the holy place (Ps. 84). Any worship that does not drive home the response of total self-giving, total servanthood to so kind a Lord knows little of the cost, and therefore little of the joy, of biblical spirituality. "Therefore let us be grateful for receiving a kingdom that cannot be shaken," and in response let us offer to God "acceptable worship, with reverence and awe; for our God is a consuming fire" (Heb. 12:28-29).

The Dynamics of Worship

From all this it is not difficult to discern two of the main dynamics of Christian worship.

The *activating motive* is gratitude to God for all he is and all he has done for us. Our services must be marked by a strong note of praise and adoration, issuing in practical service of our fellow men out of love for God. If our worship brings us in touch with the God outlined above, we cannot emerge from our worship unchanged. We take on something of the God we worship.

The *controlling motive* of worship is reverence and awe. There is nothing drab about it: but something rather exciting as we wait for God to move. There is nothing clerical about it: every member is involved. There is nothing verbose about it: silence can be golden. "There was silence in heaven for about half an hour" when the ascended Jesus disclosed himself (Rev. 8:1). Time after time I have known a divine stillness fall upon a congregation when the Spirit of God has been active in it. Nobody moves. Nobody wants to go. Sometimes it is total silence. Sometimes it leads into informal praise. But everyone knows that the Lord has made his presence felt.

The Style of Worship

The style of worship is really immaterial. It is the inner reality that counts. The first Christians could worship in the temple — but also in prison or by the riverside. They were liberated from externals — and yet

8

they used them as they were available. "We have no priests," exulted the second-century writer Felix Minucius[1] — and yet we are told that the apostle John wore the high priestly robe, *petalos*.[2] "We have no altars," they cried — and yet sacrificial language was used very early of the Eucharist: the second-century literature is full of the eucharistic application of Malachi 1:11. "We have no temples," they asserted; yet they were happy to keep the Sabbath, the Jewish feasts, even the ritual vows. Manifestly, the style of Christian worship was very flexible, but the essence was guarded with great care. It was nothing less than wholehearted response to the God of all grace, who calls us all to be a people for his own possession. What a challenge!

Our worship is all too often spoiled. It is spoiled by the *tradition* in which we have been imprisoned. It is spoiled by the *externals* we venerate — while we often miss the inner reality. It is spoiled by the *mind*, which is fearful of mime and dance, color and ceremony; fearful of emotion; above all, fearful of God breaking in. It is spoiled by *clericalism*, which ruins almost all the churches whatever their professed ecclesiology. It is spoiled by the *clock*, the plague of Western man. We have something to learn from "African time." It is spoiled by the *building*, which so often militates against real fellowship among Christ's people. It is spoiled by our *fear of the body*. Many Christians are suspicious of kneeling, or of arms raised in worship, or of dance or of drama. We have no need to be fearful about physical gestures. After all, it is God who gave us our bodies!

The Characteristics of Worship

The style of worship among the first Christians was indeed flexible, but four characteristics are clearly discernible.

It was liturgical. There is, in the Christian worship preserved in the New Testament, a massive use of the Old Testament scriptures to declare God's mighty deeds. It had a form with which ordinary worshipers

---

1. Felix Minucius, *Octavius*, 10. This and other quotations are from *The Ante Nicene Fathers*, ed. Roberts and Donaldson (Grand Rapids: Eerdmans, 1985).

2. Eusebius, *History of the Church*, 3.31, trans. H. J. Lawlor and J. E. L. Oulton (London: SPCK, 1928).

could easily identify. Hence the words of institution, the Lord's Prayer, psalmody, and the gradual emergence of a creed (prior to A.D. 150), the snatches of hymns or creeds reflected in Romans 1:3-5, Ephesians 5:14, 1 Timothy 3:16, Revelation 4:8, 11, 5:9-10, point in the same direction. Liturgy was not a form of words in these early days; but it was a recognizable sequence of elements.

It was charismatic. Prophecy, tongues, intervention by the Holy Spirit are common, and they could be introduced through any member who had been so gifted (Acts 11:27-30; 1 Cor. chapters 12 and 14).

It was spontaneous. That is clear from Acts 4:24 among many other places: "When they heard it, they lifted their voices together to God."

It was corporate. Their worship was not dominated by any one person. Many people could and did participate. That is clear from 1 Corinthians 14:26-33.

In a word, the special emphases that have differentiated the denominations in our day were all successfully held together in the churches of the New Testament era.

The Dimensions of Worship

The dimensions of worship in the earliest church were threefold.

It involved *the house meeting.* The Friday night *haburah,* or gathering for worship in a Jewish home, led to the "church in the home" of the first Christians (Rom. 16:5 etc.). This small home group facilitated love and mutual care among individual members.

It involved *the local assembly.* The Saturday synagogue was taken over into Christian worship. That is very clear from James 2:2, where the local church is still called "the synagogue" (Gk). There needed to be a local gathering of Christian believers, like the Jewish synagogue, for purposes of identity, prayer, instruction, and worship. Incidentally, the "presbyters" of the synagogue provided the prototypes for the leadership of local Christian congregations.

It involved *the great festivals.* Jews were obligated to attend at least some of the great festivals of their nation — Pentecost, Yom Kippur, Tabernacles, and the like. These were the times when God's people celebrated his mighty acts of deliverance. Participation cemented their belonging to a mighty enterprise. It is easy to recall Hebrews 12:23. "You have come . . . to the assembly of the first-born who are enrolled in heaven." Christians followed their Jewish heritage by occasional attendance at such large celebrations.

In our worship today we need all three aspects of Jewish worship. The synagogue corresponds closely to our church worship, but we are woefully weak in the area of small groups and of major celebrations. We need them all if we are to be balanced in our worship.

The Wellspring of Worship

The wellspring, the bottom line of worship for the first Christians, was that they could call God *Abba,* dear Father. It is an astonishing word, and its use was dangerous and courted misunderstanding. Yet it remains a fundamental insight if we are to think of God aright and worship him acceptably.

The Fatherhood of God

Some children idolize their fathers: some hate them. Some fathers spoil their children: some neglect them. If God is to be seen as Father, inevitably all human parenthood distorts to a greater or lesser degree what he is like. But God does intend our human parents to reflect his nature. That is why, I fancy, the command to honor father and mother comes where it does in the Ten Commandments: between the first four on our duty to God and the last five on our duty to men. It links the two strands in our relationships, the God strand and the human strand. But what distortion there has been of that image! People who have had strict fathers see God as out to punish them. Those whose father was rarely at home see God as absent. Those who experienced a father's love only with strings attached find the free grace of God almost impossible to appreciate, though they long for it with all their hearts. I am reminded of a doctor's question to a boy who had five sexual encounters in one night: "Why do you do it?" The poignant reply was, "I was looking for someone to love me."

Despite all the attendant dangers, the Bible does dare to use this word "Father" of God. It is rare in the Old Testament, occurring only some fourteen times. It points to God as Creator (Deut. 32:6; Mal. 2:10), and as very merciful (Ps. 103:13-14). Long before the feminist reaction against calling God "Father," Professor Jeremias had observed perceptively, "For orientals, the word Father as applied to God, encompasses, from earliest times, much of what Mother signifies to us."[3] True, for we are created male and female in the image of God who transcends both (Gen. 1:27).

Most of the Old Testament references to God as Father come in a context of human rebellion. We are all prodigals. With tenderness and weeping, like a heartbroken parent, he calls on us to return home. "With weeping they shall come, and with consolations I will lead them back . . . for I am a father to Israel, and Ephraim is my first-born" (Jer. 31:9). The mercy of the divine parent exceeds all human expectation. "Is Ephraim my dear son? Is he my darling child? . . . Therefore my heart yearns for him; I will surely have mercy on him, says the Lord" (Jer. 31:20). That is the Old Testament's last word on divine Fatherhood. Its very nature impels him to mercy and forgiveness. In those words, "I must have mercy," we see deep into the parent heart of God, and it is the most wonderful sight imaginable.

Nevertheless, God is never called the Father of any individual in the Old Testament. And never is God addressed as *Abba*. It would be unthinkable. For *Abba* is the most intimate form of family address. And how can one be intimate with the Creator of heaven and earth?

The Meaning of Abba

Jews, accordingly, never called God *Abba*. But Jesus almost always did. We find him praying like this even at the time of his greatest trial: "Abba, Father, all things are possible to you: remove this cup from me" (Mark 14:36). More than 160 times in the Gospels Jesus is recorded as calling God "Father," and the survival of the Aramaic word *abba* in the New Testament records shows that this is the intimacy he claimed and this is how he habitually addressed God — except in that terrible hour of bearing the world's sin on the cross, when he was cut off from that accus-

3. Joachim Jeremias, *The Central Message of the New Testament* (London: SCM Press, 1965), p. 10.

tomed intimacy with his heavenly Father and called out, in the words of the psalmist, "My God, my God, why have you forsaken me?" (Mark 15:34).

It is impossible to exaggerate the importance of this form of address. There is no example, in all literature, of any Jew ever calling God *Abba.* Yet here is Jesus doing it all the time. He, alone of all men, dared to call God "Daddy." And the unimaginable privilege of Christian worshipers is to call God "Daddy" too. We find it in the Pauline congregations (Gal. 4:6) and the non-Pauline congregations alike (Rom. 8:15). Christians can call God *Abba.* We can enjoy the intimate personal relationship which Jesus had with God and which nobody before him ever enjoyed. We are not only allowed to address God thus: in the opening words of the Lord's Prayer we are bidden to do so. In the Greek the very first word is this staggering loan word from Aramaic, *Abba.* What an astounding privilege! We may come to God as sons and daughters alongside Jesus himself, and call the Creator of the universe *Abba!* The only difference is that Jesus has this position by right, we by grace. Jesus was the one and only Son of God by his essential nature; we, by contrast, are adopted children. It is significant that the New Testament writers take up this notion of adoption, unknown in their Jewish heritage but common in the secular world around them: it served their purpose precisely, to show that we have no inherent right to that status whatsoever, but it has been freely lavished on us by God the Father. It is a great word to express the intimacy and the permanence of the relationship into which we have been introduced through his inexpressible generosity.

The word *Abba* takes us to the heart of the gospel, as Joachim Jeremias so clearly saw in the short (but mighty) book *The Central Message of the New Testament.* It denotes three things, all unique.

First, a *unique relationship.* The Jews said in the Talmud, "When a child is weaned it learns to say *abba* and *imma.*" *Abba* is one of the first words a baby utters. An intimate word. A family word. Jesus enjoyed that relationship with God, and he allows his followers to share it. The New Testament does not teach that all people are children of God. Jesus went to considerable pains in his teaching to differentiate between the relationship he had with God and that which his followers had. He spoke of "My God and your God, My Father and your Father" but never of "our Father" embracing himself and them. There is indeed a difference. "He came to his own, and his own did not receive him." That remains the sad truth about so many in our world, a settled rejection both of God and of his Jesus. Their names have become mere swear words, their love despised, their very existence denied. "But to all who received him, who believed in his name, he gave power to become children of God" (John 1:12). They become it, please note: they were not always "children of God," except in the very general sense of being his creatures. And the evangelist drives the wonder of this adoption home in his next words. They were "born not of blood nor of the will of the flesh nor of the will of man, but of God" (v. 13). What human parentage, human effort, and human mediation could never achieve, God has done. He has taken us into his family. We can cry, *Abba!* You will never in all the world's religions find hopes of any such intimacy held out to the worshipers, a childlike relationship with God as warm and trusting as a baby at its mother's breast or on its father's knee. It is utterly without parallel.

Second, *a unique revelation.* Most dads love to teach their kids. But with the Jews it was much more. It was the sacred duty of the father to teach his son the Law. And Jesus claims that God his Father has done just that for him. "All things have been delivered to me by my Father; and no one knows the Son except the Father, and no one knows the Father except the Son and anyone to whom the Son chooses to reveal him." Such is the claim in Matthew 11:27. He is saying that nobody but he knows God in this intimate, family way — an interesting sidelight of John 14:6, "No one comes to the Father but by me." He is also saying that just as the Father has transmitted to him the true disclosure of himself, so he can pass it on to those who trust and obey him. In that word *Abba* we see Jesus making a claim to ultimate, reliable revelation of who and what the Father is.

Third, *a unique authority.* We are not finished with *Abba* yet, for Jesus taught his disciples a prayer, the Lord's Prayer. And with breathtaking boldness he says to them, in effect, "I am giving you, too, the privilege of addressing God as nobody before me has ever addressed him. I give you the right to call him *Abba* when you pray."

And they did! The foreign Aramaic word stuck firmly in the prayer language of the Greek-speaking communities of the early church. They exulted in it. For this God whom Christians worship is not unreal, not absent, not too busy to bother, not deaf to our requests, not someone to be in fear of. He is our dear *Abba.* No wonder many eucharistic liturgies exult "Therefore *we are bold* to say 'Our Father. . . .'" No wonder the Lord's Prayer lies at the heart of many liturgies, next to the act of reception of Holy Communion. The family meal and the family prayer go together.

Yes, this little word *Abba* does indeed take us to the heart of the gospel. It shows Jesus' unique filial relationship with God. It shows his unparalleled intimacy with God. And it reveals his authority to draw those who follow him into the same relationship.

For you and I have not received some spirit of slavery to drag us back into fear and moral bondage. No, we have received the Spirit of Jesus, the Spirit who made us children of God. That same Spirit within us prompts the first cry of the baby in the family, "*Abba,* Daddy!" And when he does so, that is his witness with our spirit that we are indeed children of God. And if children, then heirs, heirs of God and fellow heirs with Christ. Of course we shall suffer with him. But equally certainly we shall also reign with him. We will share his glory. That is the thrust of one of St. Paul's most passionate and heartfelt outcries in Romans 8:15ff. That is our position if we are Christians — children in the Father's very own family. That is our confident cry, *Abba*. It speaks of his past adoption of us. It speaks of his present intimacy with us. It speaks of his future destiny for us.

Praise God for the privilege of being Abba worshipers! That assurance underlies all our worship, all our prayer and confession, our adoration and service. Nothing in all creation can rob us of that precious standing. "For I am sure," continues St. Paul in that same eighth chapter of Romans, "that neither death, nor life, nor angels, nor principalities, nor things present, nor things to come, nor powers, nor height, nor depth, nor anything else in all creation, will be able to separate us from the love of God in Christ Jesus our Lord" (vv. 38-39).

2

Disciples of Jesus

R. PAUL STEVENS

*Either we will receive into our hearts the Spirit of Jesus and be-
come, as never before, men and women of prayer, mercy and
peace, real followers of Jesus: or else, everything will disappear in
chaos. Today is the moment of Jesus.*

JEAN VANIER

*The Christian ideal has not been tried and found wanting. It has
been found difficult; and left untried.*

G. K. CHESTERTON

I was teaching street people in Boulder, Colorado, and stumbled on
the connection between knowing the Father and being disciples of Jesus. Some friends had organized food and accommodation for dozens
of homeless young people struggling with drug addiction and meaninglessness. In addition to feeding the body, they offered some nurture for
the soul. In the evening there was a voluntary teaching session from the
Bible. Most of the young people decided to stay for the soul food.

One of them, Eddie, had begun to follow Jesus. He was raised on
the streets of Detroit. He did not know who his parents were — no family, no identity, and no home.

During the teaching, Eddie started to fight with the men sitting beside him. He had a violent past and was only beginning to experience the touch of Christ. Rather than interrupt the teaching, they took him out of the room to the porch outside where, as he struggled with them physically, they pressed him to the ground and three men sat on him. As I continued unabated in my teaching, I could hear them "counseling" Eddie just outside the patio door.

Eddie responded, "I would like to pray." And this man devoid of identity and family prayed: "God! I have wanted to call you Daddy for a long, long time. Do you think I could call you Daddy tonight?"

James Packer says that the simplest definition of a Christian is someone who has come to know God as Father. Since Jesus reveals the heart of the Father and leads his followers into his own relationship with the Father, the way to the Father is by discipleship to Jesus. There are good reasons for this.

Jesus is a truly superlative person worthy of following even as a man. But his claims demand his being considered as more than a man. He claimed to have a unity with God that is essential and absolute: "I and the Father are one" (John 10:30). He claimed that our relationship with him settles our eternal destiny one way or the other (Matt. 10:32-33). He claimed to be able to satisfy our deepest needs, including our need for affection and meaning (Matt. 11:25-30). In so speaking of himself, Jesus revealed that he is either mad (a megalomaniac), bad (an imposter), or God. Yet his quality of life shows him to have been the sanest person in all of history. His claims are not only vindicated by his words and his life but also by his works, supremely his deeds of personal liberation and his ultimate act in the crucifixion and resurrection. Who would not want to follow such a person?

Why Discipleship?

Churches in the developing world or the newly industrialized world, churches that are growing like a forest fire, have much to teach the West on this matter. Dallas Willard observes:

> Multitudes are now turning to Christ in all parts of the world. How unbearably tragic it would be, though, if the millions in Asia, South

America and Africa were led to believe that the best we can hope for from the Way of Christ is the level of Christianity visible in Europe and America today. . . . The greatest danger to the Christian church today is that of pitching its message too low.[1]

Confronted as I am with that beneficent forest fire when I travel to countries where the Christian way is attractive and winsome, I keep asking, Why have we in the post-Christian West settled for Christianity without discipleship?

Being a "Christian" today is a complicated matter. The term can be used to describe those who go to church, or those who prefer not to be counted with Muslims and atheists. Many Christians use the wretched term "non-Christian" to distinguish themselves from those who do not believe as they do. A radical but intriguing proposal is to accept a moratorium on the term "Christian" for a year and to substitute the more biblical term "disciple." Let me suggest some reasons why.

Disciples and The Way

It is seldom noticed that the first Christians in the Acts of the Apostles were called Christians by not-yet-Christians who observed the total orientation of their lives around Jesus Christ. When observers could not regard the Jesus-followers as members of a sect of Judaism (Acts 11:26) they coined the word "Christian" to describe the Christ-people. Apparently believers did not describe *themselves* this way when asked about their belief and their pattern of life. Rather than using terms which would imply that they were "in" while others were "out," they directed people to their Lord by describing themselves as "disciples" (Acts 1:15; 6:1; 9:1; 13:52) and "followers of the Way" (Acts 9:2; 19:9, 23; 22:4; 24:14). Taken together the terms invite the questions, "Disciples of whom?" and "The way to what destination?" One can be a near or a far follower of Jesus and still direct onlookers to one's Lord. One can be "on the way," heading in the right direction without boasting about being "almost there" or despairing about "just having begun." The Greek word

---

1. Dallas Willard, *The Spirit of the Disciplines: Understanding How God Changes Lives* (New York: Harper & Row, 1988), p. xii.

for "disciple" communicates the same truth. It means "learner," "pupil," "apprentice," or "adherent." What if, during the year of my proposed moratorium on the term "Christian," those of us who wish to express our Christian allegiance simply answered the question "What are you?" with the simple statement, "I am an adherent of Jesus"? The fact that the term "Christian" is used only three times in the New Testament while "disciple" is used two hundred and sixty-nine times is reason enough to address the topic of discipleship. But there is an even better reason.

The essence of the Christian Way is the all-embracing and life-giving relationship of normal human beings with the living Christ who, following his death and resurrection, is as alive today as when he touched the lepers long ago. Jesus is our contemporary. So being a disciple means much more than going to church, having correct beliefs, or observing the Christian liturgy. Being a Christian involves something more than following the teachings of a once-vital but now entombed guru, or living by Christian principles. Discipleship is essentially a transforming relationship with someone who is as influential today — even more so — than he was when the first Christian disciples turned the world upside down. Christianity is Christ, and to be a Christian is simply to be a disciple of Jesus Christ. Discipleship implies growth, nurture, education, deepening intimacy, shared goals and life-direction, all facets of relationship with a person.

Joining God

Unfortunately, most people associate following Jesus with joining the church. Though, as we will suggest later in this book, joining the church is part of loving the people Jesus loves, the first step is quite different. The essential and primary invitation is to join God. We do this through adherence to Jesus who includes us in his own relationship with the Father. This is much more than joining the church. Indeed we are on the wrong track when we invite people to join the church before they have joined God. Here is why. Becoming an adherent of the church without becoming an adherent of Jesus leads almost inevitably to following followers of Jesus instead of following Jesus himself.

Following followers is almost always a disappointing experience. Inevitably these "model" followers prove to have clay feet when they reveal a discrepancy between profession and life or when they succumb to one of the triple terrors of Christian leaders — sex, money, or power. When the "model" followers fall, the followers of these followers fall with their idols. The pain of this disillusionment is excruciating and some never recover. How much healthier to associate with Jesus, and then to embrace the people he loves, no matter how well or how poorly they are following, simply because Jesus has chosen to associate himself with people such as us.

So relationship with Jesus is not the means to the end of our spirituality. Relationship with Jesus *is* Christian spirituality. By adhering to Jesus we enter the life Jesus has with the Father through the Spirit. Since the ambition of Jesus was to reveal the Father and to do the Father's will, the person who is learning from Jesus, adhering to him, and being educated by him, will, like Eddie, make the greatest of all confessions: the confession that he or she has come to know and be known by Abba-Father and belongs eternally in the family of God himself. That is the vital center of the invitation of Jesus to follow him. But the invitation turns out to be a compelling summons.

The Call to Discipleship

The Gospels reveal concentric circles around this most amazing person, each circle representing a progressively deeper response to his call. The largest circle was represented by the crowd who loved to hear him teach and observe his miraculous signs and wonders. Many of them carried on life afterwards with little or no change. The next smaller circle was occupied by the seventy disciples, who engaged in short-term missions on his behalf. Then there were the Twelve. Of these Mark records that

> Jesus went up on a mountainside and called to him those he wanted, and they came to him. He appointed twelve — designating them apostles — that they might be with him and that he might send them out to preach and to have authority to drive out demons. (3:13-15)

Within the Twelve there was a special "inner circle" — composed of Peter, James, and John — who were with Jesus at the healing of Jairus's daughter, on the Mount of Transfiguration, and in the Garden of Gethsemani. These concentric circles suggest that a person can be as close to Jesus as one wishes. But there is more to discipleship than volunteering to be close to the most important person ever to have walked across the stage of human history. There is the call.

Mark's crisp summary is helpful. Disciples are people who know themselves to be called "to be with" Jesus and to be sent out *by Jesus* to participate in his continuing work of liberating and empowering people. To be with Jesus in mission and friendship is the essence of Christian discipleship — the outstroke of action and the backstroke of reflection and relational rest. Both are dimensions of discipleship to Jesus. But both dimensions — to be with him and to be sent out — are dependent on the initiative of Jesus.

Disciples are neither volunteers for intimacy with the Son of God nor volunteers for an exciting and dangerous adventure. In the first century Jesus turned down some volunteers who did not know what they were getting into, and he did so for their own good! What makes discipleship begin and continue is the call of Jesus, not the good intentions of the disciple. So the call of the Twelve in the Gospels becomes a model for disciples in every century.

Everyone Is Called

Nineteen centuries of clericalism make it hard for us to understand the call to everybody because we have been enculturated to a clergy/lay distinction in the church. The standard argument goes like this: The call of the Twelve, as evidenced in Mark 3:13-15, is a special, one-for-all call issued to twelve special people in the first century and a few people in every generation. Most people in the first century did not leave job and family to follow Jesus but just carried on, grateful for the influence of this remarkable rabbi. In the same way, it is argued, most people today are not called to the same degree of commitment as the first disciples, but are merely called to observe the teachings of Jesus as best they can in the context of normal experiences of home and business life. But people who are *really* called like the Twelve should go into the ministry, become monks or nuns, or volunteer to serve sacrificially on the mission field.

John Calvin, the great Reformer, unfortunately popularized the idea of a "secret" call which some special Christians receive and which is a prerequisite for going into "the" ministry. Most denominations still require evidence of such a call before ordination. Arguing from the Old Testament model of priesthood of which it was said that "No one takes this honor upon himself; he must be called by God" (Heb. 5:4), Calvin spoke of "that secret call, of which each minister is conscious before God, and which does not have the church as witness."[2] Without this special call, Calvin maintained, our ministry would not be approved by God. Even the radical reformation leaders who championed the priesthood of all believers inadvertently promoted a two-level Christianity. Level one is for ordinary people who choose to follow Christ in the ordinary way. Level two is for superior Christians who are called into ordained service in the church or mission field. But there is no two-level spirituality in the New Testament. Over and again, the letters of Paul use "call" language to describe the summons of the living God to all people to live for the praise of God's glory in the totality of their lives. All are called and all are exhorted to walk worthy of the calling they have received (Eph. 4:1). The question is not whether they have been called but whether they have ears to hear!

Within this general and universal call to discipleship each person is led by Jesus to serve God in a special way appropriate to their gifts. So it is fitting to speak of being called to pastoral ministry. But it is equally fitting to speak of being called to homemaking. Martin Luther understood this matter with penetrating clarity. Even though his teaching was frequently marked with an overreaction to medieval monasticism, Luther grasped that there is no two-level system of call in the New Testament. He said:

> Monastic vows rest on the false assumption that there is a special calling, a vocation, to which superior Christians are invited to observe the counsels of perfection while ordinary Christians fulfil only the commands; but there simply is no special religious vocation since the call of God comes to each at the common tasks.[3]

Subsequent generations chose to follow Calvin who formulated the doctrine of an immediate and special call, believing the call of the

2. John Calvin, *Institutes of the Christian Religion,* ed. John T. McNeill, trans. Ford Lewis Battles (Philadelphia: Westminster Press, 1960), 2:1063.

3. Paraphrased in Roland Bainton, *Here I Stand: A Life of Martin Luther* (Nashville: Abingdon, 1978), p. 156.

Twelve in the Gospels is the obvious precedent. Speaking of the call of the Twelve, Calvin said, "The ministers of the Word ought, in a particular manner, to be directed by this example, to lay aside all other occupations, and to devote themselves unreservedly to the Church, to which they are appointed."[4] Unfortunately Calvin and his followers misunderstood *why* the call of the Twelve was placed in the record in the first place.

The Gospels record the calling of the original disciples in order to expound what following Jesus means for all disciples then and today, not to legitimate the special calling of church leaders and monks. Disciples then and today discover that following Jesus involves complete abandonment of all that holds us, at the initiative of Jesus. Simply put, to be saved involves becoming a disciple. The experience of the first twelve is the normal Christian experience. Dietrich Bonhoeffer is one of the few modern authors who refuses to let us interpret the hard words of Jesus as applying to a special category of disciple.

> When Christ calls a man, he bids him come and die. It might be a death like that of the first disciples who had to leave home and work to follow him, or it may be a death like Luther's, who had to leave the monastery and go into the world. But it is the same death every time — death in Jesus Christ, the death of the old man at his call. . . . But we do not want to die, and therefore Jesus Christ and his call are necessarily our death as well as our life.[5]

In the same way the apostle Paul describes the universal call of people to be followers of Jesus. He says to his friends, "And you also are among those who are called to belong to Jesus Christ" (Rom. 1:6). The call here and elsewhere in Paul's writings is equivalent to salvation. When Paul describes his own unique call to be an apostle to the Gentiles, as he does in Romans 1:1-7, he is careful to distinguish the call by which he became a servant of Jesus Christ (which is the normal experience of all true disciples) from the call by which Paul himself was commissioned to a unique once-for-all apostleship. Of crucial importance is the fact that Paul never uses his own call to apostleship as a model for the secret, immediate, and special call of church leaders.

---

4. John Calvin, *Commentary on a Harmony of the Evangelists, Matthew, Mark, and Luke,* trans. William Pringle (Grand Rapids: Eerdmans, 1956), 1:244.

5. Dietrich Bonhoeffer, *The Cost of Discipleship* (London: SCM Press, 1959), p. 79.

The Vocation of Vocations

Simply put, this means there are no second-class disciples. Two options are not set before us: full-timers (the clergy who are called to the ministry) and part-timers (the laity who receive the ministry of the "called" people). All are called to be with Jesus and to be sent out with him. All within hearing range of Jesus of Nazareth are summoned to complete abandonment at the initiative of Jesus and a life of overflowing fullness. Since the English word "vocation" comes from the Latin word for "call," we are entirely correct in stating that discipleship is the vocation of vocations.

A young Ph.D. student at the University of British Columbia knelt beside his bed to yield his life to Christ. He was brilliant and destined to a stunning career in India. When I noticed that he had finished his prayer, I turned to him and said words that I had not premeditated. "You now have a vocation greater than becoming the Prime Minister of India."

"How did you know?" he responded.

"Know what?"

"That my life ambition was to become the Prime Minister of India."

"Whether you do this or not," I continued, "you now have a greater vocation that embraces everything from politics to family life. You are called to be a disciple of Jesus."

Unpacking what that meant took several weeks of meeting together over the scriptures. Follow-through on this matter is crucial because there is misunderstanding not only on the subject of who is called, but on what it means *on the inside* to live as a called person.

Inside Discipleship

What is it like to be a disciple of Jesus? I was once asked by a student for permission to be followed for several days in order, in his words, "to find out what it is like on the inside." But this question is related to the one most commonly asked: "How does one become a disciple of Jesus?" Many answers are given to this but some of them while attractive are a dangerous diversion.

Imitating Jesus

One such answer is the idea that one becomes a disciple of Jesus by copying him. Thomas à Kempis's classic *The Imitation of Christ* seems to recommend this way. Kempis says: "Wherefore let our sovereign study be — in the life of Jesu Christ. . . . For whoever will understand the words of Christ plainly and in their savour must study to conform all his life to his life."[6] A popular book invites us to ask in every situation: What would Jesus do now? It is a good question. But it is also a depressing question.

On one hand the idea of imitation is implicit in discipleship. It is literally true that we become like the person we follow. Jesus said so. "A student is not above his master but everyone who is fully trained will be *like* his teacher" (Luke 6:40). Children inevitably copy their parents in ways that become an embarrassing self-revelation to the parents themselves. Like discipling, parenting is literally an imitation process. The learner does not usually get to know what the master knows. More important, the learner becomes *like* the master. We become like the people with whom we associate. But to imitate the only flawless person who has graced human history is an impossible ideal. The characteristic summons of Jesus to disciples was not "Copy me," but "Follow me."

At no point can we turn, as Jesus did to those scrutinizing his life, and say, "Which of you convicts me of sin?" The struggle to imitate the perfect life of Jesus can even become a form of "works" or achievement righteousness as we strive towards an impossible ideal that becomes a supremely intolerable burden. The theologian P. T. Forsyth was right when he said that Jesus is either our supreme deliverer or our supreme burden. As exemplar he is the latter if he demanded that we copy him. Our only hope would be the possibility that he is willing to live his own life through us. But before we explore this, we must look at one more misunderstanding.

---

6. Thomas à Kempis, *The Imitation of Christ* (London: J. M. Dent & Sons, 1947), p. 1.

Obeying Jesus

Some think that the disciple is not one who copies the master but rather does what the master requires. There is profound truth in this. Following Jesus is both an experience *and an ethic.* But one wonders whether those who promote this as the essence of discipleship have understood the Gospels. The Sermon on the Mount (Matt. 5–7) calls disciples to live with (1) extraordinary righteousness (exceeding that of the scribes and Pharisees — 5:20); (2) extraordinary respect for people (renouncing hatred — 5:21-26); (3) extraordinary sexual fidelity (allowing no lust to enter our hearts — 5:27-30); (4) extraordinary covenant loyalty (no divorce — 5:31-32); (5) extraordinary integrity (being utterly reliable in our words, not needing oaths — 5:33-37); (6) extraordinary generosity (through doing more than your duty and practicing massive non-retaliation — 5:38-42); (7) extraordinary hospitality (welcoming and loving our enemies and persecutors — 5:43-48); and (8) extraordinary generosity (giving generously *in secret* — 6:1-4). After reading this, one not-yet-Christian concluded: "As society is presently constituted literal obedience to the commands of Jesus would mean instant death. The meek do not inherit the earth, at least not our kind of earth." That is an overstatement, but one that is closer to the truth than pious comments about "simply living by the Sermon on the Mount."

There is no escape from the radical ethic of Jesus by taking refuge in the view that the teachings of Jesus are meant for some ideal kingdom age in the future. Jesus concludes the Sermon on the Mount with these searching words: "Everyone who hears these words of mine and does not put them into practice is like a foolish man who built his house on sand. The rain came down, the streams rose, and the winds blew and beat against that house, and it fell with a great crash" (Matt. 7:26-27). The ethics of Jesus demand a complete transformation. While perfection is never complete in this life, we must at least *start* being perfect because we are children of God (5:48). Indeed, unless we are children of God by entering into a transforming relationship with Jesus, we cannot even start. But this is the point: without relationship with Jesus the commands of Jesus are simply an impossible burden.

One could zealously imitate Jesus and attempt to obey his commands without being a disciple. Like the elder brother in the parable of the two prodigals, one could say self-righteously to the father, "Look, all these years I've been slaving for you and never disobeyed your orders" (Luke 15:29). The supreme tragedy of that "good" man was that he worked hard and lived by the commands of the father, *but did not know the father.* As an example of an "almost Christian," the older brother shows us there is more to discipleship than imitating and obeying. There is knowing and being known in a relationship of belonging. I cannot think of any worse tragedy than to come to the end of one's life and be confronted with these devastating words of the God of the universe: "I never knew you" (Matt. 7:23).

Experiencing Jesus

Discipleship is a relationship with Jesus in which we taste some of his experiences and allow him to share ours. His life shapes ours. We live because he lives in us. For the disciple this involves tasting incarnation, transfiguration, crucifixion, and resurrection.

In the Incarnation God became a human being; the Word became flesh and dwelt among us. God in Jesus went through a complete human experience from conception to resurrection. So Jesus meets us in the realities of our bodily life, work, leisure, family, and even our sleep. Christian spirituality discerns a transparency in the world and refuses a sacred-secular segmentation of life. We live for Jesus and he lives in us, at the very center rather than at the religious perimeter of our lives. Jesus has placed himself irrevocably at our disposal, so much so that we actually minister *to him* when we open our hearts to the poor, the stranger, and the imprisoned (Matt. 25:31-46).

"As the father has sent me, I am sending you" (John 20:21). This is the interior spirituality of the outgoing dimension of discipleship. Disciples are called to be "with him" and "to be sent out." But the sending out is shaped by the Incarnation. Just as Jesus went out with all the resources of the Trinity to become enfleshed, embodied, and earthed, so he sends us out *with him* to present our whole lives as a living and spiritual sacrifice (Rom. 12:1-2). Just as Jesus emptied himself of power and privilege to identify with the least, the last, and the lost, so the Christian disciple will experience self-emptying as he or she lives in Christ (Phil. 2:1-11). But there are some important differences.

When Jesus identified with us, he went down. He, as a divine, sinless being identified with humankind and with sinners. But when we identify with others, there is nowhere farther down to go. We are already human beings and sinners. A friend with whom I worked in the inner city of Montreal, where we tried to "identify" with the poor, expressed the difference eloquently.

> Identification for us is not so much a matter of going up or down to the level of another, but rather *conformity to the mind of Christ.* We are to seek identity not with men but with Christ. . . . Gazing into his face the Christian is changed into his likeness (2 Cor. 3:18). . . . While we talk about identifying with a class of people, we flee the yoke of Christ. Our identification with man is less of identification and more of condescension and self-congratulation. The problem then is not identification but humility. . . . Through the power of the love of Christ working in and through us, *our* pride can be transformed into *his* humility.[7]

Incarnation is the first pattern of discipleship. The second is transfiguration. In his Transfiguration (Luke 9:28-36) Jesus communed with the Father in such a way that his very being glowed with beauty. This too is a pattern of our relational harmony with Jesus. As we follow Jesus we experience the transformation (Rom. 12:1-2; 2 Cor. 3:18) of our persons from inside out, often without our knowing this is happening. This comes as we behold his glory; others then behold his glory *through* us, like light passing through a Kodachrome transparency. When people look at us they may see little more than what is seen when someone looks at a colored transparency. But when we live without mask or pretence and are held to the light of Christ, people can look *through* us to see something of the image of Christ. Paul referred to this in 2 Corinthians 3:18. "And we, who with unveiled faces all reflect the Lord's glory, are being transformed into his likeness with ever-increasing glory, which comes from the Lord, who is the Spirit." The disciple of Jesus is more like Jesus on the Mount of Transfiguration than he or she is like Moses on Mount Sinai, his face glowing temporarily with the presence of God (Exod. 34:29-35). Within the Orthodox tradition, icons of the Transfiguration are the most treasured, forming as they do a model for the spiritual life.

7. David McLean, unpublished notes, Montreal, PQ, July 1962.

In the crucifixion Jesus gave up his life for others, bearing in his own person the sins of us all. As we follow Jesus we identify with his suffering for the sake of his body, even "filling up that which remains of his suffering" (Col. 1:24). Cross-bearing (Matt. 16:24) is the Christian experience of life through death, though neither as martyrdom nor suicide. Rather it is discovering through identification with Jesus and his interests that reality of divine strength through weakness: "For to be sure, he was crucified in weakness, yet he lives by God's power. Likewise we are weak in him, yet by God's power we will live with him to serve you" (2 Cor. 13:4; 12:9-10). By "living on a personal cross" the disciple inverts the world's definition of success (Phil. 3:10; Col. 1:24).

Thomas à Kempis reflects deeply on the place of the cross in the disciple's life.

> Jesu hath many lovers of the kingdom of heaven but few bearers of the cross; he hath many who desire consolations and few desiring tribulations: he findeth many fellows of the table and few of abstinence.
>
> All desire to joy in him; but few will suffer any pain for him.
>
> Many follow Jesu unto the breaking of bread, but few unto the drinking of the cup of his passion.
>
> Many worship his miracles but few follow the reproof of the Cross.[8]

Crucifixion is followed by resurrection, ascension, and enthronement. As we follow Jesus we experience his lordship and permit his power to work through us (Eph. 1:19-21), demonstrating that the new age has begun and anticipating our own resurrection, and the renewal of all things in Jesus in the age to come. The glorified scars on the resurrection body of Jesus are powerful symbols of what Christ will do to our own personal and emotional scars by his resurrection power as he makes all things new. This vision of the exalted Christ (and *not* the need of the world) is the primary source of Christian ministry and mission (Isa. 6; Acts 26:19; 7:56).

What a revolutionary life the disciple is summoned to embrace! Dr. Hocking was once professor of philosophy at Harvard University. He tells how, when he was an aspiring teacher of ethics, a student re-

---

8. Thomas à Kempis, p. 85.

minded him, "You cannot prove that a man ought to love his neighbor and if you could prove it, that would not in the least help him to do so." The sequel to the question was an even keener thrust, Dr. Hocking admits. "I can understand," the student went on to say, "how Jesus or a Nietzsche could turn the world upside down. But I cannot understand how a college professor could turn the world upside down." Dr. Hocking agreed that the student was essentially right. It is precisely the business of Christianity to turn the world upside down by making revolutionary demands on motivation.[9] What we have learned in this chapter is that the revolutionary demands are not made by standards, example, or commands, but by the explosive power of a new affection, by the inundation of our ordinary existence with the presence of the living Jesus. Only when I am certain that I am a disciple of Jesus and not a follower of followers, or an adherent to Christian principles, is it safe for me to hear the challenge of Thomas à Kempis's words to become an imitator of Jesus.

With incredible courtesy Jesus stands at the door of the last sanctuary of our lives, the will. He gives us an invitation rather than a demand. Within certain limits we can do what we want with our lives. We are free to be engaged in a vocation that transcends all other vocations and makes revolutionary demands on our mind, heart, and will. To neglect this person at the door is also to decide. And Jesus warns us that the life out of harmony with the Creator of the universe will be as costly, indeed even more costly, than the invitation to take up our cross and follow. Kierkegaard once said that "It costs a man just as much or even more to go to hell than to come to heaven. Narrow, exceedingly narrow is the way to perdition!"

So what do we get out of following Jesus? The primary gain for the disciple is simply to be with Jesus and to be sent out with him! All the references to exchanging a lower life for a higher one (Matt. 16:25), gaining treasure in heaven (19:21), gaining shared leadership with Jesus (19:27-30) and eternal life (Mark 10:28-31) are ways of expressing the benefit of being with Jesus. The disciple has his or her wish: to know Christ and to make him known.

9. Quoted by Dr. H. Waters in an unpublished sermon, McMaster University, Hamilton, Ontario, 1959.

Bonhoeffer calls this costly grace and compares it with the cheap grace of easy Christianity.

> Cheap grace is grace without discipleship, grace without the cross, grace without Jesus Christ, living and incarnate.
>
> Costly grace is the treasure hidden in the field; for the sake of it a man will gladly go and sell all that he has. It is the pearl of great price to buy which the merchant will sell all his goods. It is the kingly rule of Christ, for whose sake a man will pluck out the eye which causes him to stumble, it is the call of Jesus Christ at which the disciple leaves his nets and follows him.
>
> Such grace is *costly* because it calls us to follow, and it is *grace* because it calls us to follow *Jesus Christ*. It is costly because it costs a man his life, and it is grace because it gives a man the only true life.[10]

---

10. Bonhoeffer, *The Cost of Discipleship*, pp. 35-36.

3

Temples of the Holy Spirit

MICHAEL GREEN

The date is probably A.D. 49. The apostle Paul is writing what may well have been the first New Testament letter. And he asks the Galatians, a mix of Jews and Gentiles who have become believers in Jesus, a most arresting question. "Let me ask you only this: Did you receive the Spirit?" (Gal. 3:2).

He is clearly talking about the essence of being a Christian. Did you receive the Spirit? Are you sure of it? Many moderns are not at all sure of it, and they would regard the question itself as impertinent. For their part, the Galatians had been bewitched. They apparently thought they could live the Christian life by *doing* something, what Paul calls "the works of the law." They were regular in worship, orthodox in belief, moral in behavior. Surely that will do. No doubt this is what they felt, along with many a modern churchman. And Paul burst in, No, it will not do. You foolish Galatians. To be a Christian is not primarily to *do anything*. It is to *receive someone,* the lifegiving Spirit of God. He is the indispensable gift that nobody can earn, yet all true Christians must possess.

Paul is unambiguous on the matter. The indwelling Spirit of God is the hallmark both of the individual Christian and of the Christian assembly. In 1 Corinthians 6:19 he tells these converts from a very murky past that their bodies are the temples where the Spirit lives; while in 3:16 it is the church that he describes as the dwelling place of the Spirit. If anyone does not have the Spirit of God, he is not a Christian, according to Romans 8:9. Thus the individual is the place where the Spirit dwells. But equally "the whole structure [of the Ephesian church] ... grows into a holy temple in the Lord; in whom you also are built into it for a dwelling place of God in the Spirit" (Eph. 2:21-22). The indwelling of the Spirit is the one indispensable essential both for the Christian and the church.

That claim was mind-boggling to Greeks and Hebrews alike. The Greeks could hardly imagine what was meant by the Spirit of God. For the Jew, it was beyond one's wildest imaginings. Yet to the Christian it has become the bottom line. How could that be? Let us start at the beginning.

The Spirit in the Old Testament

The word used for "the Spirit" in the Bible is significant, both in Hebrew and Greek. The same word does duty for "wind," "breath," and "Spirit." The Spirit is God's life-giving breath without which man is inert. It is God's mighty, mysterious wind, which you and I like Nicodemus cannot understand let alone harness or organize. But we can feel and recognize its impact.

We can sharpen our picture of the Spirit in the Old Testament when we see what it is not.

It is not the same as the human spirit. There is a perfectly good word in Hebrew for that: *nephesh*, the "spirit" that differentiates a live person from a corpse. But the "Spirit of God," the *ruach Adonai*, is quite different from that.

Nor is it to be found in other religions. Attractive though that hypothesis is to many, it is nowhere taught in the scriptures. They do not deny that there is some light in other faiths. But they never call that light "the Spirit."

No, we have to do with nothing less than the Spirit of the living God, Yahweh himself. There are a few places where the Spirit may be associated with Yahweh in creation, such as Genesis 1:2 and Psalm 104:30; but these are all questionable. The main emphases about the Spirit in the Old Testament are as follows.

The Spirit is always God's gift. It is never an inherent quality in man himself. It comes on him from *outside,* from beyond.

Accordingly, it is often used of *empowering*. Gideon was a very ordinary man until the Spirit of the Lord came upon him (Judges 6:34). Samson's strength was nothing out of the ordinary until the Spirit of the Lord came upon him (Judges 14:6). Bezalel was nothing to write home about until the Spirit came upon him, and he then became a fantastic craftsman (Exod. 31:3).

But it was not just in power but in *revelation* that the Spirit was active. The word of the Lord *(dabar)* and the Spirit of the Lord *(ruach)* work together. God's Spirit is in the communication business. Thus "The Spirit of the Lord speaks by me, his word is upon my tongue" (2 Sam. 23:2). It is because of this essential link between the word and the Spirit of the Lord that the prophets claimed inspiration by God's Spirit as they spoke God's word (Isa. 48:16; Micah 3:8; Zech. 7:12).

There were three aspects of the Spirit's activity in the Old Testament that concern us particularly, since they anticipate both Jesus and the church.

The first is *servanthood*. The Spirit of the Lord was especially promised to the Servant of the Lord in those four great Servant Songs in Isaiah. "Behold my servant, whom I uphold, my chosen in whom my soul delights; I have put my Spirit upon him" (Isa. 42:1), or a similar passage outside the Servant Songs, "The Spirit of the Lord God is upon me, because the Lord has anointed me to bring good tidings to the afflicted . . ." (Isa. 61:1). Jesus claimed to fulfill both those passages in his ministry. He, the supreme Servant of the Lord, was uniquely equipped by God's Spirit.

The second is *kingship*. The king of Israel might expect to have God's Spirit (1 Sam. 10:1, 6; 16:13), and although some kings were notably deficient in this area, the hope of Israel was that her coming great king would be equipped with God's Spirit to a remarkable degree. This hope had been there a thousand years before Christ (2 Sam. 7:14-16 was a much treasured text) and it persisted, not only through the prophets (cf. Isa. 11:1) but into the intertestamental period. "God will make the Messiah mighty in the Holy Spirit," sang the *Psalms of Solomon*[1] in the first century B.C. The kings of Israel had often disappointed. This king would not.

---

1. Trans. R. H. Charles, *Apocrypha and Pseudepigrapha of the Old Testament*, vol. 2 (Oxford: Oxford University Press, 1913), 13:7.

The third is *people.* In Old Testament days you had to be rather special to have the Holy Spirit given you. A prophet, a king, a very wise man, perhaps. But the Spirit was not for the common man. Yet there was a hunger for the gift of the Spirit to be poured out on all God's people. Many a Jew must have felt how great it would be if Moses' hope could be fulfilled: "Would that all the Lord's people were prophets, that the Lord would put his Spirit upon them!" (Num. 11:29). And that is precisely what some of the prophets foresaw for "the last days." Thus Joel's prophecy (2:28) about the universality of the gift of the Spirit came strikingly true on the Day of Pentecost, and those present were well aware of it (Acts 2:17-18). Jeremiah cherished much the same hope, as did Ezekiel. God's covenant with Israel kept getting spoiled because Israel kept breaking it. So Jeremiah and Ezekiel looked for the day when God would not only keep his side of the covenant but empower Israel to keep hers. It would be a day when they all knew God personally, when they were aware that sins had really been forgiven, and when they received the gift of the Spirit to internalize God's law on their hearts so that obeying him would become like second nature (Jer. 31:31ff.; Ezek. 36:25ff.). That was what was wanted: a new covenant, where a new experience of God's Spirit within us would warm our heart to want to go God's way, and empower our will to do it. In due course, all of that came true.

But in the meantime there were three great disadvantages in human experience of the Spirit in the Old Testament.

First, the Spirit was sub-personal. It was naked power, wild, untamed, like the winds that roared down the desert wadis.

Second, the Spirit was impermanent. It could be not only bestowed but removed, as both Samson and Saul discovered (Judges 16:21; 1 Sam. 15:26; 16:14).

Third, the Spirit was restricted. It was a gift for some of God's people, not all. The hope was that on God's great day of deliverance for his people the Spirit would be universalized.

The Spirit and Jesus

Jesus fulfilled all the Old Testament expectations and longings for the Spirit.

Jesus was *the unique man of the Spirit.* The Spirit "rested" upon him at his baptism and stayed with him all his life (cf. John 1:32). In his baptism Jesus received the calling to be both the Son and the Servant of God, and for those dual roles he was mightily equipped by the gift of the Spirit coming upon him like a dove. The Spirit did not rest upon him in any limited way: he was filled with the Holy Spirit (Luke 4:1). No wonder this was unprecedented, for he was the messianic king. He was the suffering servant. He was the prophet like Moses. All three strands of Old Testament prediction came to a head in him. In his own person he embodied the prophet, priest, and king who had been most commonly recipients of the Spirit under the old dispensation.

Jesus was also *the unique dispenser of the Spirit.* John the Baptist saw this. He realized that Jesus would baptize people with the Holy Spirit (Mark 1:8 and parallels). "Receive the Spirit," Jesus says to his disciples in John 20:22. The Spirit who had so notably filled him is now to be given also to his disciples. The mission committed to him by the Father becomes their mission now — and they are going to need the Spirit without whom it cannot be attempted. For the mission and the Spirit belong together. And that is what John 20 and Acts 2 stress in their very different ways. If the Spirit is not in us, we cannot evangelize. If he is, we must.

The Spirit and the Church

When the Spirit came upon the earliest church on the Day of Pentecost, it became clear that the restrictions and disadvantages under the old covenant were gone.

The Spirit that in the Old Testament days had appeared as subpersonal, almost naked power, was now seen to be clothed in the person of Jesus of Nazareth. The Spirit was "the Spirit of Jesus."

The Spirit that in the Old Testament days had been reserved for special people was now made universally available: the wide variety of people from across the world who were present at Pentecost is a notable feature of the account. The days of restriction are over.

The Spirit that in Old Testament days would come and go, dependent upon the recipient's spiritual state, was now a permanent resident in the lives opened up to him. He would never be withdrawn.

It is this Spirit — divine, personal, unwithdrawn, and universally available — which was the parting gift of the ascended Jesus. The giving of the Spirit to his followers was the fruit of his death, resurrection, and ascension. In the days of his flesh, "the Spirit had not been given [to believers], because Jesus was not yet glorified" (John 7:39). But after his passion and Pentecost, the gift of the Spirit came to indwell the hearts and lives of all believers, as Jeremiah, Ezekiel, and Joel had predicted so long ago.

Think of what that implies.

- *It means that your body is the shrine that God inhabits.* The *shekinah* glory that was absent from the second temple was wonderfully present in Jesus (John 1:14) and shines progressively in you and me (2 Cor. 3:18). It means that the Christian church at worship is the place where the Holy Spirit is longing to make himself known (Eph. 2:22).
- *It means that God's new and everlasting covenant with men and women is in operation, and the hopes of the prophets of old have been fulfilled* (Jer. 31:31-34). Sins forgiven, God known personally, and his *torah* interiorized. Our Teacher dwells within!
- *It means that the Holy Spirit makes Jesus our contemporary* — as real as he was to those first disciples. Jesus is God's last Word to man. What more could God add to personal self-disclosure through incarnation? And the function of the Spirit is not to give some new revelation of his own (we should distrust such pretended revelations) but to bear witness to Jesus, to make him real to us, and to draw out the implication of God's last Word. So the Spirit does for disciples all that Jesus did. He remains with them and guides them (John 14:16-18), leads them into all the truth (John 14:6, 17), and continues to teach them (John 15:26; 16:13). What is more, the Spirit continues not only to comfort the disciples but to challenge the world, just as Jesus did. As Jesus predicted, the Spirit does show men and women they are in the wrong. Wrong with their moralistic ideas about *sin* (which is not so much infringement of God's rules as rejection of God's Son). Wrong with their ideas of *righteousness* — Jesus has been shown to be in a class of his own by his resurrection to the Father's side. And wrong, too, in supposing that *judgment* is either unreal or exclusively future: the decisive

battle has been fought, and Satan is a defeated foe (John 16:7-11). In a word, what Jesus did and was, so the Spirit now is and does.

• *It means, too, that we are not worse off than the first disciples, but better off.* Jesus was with them for a limited period of time. But the Spirit remains with us all the time (John 14:17-18). And to this extent we need never bewail our lot at not having been contemporaries with Jesus: the Spirit makes him our contemporary.

• *What is more, it means that we have a foretaste of heaven.* The Holy Spirit is that part of God's future who is already present: he is a first installment of all God has in store for us (Eph. 1:13-14). He is the seal and guarantee of our inheritance until we acquire full possession of it. So we need never wait unimaginatively for the parousia. We should rather rejoice in the gift of the Spirit — the pledge that the last days, inaugurated by the first advent of Jesus, will be consummated at his return.

The Work of the Holy Spirit

Why has God chosen the amazing step of indwelling his followers through the Holy Spirit? There are at least seven answers to that question.

To Make Us Like Jesus

That is the ultimate goal. He longs for us to be so changed that we reflect his face. The Lord who is the Spirit transforms us into the likeness of God's Son, full of his life and power, his love and joy. But where is the Spirit to start on this daunting task?

To Baptize Us into Christ

That is his stated purpose in 1 Corinthians 12:13. Baptism is always an initiatory rite in the New Testament. And baptism "in" or "with" the Holy Spirit (the same Greek preposition has both meanings) is the initiatory experience for all Christians, not some high-octane spirituality into which some are initiated. There are just seven references to being "baptized in the Holy Spirit" to be found in the New Testament, and they all speak clearly of initiation. Matthew 3:11, Mark 1:8, Luke 3:16, and John 1:33 all contrast John's baptism in water with Jesus' forthcoming baptism in the Spirit. Acts 1:5 is explicit in its allusion to Pentecost, when they would for the first time be plunged into the realm of the Holy Spirit. And that was fulfilled a few days later when the Spirit who had "rested" on Jesus "rested" on them too. It was the beginning of a new life, life in the Spirit. Acts 11:16, the sixth reference, is just as initiatory. The Gentiles receive the same gift as Jewish believers had, all in fulfillment of John the Baptist's prediction. Jesus is baptizing them with his Spirit. And it is just the same in 1 Corinthians 12:13. He, he alone, baptizes us into Christ. That is why the new birth is described, in John 3:3, 5, as brought about through "water and the Spirit." Baptism is the initiatory Christian action that we receive outwardly on our bodies, just as the Spirit of Jesus is the initiatory bearer of God's life to our souls. Baptism in the Spirit, then, is never in the New Testament portrayed as a sort of "part two" initiation for some Christians. It is the indispensable prerequisite for being a Christian at all. God takes sinners and plunges them into the river of his Spirit, irrigating the parched earth of our lives with his living water.

To Produce Fruit of Character in Us

That, of course, is the thrust of Galatians 5:22-23, the famous passage about the quality of fruit the Spirit produces. Notice that these are not individual fruits: they are "fruit," or " a crop." The singular is important. For this is the crop that the Spirit will always produce in us if we allow him, and do not quench him by disobedience or neglect. Have you ever seen one of those apple trees with four or five different varieties of apples on it? The branches are grafted into the stock, but then the same sap brings them all to fruitfulness. Such is the variegated crop of virtues that the Spirit wants to grow in us by his sap.

To Enable Worship

Worship is foreign to us sinful people. And part of the function of the Holy Spirit is to enable us to enter into that eternal self-giving, or ascribing of "worth" which marks the heart of the Trinity. The supreme quality of worship is that it should be inspired by the Spirit (John 4:24). Then worshipers become in truth "a temple of the Spirit" and "a place where God dwells by his Spirit." That is one of the reasons why prayer is so vital: it opens the way for the Spirit to come into his own home and lead us in worship. That is why openness to change is so important: it leaves room for the Spirit to mold us and our worship. That is why expectancy is so important as we come to worship: it invites the Spirit to come and enliven us. Alas, there is little prayerfulness, little flexibility, little expectancy in many a church. The result? There is little evidence of the Spirit.

To Inspire Mission

Mission and the Holy Spirit are inextricably linked. The Lord knows it is so against our nature to reach out to others that he offers his own love and power, his own Spirit, to enable us to do so. Passages such as Mark 13:9-13, John 15:26-27, and Acts 1:8 make that very plain. So does Acts 10:38. "God anointed Jesus of Nazareth with the Holy Spirit and with power" for his mission in the world. That takes us back to Isaiah 61:1, which Jesus claimed he was fulfilling. "He has anointed me to preach [the] good news" (Luke 4:18). In and through Jesus, the Spirit, designed for messianic days, the days of salvation, had come to stay. He equips the disciples for their mission, as he had Jesus for his.

Thus we find it is the Spirit who initiates the Christian mission constantly in Acts. Sometimes through a committee (15:28), sometimes through a prophet (11:28), sometimes through a trance (10:19), sometimes through a community at worship (13:2), he inspires the mission of the church. He is central throughout. He alone convicts of sin. He alone makes Jesus glorious (John 16:8, 14). It is he who enables people to confess Jesus as Lord (1 Cor. 12:3). He baptizes people into Christ (1 Cor. 12:13). He brings about the new birth (John 3:8). It is he who gives assurance to the infant Christian that he or she belongs in God's family (Rom. 8:15). He helps our weaknesses and aids our prayers (Rom. 8:26-27). From first to last it is all the work of the Spirit.

Very well, then. Given the powerful link between the Holy Spirit and outreach, mission, and evangelism, two painful results follow. The modern church in the West knows so little about evangelism because it is so closed to the Spirit. And conversely, because it knows so little of the Spirit it knows so little of evangelism, for the Spirit is essentially given for that purpose. No evangelism — no Holy Spirit. No Holy Spirit — no evangelism. That is the brutal truth.

To Proffer Gifts

The Holy Spirit is the Giving Gift. It is he who gives us the equipment we need if we are to engage in the spiritual battle incumbent upon all followers of Jesus. The New Testament affords us many examples of these gifts. They are outlined for us (1 Cor. 12:7-11, 28-30; Rom. 12:4-13; Eph. 4:10-12; 1 Peter 4:7-11) and we see them operating in the Acts as the early Christians work on their calling: tongues, healings, exorcisms, discernment, administrative gifts, leadership gifts, preaching, and practical goodness of various kinds. No wonder Peter rejoices in the "variegated love gifts of God" (1 Peter 4:10).

The whole subject of the gifts of the Spirit has been bedeviled in recent decades by the use of the word "charismatic." It has not made for lucid thinking. Three things need to be made clear.

First, nowhere does the New Testament differentiate between "charismatic" and "non-charismatic" gifts. To do so is to open a Pandora's box of jealousy, pride, divisiveness, and seeking to gain certain gifts rather than seeking to live closer to the Giver.

Second, insufficient notice has been taken of the fact that the Greek word *charisma* is used by Paul of marriage and celibacy (1 Cor. 7:7). These estates, one of which most of us share, are designated "gracious gifts of God" to us. Even more impressive is Romans 6:23 where, in contrast to the wages of sin, death, we are told that the free gift, *charisma,* of God is eternal life; and that is something in which all Christians share. So "charismatic" is the last word that should ever have become the watchword of a movement!

But let us not argue about the word. Let us concentrate rather on the power, the vitality when the Spirit came. Acts 2 is as good a place to look as any.

- When the Spirit came, disciples received a new power to praise God and pray to him with confidence (2:11, 42, 47).

- When the Spirit came, disciples gained a new power over selfishness (2:44, 45). This took two notable forms. Instead of doing their own thing, they were knit together in unity. And instead of holding on to their own possessions, they shared with one another in an unparalleled way.
- When the Spirit came, they had a new insight into the coherence and relevance of the scriptures. A whole variety of Old Testament passages are quoted in that address of Peter's, and its major thrust is one of fulfillment: "this is what was spoken by the prophet . . ." (2:16).
- When the Spirit came, the gift of tongues was given (2:4). That gift continued in the church, and still does.
- When the Spirit came, the disciples gained power to heal, at least on occasion (3:7). Though Paul's "thorn in the flesh" was not healed, and he had to leave Trophimus at Miletus sick, yet there are many examples of the healing power of God flowing through the early Christians. This too continues, and has had a remarkable flowering in our day.
- When the Spirit came, he opened up afresh the gift of prophecy that he had inspired in the prophets centuries ago. This gift is much in evidence in Acts (e.g., 11:27ff.), but its prevalence is nowhere better shown that in 2:17ff. Peter is quoting Joel, but the words "and they shall prophesy" do not occur in that Old Testament passage. Yet they are seen by Peter to be such an inherent part of the new age that has dawned, that with great naturalness he includes them!
- When the Spirit came, there was a new joy and confidence in belonging to the company of Jesus' disciples. That shines out of every verse of Acts 2.
- When the Spirit came, ordinary fishermen and the like had the courage to get out on the streets and bear bold and confident witness to Jesus — something most churchmen find terrifyingly difficult. The first disciples faced fierce opposition cheerfully.

Further chapters in Acts reveal other gifts in operation. The gift of wisdom is very plain in the Apostolic Decree, and it is specifically attributed to the Holy Spirit (15:28). The gift of exorcism is powerfully at work in 16:18 and 19:18ff. The gift of divine guidance through the Spirit is very plain in 16:6-10. The gift of knowledge through a dream or a vision comes from time to time, notably in 10:1-23.

We have here a mix of what today we would call "charismatic" and "non-charismatic" empowerings by the Spirit. It all goes to show how unwise it is to suppose there are nine spiritual gifts, no more and no less, and that they are defined exhaustively in 1 Corinthians 12! To that extent the Pentecostal emphasis is misplaced. But on the matter of the vital presence of the Spirit in the church, and our need to be daily filled with him, they have put the whole of Christendom in their debt.

To Fill Us to the Full

If our body is the temple of the Holy Spirit, it is only natural for him to want to own it completely. If we are the field of the Spirit, naturally he wants to irrigate us so that we may be fertile. If we are, as some of the second-century writers put it, "the lyre of the Spirit," he wants to play all manner of beautiful tunes on us. We are meant to be filled with the Spirit, no less. Indeed, we are so commanded (Eph. 5:18). And the Greek rubs that point home: it is a present imperative, and means that we must *go on being filled* with the Spirit. It is not so much a one-off crisis as a continual dependence.

What might it look like?

The context in Ephesians is very suggestive. A person full of the Spirit is a joyful person — someone it does you good to meet (5:19), a person with deep and radiant contentment. Such a person is full of praise and thankfulness both to God and to other people (v. 20). He or she is a humble person, always putting others first, particularly those nearest and dearest, though that is often the hardest place of all (vv. 21ff.). A person full of the Spirit will always be on the lookout to introduce others to the Lord (v. 16). And those full of the Spirit will be careful to allow no hint of moral darkness to cloud their living in the light of Jesus (v. 14). That is what it might look like.

Another approach is to glance at the five places in Acts where people are said to be filled with the Holy Spirit. They are illuminating.

The first is Pentecost (2:1ff.) where profound praise and the gift of tongues are among the major characteristics.

The second concerns Peter (4:8). He needs, and receives, a new infilling with the Holy Spirit when he has to face perilous circumstances and a bold witness.

The third occasion concerns the infant church (4:31). After intensive prayer they are filled anew with the Spirit so that they may bear bold testimony in dark days.

The fourth example is Saul of Tarsus (9:17). His blind eyes are opened by the Spirit and his empty life is filled.

The fifth occasion is the Elymas incident (13:9). As Paul bears witness against this powerful exponent of the occult arts, he is filled with the power of God and brings judgment on the sorcerer.

It is clear from all this that being filled with the Spirit is not a once-for-all and unrepeatable experience. We may — and should — be filled with the Spirit often in our Christian lives. Christians should always be full of the Spirit, as Jesus was (Luke 4:1), as Stephen was (Acts 6:5), as Barnabas was (Acts 11:24), as the Seven were (Acts 6:3). There is no way that we can be sinlessly perfect in this life, but being full of the Spirit should be our normal, settled condition. Alas, it is not. We sin. We get dry. We are often blind to his offer of grace.

And the marvel of it is that the Lord invites us to come back to him and be refilled with his gracious Holy Spirit. As we have seen, he will never leave us. But he may be like a visitor politely confined to the front room in the house of our lives. When we ask him to fill us, we offer him the bunch of keys that will open every room in the house, however embarrassing its contents. Think of a fountain pen: it runs dry, and then it can no longer write. I am often like that, and the trouble is I am so blind that I fail to realize I have run out of ink. That pen does not need an entirely new start. It is not utterly useless. It simply needs to be filled anew. And so do we. Or think of a boat with drooping sails, becalmed. They need to be filled with the wind. And we need to be filled daily, hourly with the wind of God, his gracious Spirit. Surely the whole heartbeat of New Testament spirituality is that each of us is the temple where the Holy Spirit lives. Come, let us allow him to possess his inheritance, and fill the temples he has deigned to inhabit.

Part Two

Old Testament Spirituality

4

Pilgrims of Faith

R. PAUL STEVENS

Before the theologian there was the storyteller.

RAY ANDERSON[1]

The Old Testament can be divided into two parts, one short and one long. In Genesis 1 to 11 God creates God-imaging creatures and charges them to live in communion with God, to build the human community and to co-create with God through cultivating creation — this is step one of God's intent to bring his transforming rule progressively on earth. "Fill the earth . . . and subdue it [take care of it]" (1:28). From Genesis 12 to Malachi (the second section), God continues to bring his transforming kingdom on earth by choosing a people through whom he intends to bless all the peoples on earth and his entire creation, to be consummated with the coming of the Messiah. All this is in story form.

---

1. Ray S. Anderson, *The Shape of Practical Theology: Empowering Ministry with Theological Praxis* (Downers Grove, Ill.: InterVarsity Press, 2001), p. 11. In one sense Moses was the first formal theologian (to use a distinction made by Karl Barth) while Abraham, Isaac, and Jacob were the first informal theologians — extracting revelation from their real encounters with God, just as John Calvin was a formal and Martin Luther an informal theologian.

Abraham, Friend of God

Abraham and Sarah are cases in point. If we are in doubt about the pivotal role of Abraham in forming our own faith story, three New Testament references to Abraham should clear that up: "[Abraham] is the father of all who believe . . ." (Rom. 4:12). "He is the father of us all" (Rom. 4:16). "So those who have faith are blessed along with Abraham, the man of faith" (Gal. 3:9).

The bare bones of Abraham's story goes like this: Abram's father, Terah, was apparently called by God to join a migration from Ur of the Chaldeans (in modern Iraq) to Canaan. But Terah settled halfway at a place called Haran (on the southeast border of modern Turkey). Terah died there, but the Lord renewed the call to Abram and his barren wife Sarai. Along with the call God gives a promise that had several parts: first, he would be the father of a nation (having lots of children — amazing for a childless couple); second, he would be profoundly blessed (a positive transmission of spiritual good); third, all peoples on earth would be blessed through him (he was elected to be part of a global mission).[2] Abram believes God, and with his wife and an entourage that included his nephew Lot, they set out, not fully knowing where they are going but knowing that God is leading. Abram settles briefly in Shechem, then pitches his tent near Bethel, but when famine hits, he makes his way to Egypt, persuading his beautiful but barren wife to say that she is "Abram's sister" in order to save his own skin — fearing they would kill him to get Sarai. This leads to a disaster with Pharaoh, who wanted Sarai for himself.

So they leave Egypt the richer for this escapade but possibly not the wiser. Meanwhile back in Canaan his nephew Lot and he separate because their herdsmen are quarreling over rights to the pasture land. Abram lets Lot choose the best part. E. F. Kevan observes, "Lot was as materialistic as Abram was magnanimous."[3] Immediately after this gracious act, God confirms to Abram that he will have children. Then God

2. The progression and expansion of God's promise to Abraham goes like this: Abraham will be a great people (12:2); Abraham will be blessed (12:2); all the peoples on earth will be blessed through him (12:3); Abraham will have a large family from his own seed (15:4); Abraham will be given the land (15:7).

3. E. F. Kevan, "Genesis," in F. Davidson et al., eds., *The New Bible Commentary* (London: Inter-Varsity Fellowship, 1961), p. 88.

48

adds that the land is his too. A local war erupts. Lot is taken captive and Abram rescues him, defeating the enemy kings and, surprisingly, refusing the spoils of war offered to him by the king of Sodom. Here too we meet Melchizedek, king of Jerusalem (Salem) and "priest of God most high," whose offering of bread and wine is accepted by Abram and his men. Immediately after this God tells Abram that God is Abram's "shield" and Abram's "reward." What a reward!

Were that not enough encouragement, Abram "takes God on" by reminding God that he still has no child. Abram asks how he can possibly be the father of a great nation. God takes him out for a night walk, and tells him that he will have more children than stars in the sky. Abram "believed the Lord, and [the Lord] credited it to him as righteousness" (15:6). To fortify Abram's faith God makes a unilateral (one-sided) covenant with him in a nighttime ceremony by passing between the halves of Abram's sacrifice, sealing the agreement for good. All well and good. But Sarai doesn't believe, and she arranges for Abram to conceive a child by her Egyptian maidservant Hagar. So Ishmael is born. Nevertheless God does not give up on Abram and now asks him to do something about the covenant; he is to circumcise all the males. Significantly Abram does this right away. At the same time (significantly) God promises that Sarai will have a child by the next year. Understandably Abram laughs. And as a further joke — really a comic prophecy — God changes Abram's name to Abraham (father of a multitude!) and Sarai's name to Sarah (princess of many). At this point something beautiful happens.

God shows up again, but this time through three angel-visitors. At first Abraham just thinks they are strangers and offers them hospitality. These three visitors, the subject of a famous icon in the Orthodox tradition, are the presence of the Triune God.[4] We are in gospel territory. There is a mutual welcome. Abraham welcomes the strangers and so invites the Lord into his house; the Lord welcomes Abraham and Sarah as

---

4. The passage begins by stating that "the Lord appeared to Abraham" (18:1). While the "angel of the Lord" is not explicitly mentioned, the speech and manner of the spokesperson "are precisely those of the 'angel' who is named on other occasions. The language of verses 10, 13, 14, 17-22, and the great intercession of 23-33, together with the employment of the word 'angels' in xix.1, corroborate the suggestion that here we have to do with the 'angel of Jehovah'. . . . [T]he angel may be identified with the Second Person of the Trinity." Kevan, "Genesis," p. 91.

the visitors confirm that Sarah will have a child within the year. Abraham and Sarah are included in the house of God's love. This time Sarah laughs, though when challenged she denies it. Not surprisingly, when little Isaac is born he is named Laughter, for that is what "Isaac" means.

But the great and God-saturated birth doesn't happen until, once more, Abraham pleads for the preservation of whatever righteous people the sinful city of Sodom might contain. He is told by the Angel of the Lord about the impending doom of this debased-sex society not because he has a relative living there — Lot — but because the nations of the earth were to be blessed by him. Lot and his daughters are saved, though Lot's wife looks back to her own demise, showing that what was needed was not only a physical forsaking of evil but the full turning of the heart. Then Abraham himself backslides by passing off his beautiful (but barren) wife once again as his sister, this time to Abimelech, narrowly avoiding another domestic disaster. Avivah Zornberg notes the special way the Jewish midrashim put into the mouth of Sarah her dilemma, as she awaits rape in Abimelech's palace. "All that night, Sarah lay on her face and said, 'Master of the Universe, Abraham lives on promises, while I live on faith alone. He is outside the prison, while I am placed inside the prison." Sarah's is a more difficult faith than Abraham's.[5]

Then Sarah gets pregnant. This was not a virgin birth. This old post-menopausal couple must make love — faith in action. The upshot is that Sarah now sends away Hagar and Ishmael (the child of Abraham by Hagar). But they are sent away with a promise of God that the children of Abraham through Hagar would also be a great nation (the Arabs). Sarah dies and is buried in the one piece of land that Abraham owns, a field and cave he purchased near Hebron. Abraham, anxious that his son Isaac should not marry one of the women of the land, sends his servant to their old homestead in Haran and finds Rebekah. Then Abraham himself dies.

So that's the story — or rather the husk of it. The heart is laden with the revelation of God and the invitation to become, as Abraham was, a friend of God.[6] Things decline with the next patriarch except, it seems, for his early life.

---

5. Avivah Gottlieb Zornberg, *The Beginning of Desire: Reflections on Genesis* (New York: Doubleday, 1995), p. 113.

6. 2 Chron. 20:7; James 2:23.

Isaac, the Sensuous Saint

As we read the story of Isaac in Genesis the indelible image etched in our minds is the young teenager carrying the wood up Mount Moriah, with his father carrying the fire and the knife for his sacrificial execution. He allows himself to be bound and placed on the altar, so much did he trust his father and his father's God. But that is not the most significant moment of faith for Isaac. Remarkably, the author of Hebrews 11 in cataloging the pilgrims of faith chooses an event at the end of Isaac's life, the blessing of Jacob and Esau by faith "with regard to their future" (Heb. 11:20). This is all the more surprising in that the event is laden with duplicity and self-interest. Isaac and Rebekah each had a favorite son. Isaac loves Esau because Isaac "had a taste for wild game," and Esau was a hunter; Rebekah loves Jacob because Jacob was "quiet man staying among the tents." While God had prophetically announced the reversal of the normal course — the younger instead of the older son carrying the leadership of the family and the promise — Isaac contrives to bless his favorite son anyway. Jacob, dressed up in his brother's clothes and wrapped in animal skins to simulate his brother's hairy skin, presents himself as a charade and is blessed "by mistake." Significantly the almost blind Isaac, confused by the voice of Jacob but sensing the smell and feel of Esau, goes with his nose and hand. Esau then comes in from the hunt and discovers that he has been upstaged by his cheating brother. At this point Isaac trembles violently (27:33) because he sees that what he has done with the wrong motive is in fact what God really wants — that the older would serve the younger.

Isaac was a sensuous, self-indulgent man whose spiritual appetite was jaded by his love of wild game. It could truly be said that the way to his heart was through his stomach. He lived for pleasure. The high point of his life appears to have been in his childhood, when he voluntarily submitted to his father's extraordinary obedience in offering him on the mountain (Gen. 22:1-18), though Isaac was the only observable means of fulfilling the promise given to Abraham. It was downhill from that point on. So much was it, that the famous Bible biographer Alexander Whyte concludes, "as we follow out the sad declension of Isaac's character to the end, it is forced upon us that it would have been well for Isaac, and for all connected with Isaac, that Abraham's uplifted hand had not been arrested by the angel of the Lord."[7] Whyte further comments:

> When I read Isaac's whole history over again, with my eye upon the object, it becomes as clear as a sunbeam to me that what envy was to Cain, and what wine was to Noah, and what lewdness was to Ham, and what wealth was to Lot, and what pride and impatience were to Sarah — all that, venison and savoury meat were to Isaac.[8]

Like his father, Isaac passes his wife off as his sister in order to save his own skin. But there is much to be said for Isaac. Isaac believes he is mediating God's irrevocable blessing and that he speaks (what he thought was to Esau but was actually to Jacob) in the power of God, and for God's purposes. The blessing cannot be undone and he has "made [Jacob] lord over" Esau, sustaining Jacob with grain and wine (27:37). There is irony in this.[9] As Waltke says, "Isaac and his vice are treated as a joke, but God and virtue have the last laugh."[10] Can we learn from this sensuous saint something more than the spiritual danger of living for sensuous pleasure? The next generation provides a surprising reversal. Jacob was an outstanding sinner, but he was a person so passionate for the blessing of God that he would lie and cheat to get it. In doing so he extracted revelation from God.

Jacob the Heel-Grabber

Significantly God wants to bless Jacob but he cannot until he comes to himself. But Jacob also needs to come to his brother. And in these

7. Alexander Whyte, *Bible Characters: Adam to Achan* (Edinburgh: Oliphants, Ltd., n.d.), p. 151.

8. Whyte, *Bible Characters,* p. 158.

9. Bar-Efrat explains the function of dramatic irony in Hebrew narrative: "Dramatic irony has a variety of functions, such as expressing criticism, stressing a shocking event or emphasizing a tragic situation. . . . Dramatic irony sometimes serves as a vehicle for the view that everyone received just deserts, in contrast to the view held by the character concerned." Simon Bar-Efrat, "Narrative Art in the Bible," *Journal for the Study of the Old Testament,* Supplement Series 70, Bible and Literature Series 17 (Sheffield: The Almond Press, 1989), p. 125.

10. Bruce K. Waltke, "Reflections on the Life of Isaac and Retirement," *Crux* 32, no. 4 (December 1996): 13.

"comings" Jacob comes to God. It all started with the way he was born.[11]

He came from the womb grabbing the heel of his twin brother, Esau. So they named him Jacob, which means "he who grabs by the heel,"[12] as a wrestler pulls his opponent off balance by grabbing his heel. Cheater. Manipulator. Schemer. Imagine introducing yourself to a beautiful young woman when you have a name like that. True to his name Jacob manipulated his brother out of the birthright, by which the oldest son would inherit two-thirds of the estate. Then he cheated him out of the blessing by which the promise of God's family would be passed on. He schemed to get the best of his father-in-law's flocks and herds by some dazzling genetic engineering. He tried to soften up his estranged brother with gifts. Jacob always had a plan, a scheme.

But God has a plan too. There is gospel in this story. God wants to bless Jacob but he cannot do this until Jacob comes to terms with himself. And to set Jacob up for this gift, God has to plot a series of scenes to hold up mirrors to his life:

Scene 1. God confronts Jacob with his own identity through his father's question: "Who are you, my son?" Jacob replies, "I am Esau your firstborn" (Gen. 27:19). He plays a role (complete with costume contrived by his mother Rebekah) to help him trick his father, Isaac, into blessing him. When Esau finds his blessing has been stolen, he wants to kill his brother. Exit Jacob.

Scene 2. Enter Rachel, a beautiful young woman by the well in the land to which Jacob has fled. Jacob will not tell Rachel his name. He tells Rachel that he was a relative of her father and a son of Rebekah (29:12). If my name was Cheat, I would not mention it either. Jacob does not admit his character to anyone. Yet.

Scene 3. Enter Laban, Rachel's father, whose behavior mirrors his own. While Jacob thinks he is marrying Laban's younger daughter, Rachel, Laban slips in weak-eyed Leah behind the veil. Perhaps he had

---

11. Some of these thoughts on Jacob were first published in *Disciplines of the Hungry Heart* (Wheaton: Harold Shaw, 1993), pp. 43-46, and more extensively developed in *Down-to-Earth Spirituality: Encountering God in the Ordinary, Boring Stuff of Life* (Downers Grove, Ill.: InterVarsity Press, 2003).

12. The name can also mean "God is at my heel" or "God is my rear-guard." It is quite apparent that while the naming was innocent and based on the accident of birth, Jacob chose to embody the more sinister meaning of his name.

plied Jacob with wine to facilitate the deception. Just as Jacob dressed up in skins to imitate his brother, so Laban covers Leah to make Jacob think he has married Rachel. "What is this you have done to me?" (29:25) is equivalent to "Why have you been a Jacob to me?" Jacob meets another Jacob — a replay of the steal-the-blessing-from-your-brother act. Usually when we run away from home we end up pulling at the same old weeds in someone else's garden. This should give some pause to someone escaping into marriage.

Scene 4. Jacob has to face the music. God calls him to return to his homeland (31:13) — which means reuniting with Esau. Twenty years ago Esau wanted to kill him. Now Esau comes with four hundred men. Jacob prays! But he does some scheming too, as usual. Alone in the night, Jacob wrestles with God in the form of a man. He will not let God go until God has blessed him. But in the process his thigh is touched. Jacob is now a broken man. He has come to terms with himself. The God-man asks him the question he has been avoiding for twenty years: "What is your name?" (32:27). And Jacob, for the first time in the entire account, speaks his own name.

"'Jacob,' he answered" (32:27). It sounds too simple. But Jacob must be *himself* before God, not his brother, and not even the Jacob he would like to be. No more role-playing, no vows or promises, no schemes and plans — just "Jacob." He has to let God deal with the real Jacob, the self whom God so patiently directed twenty years of conflicts to show him. Like the prodigal in Jesus' tale, Jacob can only come to the Father if he comes to himself. And like the New Testament prodigal Jacob can only come to himself because he has a Father to whom he can return. So the heel-grabber is no longer called Jacob but Israel. No longer "cheater," but "he who strives with God" — a new name and a new person, limping and broken but knowing that he belongs to God. Even the bruise becomes transfigured as a daily reminder that Jacob's weakness takes him to the God who makes his strength perfect in weakness. Jacob has experienced the gospel.

There are four dimensions of this story that illuminate our spirituality: mission, the promise, the covenant, and the gospel.

People on Mission

Abraham is, in a sense, the first missionary in the Bible. And all who are children of Abraham through faith in Jesus are called to be part of a grand mission project, not just pastors and missionaries. This includes homemakers, business executives, lawyers and stockbrokers, police-persons and soldiers. Biblical spirituality is mission spirituality. The reason for this is in the nature of God himself. Within the Triune God there is a sender, a sent-one, and a sending, just as Augustine once said that God was lover, beloved, and love itself. This sending within God and by God and from God is well attested in the words of Jesus who said in his own prayer to the Father, "As you sent me into the world, I have sent them [the disciples] into the world" (John 17:18). What a difference this makes!

Mission does not start with human obedience to a command, such as the Great Commission in Matthew 28:19-20, which sometimes has the effect of reducing mission to a duty. Rather mission starts with God himself, with God's outgoingness, with the ecstatic life of God. We like Abraham are sent into the world not with a command and a set of how-to cassette tapes; we are sent with the resources of the Triune God. God goes before us. God goes through us. God goes in us.

That being the case, any friend of God will get involved in reaching neighbors near and far and caring for creation, participating in the transformation of the world. That was God's intention from the beginning. Adam and Eve were forced out of the garden to "fill the earth and subdue it." The people of Babel were compelled to disperse in order to "fill the earth" (since they wanted to homogenize their own little world into a bland unity). And then, immediately following the Babel story (this is the beginning of the second part of the Bible) God elects one family (Abraham), one people (Israel) with the purpose of reaching out in blessing to the entire human family and the whole creation. Though long down the road, those who follow Christ, the universal people of God, all share in the missionary call of God.

Responding to this call involves both relinquishment ("leave your country, your people, and your father's household," Gen. 12:1) and movement ("go to the land I will show you"). Each of the matriarchs also had a call to "leave" and "go" — Sarah to leave her country and family, Rebekah to leave Haran with a complete stranger to marry a man she had never met, Rachel and Leah to leave Haran and go to the Promised Land. Biblical spirituality calls us to relinquishment and movement: relinquishment of comfortable securities, and movement to our neighbor. This may be neighbor far or near, to an unreached people group in a far-away country, or the person in the next office. But while the center of the call is to evangelism, the circumference includes the whole of life and creation itself, thought-forms in society, culture, and organizations, in the stewardship of creation. But there is more.

People of the Promise

We live as promised people. The promise delivered first to Abraham, then to Isaac and Jacob now comes to all who put their faith in Jesus. Put differently, we are people that God is determined to bless and through whom God is determined to bless others. In the case of Abraham the promise has three parts (expanded in his frequent encounters with God): the family, the land, and the blessing of the nations.

Ultimately the promise is fulfilled in Jesus, provisionally in his first coming and finally in his second coming with the full consummation of the kingdom. The blessing of the family becomes in Christ the people of God composed of Jews and Gentiles in a new humanity (Eph. 2:15-16). The blessing and inheritance of the land becomes in Christ restoration of the creation mandate, the blessing of the Spirit of God (Gal. 3:14) and "every spiritual blessing" (Eph. 1:3), consummated ultimately in the new heaven and the new earth (Heb. 11:13-16) — a fully human and creational blessing. The blessing of the nations (which in Abraham's case included Ishmael — Gen. 16:10; 17:20) becomes in Christ participation in God's grand plan of gathering all under the headship of Christ (Eph. 1:22), a mission that is evangelistic, global, international, interracial, creational, and cosmic.

Fundamental to being a promised people is obedience, alignment with the word and purpose of God. And the old saying that obedience is the organ of revelation was manifestly shown in the case of Abraham. After each obedient step this pilgrim of faith got more of God: more promise, more blessing, more maturity. But one step of obedience was especially excruciating.

Abraham's ultimate test was the call to offer up his son Isaac (Gen.

22:1-19). The first call of God was to go to the land. God's last call is to go to the region of Moriah. Understandably this is one of the most complex parts of the story. How could God call Abraham to offer up the only visible means of fulfilling the promise? And could God have called him to take innocent human life, something that was absolutely prohibited in the Ten Commandments? He is called to do something he is told not to do.

The Talmud, wrestling with how God could ask this of Abraham, suggests that it was Satan's idea, much as we see Satan testing Job. The Jewish philosopher Avivah Zornberg puts it this way:

> Satan said to God, "This old man — You granted him fruit of the womb when he was a hundred years old. And yet of all the feasts that he made, he did not have a single turtle dove or a young bird to sacrifice for you!" God answered him. "He has done nothing that was not for his son — and if I were to say to him, 'Sacrifice your son to Me,' he would immediately obey." Immediately after that, God tested Abraham.[13]

Kierkegaard wrestled with the text and found God's command illogical and absurd. It called for radical trust, not reasonable faith. There is some truth in this, a matter thoughtfully considered by Mike Mason in his insightful reflection on another person of radical obedient faith — Job.

> [T]o know Him is to know continual, exponential growth in one's capacity to live with contradiction. . . . Yet it is right here, in the turbulent waters of divine contradiction, that faith must perform its strange navigation. By steering a course between the Scylla and Charybdis of two utterly contradictory words from the Lord, Abraham was established as the father of faith.[14]

The point is that "testing" is not enticing to do wrong but challenging and proving to see whether one has integrity. Its purpose is to deepen faith.[15] Significantly, Abraham tells the servants as they proceed to the

13. Avivah Zornberg, *The Beginning of Desire,* p. 97.
14. Mike Mason, *The Gospel According to Job* (Wheaton: Crossway Books, 1994), pp. 133-34.
15. It is used this way in 1 Kings 10:1; 2 Chron. 9:1; Dan. 1:12, 14.

mountain that "we" will worship and then "we" will come back to you (22:5). It is for this reason that Hebrews 11:17-19 sees Abraham as expressing a type of resurrection faith. Somehow he believed that Isaac would be brought back from the dead, or that he would be brought back from the brink by the provision of a substitute (which is what actually happened). And the New Testament clearly presents Abraham as a model of faith in the resurrection of Jesus from the dead (Rom. 4:16-25).[16]

And Isaac? This story tells us, on one hand, to see how preoccupation with sensuality can cloud one's spiritual judgment and corrupt faith. On the other hand, we see that living as people under a promise means that even when we fail, as Isaac surely did, God will still be God. And God will not divorce us.

People of the Covenant

A covenant is not like a service contract. A contract is an agreement to exchange goods and services upon certain terms. If the terms are not met the contract is broken. Many people have a contractual view of their relationship with God: God gives eternal salvation in exchange for a lifetime of sacrificial service. People who take this view, often at a subconscious level, never feel they have "done enough." The church pews are filled with such people. In contrast, a covenant is not about *doing* so much as *being*. Like the marriage covenant the relationship of God with

---

16. Waltke's theological reflection on the story is as follows: The obedience of Isaac and Abraham is a type of the Son of God, the true Suffering Servant. Like Isaac, Christ is a lamb led to the slaughter, yet he does not open his mouth. Just as Isaac carries his own wood for the altar up the steep mount, Christ carries his own wooden cross toward Golgotha (see John 19:17). Just as Abraham sacrificially and obediently lays Isaac on the altar (Gen. 22:9), so Christ sacrificially and obediently submits to his father's will (Rom. 8:32; Phil. 2:6-8; 1 Peter 2:21-24). Abraham's devotion ("You have not withheld from me your son, your only son") is paralleled by God's love for us in Christ as reflected in John 3:16 and Romans 8:32, which may allude to this verse. Symbolically, Abraham receives Isaac back from death, which typifies Christ's resurrection from the death of the cross (Heb. 11:19). In taking an oath to bless Abraham and all nations through him, God guarantees the promise to Abraham's offspring (Gen. 22:15-18). Abraham's obedience prefigures the active obedience of Christ, who secures the covenantal blessings for Abraham's innumerable offspring. Bruce Waltke, *Genesis: A Commentary* (Grand Rapids: Zondervan, 2001), p. 311.

a believer has a similar bearing: I take you to *be* my wife/husband, not to *do* domestic chores, to meet my sexual needs, and to provide for the family. It is essentially about belonging. And far from being a relational prison, the covenant provides hope even when we fail (as Abraham did with his wife Sarah, as Isaac did over and again, as Jacob persistently did). David Atkinson defines covenant as "an agreement between two parties based on promise, which includes these four elements: firstly, an undertaking of committed faithfulness made by one party to the other (or by each to the other); secondly, the acceptance of that undertaking by the other party; thirdly, public knowledge of such an undertaking and its acceptance; and fourthly, the growth of a personal relationship based on and expressive of such a commitment."[17]

At the heart of Abraham's relationship with God is the covenant, sealed on God's side by the presence of the smoking pot and flaming torch passing through the sacrificial animals (15:17), and sealed on Abraham's side by his obedient circumcising of all the males in his household (17:23). Isaac knew that he belonged to God and was, in spite of all his flaws, still empowered by the covenant to rest in God's grace and purpose. Jacob the struggler who heard God say to him, "I am with you" (Gen. 28:15), came finally to believe in the gratuitous love of God — which is covenant love.

God has committed himself irrevocably to us. There is nothing we can do to make him stop loving us. He will never divorce us. We are a covenant people. We are, as Chaim Potok described the Jews, a "covenanted rabble."[18] God says to us in Christ, "I take you." And we respond by saying, "We take you." Our salvation is nuptial. This is the romance of the Bible. God's covenant is a love "that will not let me go."

Martin Luther expounded brilliantly the profound implications of this for our spiritual life. He asks, when a husband and wife truly love each other, who teaches them how to behave, what gifts to give? Confidence alone. They are confident in their relationship so it does not matter whether the husband does a little thing or a big thing, gives a big gift or a little one. But if they do not have this confidence, the husband is a

---

17. David Atkinson, *To Have and to Hold: The Marriage Covenant and the Discipline of Divorce* (Grand Rapids: Eerdmans, 1979), p. 70.

18. Chaim Potok, *Wanderings: Chaim Potok's History of the Jews* (New York: Fawcett Crest, 1978), p. 111.

tortured man, trying to imagine the one deed or one gift that will win the affection of his wife. In the same way, argues Luther, a person who has confidence with God may do anything — be a cobbler or an apostle, preach a sermon or make soup — because it springs from confidence. But if one does not have gospel confidence he is tortured. "Thus a Christian man who lives in this confidence towards God knows all things, can do all things, ventures everything that needs to be done, and does everything gladly and willingly, not that he may gain merits and good works, but because it is a pleasure for him to please God in doing these things . . . with no thought of reward, content that his service pleases God."[19] The heart of biblical spirituality is gospel confidence. This becomes manifestly clear in the story of Jacob.

People of the Gospel

Significantly the weakness and burden that carried Jacob constantly to God is part of the event that the author of Hebrews selects as an example of faith. It is at the end of Jacob's life. He has discovered that his son Joseph, once thought to have been mauled by a wild animal, is actually alive and invested as second-in-command in Egypt. So he goes to Egypt and settles there (again at God's command) and on his deathbed blesses two of his grandchildren, the sons of Joseph, Manasseh and Ephraim. But he does so, as Hebrews says, worshiping "as he leaned on the top of his staff." He still has his limp. And even more remarkable, as Hebrews points out, Jacob blesses them in faith. That is, he expresses the gospel in the way he adopts these two half-Egyptians into his family and blesses them. At the critical moment when Joseph brings the oldest, Manasseh, to Jacob's right hand, the position of prominence, Jacob crosses his hands and puts the younger, Ephraim, under his right hand. Joseph protests that Manasseh is the older. But Jacob says, "I know, my son, I know" (48:19). What does Jacob know? And what can we learn from this gospel-inundated cheat?

"I know" is full of irony. Jacob had inveigled the blind Isaac to bless him without Isaac's "knowing" it. But now Jacob, himself almost blind,

19. Martin Luther, "Treatise on Good Works," trans. W. A. Lambert, ed. James Atkinson, *Luther's Works*, vol. 44 (Philadelphia: Fortress Press, 1966), pp. 26-27.

"knows and deliberately follows God's unconventional plan." As Bruce Waltke says, "If Isaac's unwitting blessing could not be reversed, how much more this conscious blessing."[20] Jacob knows that grace does not follow natural preeminence, natural gifts, position in family, and human prominence. God loves without partiality. His love is gratuitous — without human cause or predictability. Jacob knows from experience that being the younger is not a position of disadvantage. Jacob knows that God looks on character, not on privileged position. Jacob knows that God's ways are not our ways and that we cannot control God, cannot manipulate grace, cannot force God's hand, cannot make the blessing happen. God is totally surprising. God is beautiful.[21] Jacob knows the gospel. His crossed hands symbolize what, under the new covenant with Jesus, came to be expressed as "at just the right time, when we were still helpless, Christ died for the ungodly" (Rom. 5:6).

Such love will not let us go. While we, along with Jacob, tell God we will not let him go until he blesses us, God assures us that he will keep his prodigal children forever. He will keep finding us in our everyday life and all of life's passages. This is beautifully expressed by Calvin Seerveld when he reflects on the alabaster sculpture of "Jacob and the angel" carved by Jacob Epstein, a Jew, in 1941 in the middle of World War II and the holocaust. The angel and Jacob are locked in an embrace, their bodies meaty and muscular. They are toe-to-toe, shoulder-to-shoulder, head-to-head, cheek-to-cheek. It is a real fight. But it is also a deep embrace. The angel's hands are strong, tightly clenched. But Jacob's arms are now limp, hanging downward in submission. So, says Seerveld, "The Holy Scriptures invite us treacherous, deceitful people to take hold of God and pull for blessing. When we finally give up our self-sufficient pride then the Angel of the Lord, whom we know as Jesus Christ, will hold us tight in an embrace of love from which nothing can separate us."[22]

Through the story of these pilgrims of faith Lesslie Newbigin says

We get a picture of the Christian life as one in which we live *in* the biblical story as part of the community whose story it is, find in the

---

20. Waltke, *Genesis*, p. 600.

21. This wonderful phrase comes from the theologian Karl Barth.

22. Calvin Seerveld, *Take Hold of God and Pull* (Carlisle, Cumbria: Paternoster, 1999), p. 218.

story clues to knowing God as his character becomes manifest in the story, and from that indwelling try to understand and cope with the events of our time and the world around us and so carry the story forward.[23]

Call and promise, covenant and gospel are the marks of the experience of the pilgrims of faith. Without the faith of Abraham, Isaac, and Jacob we could simply be religious workaholics, well scrubbed and apparently pious, but no friend of God.

23. Lesslie Newbigin, *The Gospel in a Pluralist Society* (Grand Rapids: Eerdmans, 1989), p. 99. Newbigin asserts that the Bible gives us a "plausibility structure."

5

People of the Burning Heart

R. PAUL STEVENS

The kind of work God usually calls you to is the kind of work that you most need to do and the world most needs to have done. . . . Thus, the place God calls you is the place your deep gladness and the world's deep hunger meet.

FREDERICK BUECHNER[1]

Archbishop Bernard Malango journeyed to our parish in Vancouver from Central Africa to help in a church crisis involving a bishop and several other churches wishing to bless same-sex marriages. "Why did you come?" asked our pastor in a short interview Sunday morning. He replied, "When you see your neighbor's house on fire you have an obligation to go to him and tell him, 'Your house is on fire!'" There was a long and thoughtful pause. He continued, "If your neighbor says, 'I *like* my house on fire,' then at least you save the children!" But then he added, "You can't ignore the fire. Your house might be next!" That is prophetic spirituality — awakened by the passion of God and concerned for righteousness in the people of God and the world. It is a love-passion for the people of God.

---

1. Frederick Buechner, *Wishful Thinking: A Seeker's ABC* (San Francisco: HarperSanFrancisco, 1993), p. 398.

The Prophets

Mention the word "prophet" and one calls up images of strange people dressed in hair shirts, thundering withering denunciations on the rich and powerful — people like Amos holding a plumbline to Israel and saying it is a tilted wall about to collapse. Not easy reading. Nor easy hearing. Would one want to be near them or be their friend? Would one want to be like them? King Ahab called Elijah a "troubler of Israel" because Elijah condemned Ahab's actions in killing a landowner to get his lush vineyard. The prophets did call down God's judgment. But they also cared deeply enough for the people of God and for the world to do so. Their hearts were not hard but wonderfully tender — velvet-covered rocks. Sometimes, as one reads the prophets of the Old Testament one thinks that they were not just thin-skinned, feeling things more deeply than others, but without skin at all. Their nerves were on the surface. Hosea's heart broke for his wayward wife (who became a prostitute) and at the same time his heart broke for prostituting Israel. Jeremiah was so sensitive that he wanted to get away from it all to a "wayward place" where he could be alone and not have to deal with the unfaithfulness of the people he loved — seemingly he cared almost too much while his heart pounded within him (Jer. 8:18–9:2). Elisha cared enough for the lovely woman who provided a "prophet's chamber" for him when he passed through from time to time, that he raised her dead son to life in what appears, from the text, to be mouth-to-mouth resuscitation.

Their work was not easy. King David seduced another man's wife (Bathsheba) and, when she got pregnant, he arranged to have the husband killed. Nathan the prophet was raised up by God to confront David with his sin. He did this by a parable not unlike the one Archbishop Malango used in our home church. Imagine telling the king he was a sinner and needed to repent. The prophet Elijah had to confront Queen Jezebel for her employment of prophets of Baal and her indulgence in syncretism. Elijah challenged the prophets of Baal to a definitive contest to see which God was actually alive — and won! But the spin-off of this was that Jezebel was after his skin. Elijah ran away and pouted in a cave, feeling he was the last living faithful worshiper of God, and slipping into a deep depression. God confronted him twice with an illuminating question: "What are you doing here?" The Jewish theologian Abraham

64

Heschel says, "The situation of a person immersed in the prophets' words is one of being exposed to a ceaseless shattering of indifference, and one needs a skull of stone to remain callous to such blows."[2]

The prophetic experience is simply being gripped with the passion of God. This was not something they worked up within themselves. It didn't get educated in them by joining one of the "schools of the prophets." It came from being personally connected to God in an emotional solidarity that led to having a heart like that of the living God. As we shall see, all Christian believers are joined to God in a living relationship and are meant to be people of passion. Perhaps one of our worst sins is apathy — lack of passion.

Who Were the Prophets?

The English word "prophet" comes directly from the Greek noun *prophetes,* which means "one who speaks for another." The Hebrew prophets have the dual role of speaking "before" in the local and the temporal sense of being "forthtellers" and "foretellers," the former being the primary way they served the living God.[3] So the essence of the prophetic ministry was speaking God's word with immediacy and directness.[4] In the Old Testament there were non-writing prophets whose ministry is described but who left no written records, for example Miriam (Exod. 15:20), Eldad and Medad (Num. 11:24-29), Jehu (1 Kings 16:1, 7), and Elijah (1 Kings 17:1). In the case of the writing prophets Scripture contains the record of their prophecies. The Hebrew Bible is divided into the Former Prophets (Joshua, Judges, Samuel, and Kings) — books that are really a prophetic interpretation of history — and the Latter Prophets (Isaiah, Jeremiah, Ezekiel, and The Twelve — Hosea to Malachi). The Christian arrangement of the Bible, based on the Greek translation, considers as "prophets" Isaiah to Malachi, including Daniel.

---

2. Abraham J. Heschel, *The Prophets* (New York: Harper & Row, 1962), I, p. xii.

3. Some of this analysis has been provided by Sven Soderlund in his lecture at Regent College, "The Spirituality of the Prophets," February 5, 2001.

4. Foretelling is an essential ingredient of the prophetic role as noted in Deut. 18:22; Isa. 41:22; 43:9, but essentially the prophets were speaking the word of God for the here and now and when they did prophesy about the future it was to expose the divine perspective on the present.

The Prophets is the last section of the Old Testament following the Pentateuch, the Historical books, and the Wisdom books.

The prophets were people who encountered the living God (Isa. 6:8-13; Jer. 23:18). They stood in the counsel of God. "Surely the Sovereign LORD does nothing without revealing his plan to his servants the prophets" (Amos 3:7). But this dynamic relation with God is not one of passivity, complying with the will of God. When the lives of people were at stake, their word was not "Thy will be done" but "Thy will be changed."[5] The theologian P. T. Forsyth once said that "we say too often, 'Thy will be done'; and too ready acceptance of a situation as his will often means feebleness or sloth. It may be his will that we surmount his will." Forsyth continues, "does not Christ set more value upon importunity than on submission?" Forsyth is referring not only to Jacob wrestling, but to the parable of the unjust judge, the incident of the Syrophoenician woman, Paul beseeching the Lord thrice, Abraham pleading, yes haggling with God for Sodom, Moses interceding for Israel. "We have Job facing God, withstanding him, almost bearding him and extracting revelation. . . . So the prayer that resists his dealing may be part of his will and its fulfilment. . . . It is a resistance that God loves."[6]

Elaborating on this dynamic relationship, Abraham Heschel notes that "in the presence of God [the prophet] takes the part of the people. In the presence of the people he takes the part of God."[7]

Prophets were people summoned by God to an irrevocable calling (Ezek. 2:1-2, 3, 8), people whose life was bathed in prayer (Dan. 9:4-16), people of great courage confronting kings and queens and false prophets at the risk of their lives (Isa. 22:11-12; Ezek. 34:1). They also had honest doubts and sometimes complained to God (Jer. 4:9-10). They were deeply disturbed by the sins of their day — mainly the big three: idolatry, immorality, and injustice. But supremely the prophets were people of pathos and passion, a theme developed superbly by Heschel in his two-volume work on the prophets.[8]

---

5. Heschel, *The Prophets*, I, p. 22.

6. P. T. Forsyth, *The Soul of Prayer* (London: Independent Press, 1984), pp. 86-88.

7. Heschel, *The Prophets*, I, p. 24.

8. See Heschel's study of the history of the word "pathos" and how it has come to mean, unfortunately, a painful emotion or pity. Heschel uses it to mean an emotional solidarity with the feelings of God. *The Prophets*, II, pp. 269-72.

It is this passion that is our link with the Old Testament prophets as we explore a prophetic spirituality. Spirituality, as we have seen, is our lived experience of God in the multiple contexts of life in which the seeking Father finds us. This being so, our expanding experience of God will include gaining the heart of God and being gripped with the passion of God, as were the prophets under the older covenant. Now that Christ has come and the Spirit has been poured out on all flesh, maidservants and menservants, old and young (Acts 2:17) are prophets. The prophetic spirituality is the gift and experience, at least potentially, of all believers. But what does this mean?

The Burning Heart

Aflame for Justice and Righteousness

The prophets do not take us to church except sometimes to see the hypocritical worship of those who tilt their hats to God on Sunday and live like baptized pagans the rest of the week. Rather, we are taken to the slums to see widows and orphans grinding out their living and the poor sold for the price of a pair of sandals. The primary way of serving God, the prophets insist, is not in ritual but rather through love, justice, and righteousness. Take Amos for example. At the time Amos prophesied to the northern kingdom Israel, that nation was flourishing in pride and arrogance. The rich had winter and summer homes adorned with costly ivory. They rested on silk pillows and drank wine from bowls of gold. They anointed themselves with expensive perfumes. Business people observed Sabbath but couldn't wait for the day to end to get on with their business. The poor were exploited. Judges were corrupt. The rich ate gourmet meals. Drawing on an image from Genesis where the brothers of Joseph sat down to a picnic at the edge of a cistern while Joseph cried for help in the pit they had cast him into, Amos thunders, "but you do not grieve over the ruin of Joseph" (Amos 6:6).

With great depth Heschel describes just what justice means in the Bible. It is not simply keeping the law or following the rules. It is primarily relational rather than behavioral. "Justice as an interpersonal relationship, involving a claim and a responsibility, a right and a duty, applies, according to the Bible, to both God and man. In its fundamental meaning, *mishpat* refers to all actions which contribute to maintaining the covenant, namely, the true relation between man and man, and between God and man. Thus justice in the Bible must not be taken in a legal sense as the administration of law according to the rules of law by a judge." Here Heschel quotes Johanus Pedersen who says, "One constantly 'judges' in the daily life, because one must continually act so as to uphold the covenant, i.e., the whole of the common life of the community. Everything in which this kind of judging manifests itself is called *mishpat*."[9] When Cain murders Abel, God does not say, "You broke the law." But rather he asks, "Where is your brother?"

This is critical for knowing God. How does God manifest himself? Isaiah says, by filling the world with justice and righteousness (Isa. 33:5-6), and this is especially demonstrated in concern for the needy, the marginalized, and the poor. "You have been a refuge for the poor, a refuge for the needy in his distress" (Isa. 25:4). To have a prophetic spirituality means to be passionate about justice in the church and the world. But justice without love is less than the passion of God.

In Love with the People of God

It might appear that the prophet was a specialist in judgment, like Jonah, the reluctant missionary who was disappointed when the Ninevites repented and God turned from wreaking devastation, having compassion on the people and even on the animals. But the prophets were gripped by the love of God. Indeed the heart of their message was the concern for the breach of covenant love towards God. At the same time they were aware not only in their heads but in their hearts that God would not stop loving his even adulterous people. Hosea is the prophet who, even more than the others, communicated that God could not give them up, would keep on loving even when they turned their love towards idols. "How can I give you up, Ephraim? How can I hand you over, Israel? How can I make you like Zeboiim? My heart is changed within me; all my compassion is aroused" (Hos. 11:8).

Hosea's own marriage to Gomer proved to be the incarnational medium through which he was able to give and receive a message about

---

9. Heschel, *The Prophets,* I, p. 210.

covenant love. His marriage was like looking through a pair of binoculars from both ends, seeing on one hand a larger-than-life image and on the other a smaller. From the perspective of his love for his wife he caught a glimpse of the large heart of God and also from the perspective of the unconditional love of God he looked into his own heart, sorrowing over an impossible marriage. His wife Gomer became a prostitute. God had called him a second time to love her (3:1). So he bought her back from the slave market and wooed her back, just as God was wooing back his adulterous nation. Israel had abandoned the worship of Yahweh and worshiped the gods of the land with temple prostitution (4:14) and intoxication. Once again, God is not the detached ruler but, as Heschel says, God is "the sensitive Consort to Whom deception comes and Who nevertheless goes on pleading for loyalty, uttering a longing for a reunion, a passionate desire for reconciliation."[10] God is tender as a mother (1:6-8; 2:3, 6, 21, 25; 11:1), as tender as a husband wooing his beloved and winning a new betrothal with a dowry, righteousness, justice, kindness, and mercy.

This is what it means to know God. The frequently used term *daath elohim,* usually translated "the knowledge of God," means much more than intellectual knowledge. It involves engagement, attachment, affection, feeling, soul connection — pathos.[11] For Hosea knowing God means betrothal and marriage and, when there is apostasy and betrayal, it means courting, betrothal, and the renewal of the marriage covenant. The word used for this covenant love, the love that is the glue of the covenant, is *hesed.* "For I desire mercy [*hesed*], not sacrifice, and acknowledgment of God rather than burnt offerings" (6:6).

In the same way, under the New Covenant, we are being infused by God with a passionate love for the people of God. We go on continuously and plurally being filled with the Holy Spirit (Eph. 5:18). The effect of this inundation with God is not only our capacity to sing spiritual songs and hymns but also our love for the church (Eph. 5:23). The church is not the corpse of Christ or a body of Christians. It is the body of Christ. It is impossible to be in Christ without being in his body, with whom Christ the Head is intimately joined. Thus not only are individual Christians impossible but it is impossible to be in Christ with-

10. Heschel, *The Prophets,* I, p. 48.
11. Heschel, *The Prophets,* I, p. 57.

out caring for Christ's body, caring about its disobedience and caring for its growing into the maturity of the manhood of Jesus. Love for the people of God leads us to go to our neighbor and say, "Your house is on fire." Prophetic spirituality is passion for justice and love for the people of God.

Empowered by the Praying Imagination

Much of the prophetic literature is a record of how the world looks to a person in the Spirit. It is as though the veil that keeps us from seeing things as they really are is drawn back — the principalities and powers at work, the real meaning of sin, and the awesome sovereignty of God. It is an exposé. Heschel says, "The prophets were the first men in history to regard a nation's reliance upon force as evil" (Hos. 8:14; 10:13; 8:9-10; 5:13).[12] "'Not by might nor by power, but by my Spirit,' says the LORD Almighty" (Zech. 4:6). The prophets saw that the seeming enemies of God's people were sometimes God's cleansing agents. Assyria is the rod of God's anger (Isa. 10:5). The king of Babylon is "my servant" (Jer. 25:9). In a sense they were exegetes of the contemporary situation, seeing into it and not merely looking at it. They foretold. But mainly they told forth. To do this the prophets used imagination. What we need to worship God, to see the world rightly and to live righteously in the church and world, is not mere information but the provisioning of our imaginations. And it is this that the prophets did, especially Ezekiel.

Ezekiel had an important reason to frame his message in allegories, metaphors, and parables. His message was one of judgment and hope for Jerusalem, the church of his day. It would be hard to hear. The people who remained in Jerusalem after the first deportation to Babylon (which took Ezekiel and his wife to Babylon in 597 B.C.) were given to idolatrous and perverted imaginations (the subject of chapter 8). The people were like an unfaithful spouse (16). The leaders no longer led but were shepherds who fed themselves from the sheep (34). The nation was like a valley of dry bones (37). To communicate the tragedy of this as well as the hope, Ezekiel becomes an incarnated audiovisual aid when he lies on his side for a year outside his house for part of each day, makes

12. Heschel, *The Prophets*, I, p. 166.

models of Jerusalem with siege works, and foregoes mourning the death of his wife (24:15-27).[13]

The underlying pathos for Ezekiel was for the glory of God. "That you may know," says God over and again, "that I am the LORD" (37:6, 13). Ezekiel was far away from home, longing for his true homeland and distressed at the tawdriness of the community that presumably bears God's glory on earth. He wondered what would come of it all. The word they needed — and we need — is not a word but a vision of the magnificence of God who is determined to glorify himself and be known. The primary motive for mission and ministry is not the need of the world but the glory of God.

While Ezekiel's experience is not transferable to other human beings, its universal elements can still awaken our faith, not just the concept of God's glory but rather a whole panoply of inspired word pictures. Bathed in the presence of God through prayer, our imaginations may thus provision our wills to persevere, the very thing that a prophetic spirituality encourages.

Focused on the End

What our imagination allows us to do is to complete the story. We have a profound need to see the conclusion of it all, especially what will come of God's people. It is impossible for God to tell us the future. So he shows us. And he does so through empowering pictures that so capture our spiritual persons that we ourselves are able to live the metaphor in the here and now. In the famous vision of the dry bones coming to life (Ezek. 37), God is helping us envision not only the restoration of Israel but also to see the formation of the spiritual Israel in Christ. In the last section of Ezekiel (40–48) we are invited to experience pure contemplation — attending to God himself, not just the "things" of God. The vision of the restored temple, the ideal Jerusalem, and the renewed creation takes us beyond "the things of God" to God himself. The vision of the last book of the Bible (the Revelation) has the same empowering ef-

---

13. The first half of the book, written before Jerusalem fell, can be summarized by the phrase "God will destroy," the second half of the book by the phrase "God will rebuild."

fect on our faith. Our ultimate destiny is a completely renewed creation, with the people of God and the presence of God everywhere. Ezekiel is a missionary artist, a missionary poet. It may seem pointless to throw a poem to a drowning person, but if that person is dying in meaninglessness, addicted to the present moment because there seems to be no future and inventing meaning like a magician, then a poem might just be the best thing to throw at him. This is what Ezekiel and the other prophets do. Lesslie Newbigin once said that our generation is without any worthwhile end to which the travail of history might lead. The prophets show us that there is a worthwhile end.

The Pathos

Analyzing the prophetic experience with great depth, Heschel notes that the pathos or passion of the prophets was a real kinship between God and God's people, an interweaving of concern expressed in judgment, disappointment, mercy, and sometimes even indignation. "The basic features of pathos and the primary content of the prophet's consciousness is a divine attentiveness and concern. . . . The prophet cares for God's care."[14] This is precisely so because God is not impersonal or abstract but profoundly personal, the most personal being in the universe. Heschel compares the image of justice, a blindfolded virgin impartially administering justice, to the passionate way that God make things right and maintains the covenant.[15] Heschel says, "Divine ethos does not operate without pathos. . . . God is all-personal, all subject. His ethos and pathos are one."[16] And those, like the prophets, who come into personal relationship with God are gripped with God's person and obtain an emotional solidarity with God. So the task of the prophet was not merely to deliver information but to deliver the pathos or feeling that God has about the situation. This is revelation strained through personality — for the prophets were not mere microphones. These are words fired with sympathy, sympathy with God and sympathy with humankind.

14. Heschel, *The Prophets,* II, pp. 263-64.
15. Heschel, *The Prophets,* I, p. 215.
16. Heschel, *The Prophets,* I, p. 218.

What does this means for those today who have joined the prophethood of all believers through faith in Jesus? Simply this: each of us is equipped to bear God's word to others not merely as "words," information that can be digitalized and processed, or reduced to an impersonal message delivered by billboards, floppy disks, CD's, and printed pages. Much more, we are equipped to deliver God's word with sympathy. More than that, in the extraordinary privilege of the new covenant by which, as Jeremiah prophesied, "we all know the Lord, from the least to the greatest" (Jer. 31:34), we ourselves are being moved by God, gaining an emotional solidarity with God, having a heart increasingly "after God's own heart." It remains to consider how we gain a heart like God's.

Prophetic Spirituality

How does this come about? Simply through the Spirit and the Word. We are living in the "last days" (Acts 2:17) when the Spirit has been poured out universally on the whole people of God, not merely the leaders or selected "prophets" as under the Old Covenant. This means that each of us is being inundated with at least a fraction of the heart of God, like one color of the spectrum as it passes through the cloudy atmosphere. None of us can contain the fullness of God, though together we may show the full white light of Christ to the world, as though the spectrum were recomposed into white light through the togetherness of all the believers. Further, our hearts are shaped by the Word of God. Jesus, quoting Deuteronomy 8:3, said that "Man does not live by bread alone but by every word that proceeds from the mouth of God." As we live into the story of God's Word, we are being shaped and sensitized, plowed up and resown with the very heart of God.

This is not merely allowing our minds to gain intellectual information about God and God's purpose, as though we could "save" this information for future use the way a computer saves data. To live by the word that comes from the mouth of God is to feed on God's self-revelation, to be in a loving, receptive, and responsive relationship with the one who speaks forth himself through speech.[17] We do this as we daily read Scrip-

17. M. Robert Mulholland, *Shaped by the Word: The Power of Scripture in Spiritual Formation* (Nashville: The Upper Room, 1985), p. 90.

ture and take it into our hearts, allowing the whole story to shape our story, meditating on the word until it is inwardly digested and becomes our prayer. The result of this ingestion of Word and Spirit is that our hearts are given a passion. But it is a passion that is unique to each person. As Frederick Buechner said above, each of us is called to the place in the world and the church where our own deep gladness (and we could add, our own deep concern) and the world's deep need meet. Discerning this passion is one of the most important tasks in our lives since it is in reality the discernment of our personal vocation and mission.

Richard Bolles says that in general terms each of us has three missions: (1) to stand hour by hour in the conscious presence of God, the one from whom your mission is derived; (2) to do what you can, moment by moment, day by day, step by step, to make this world a better place, following the leading of God's Spirit within you and around you; (3) to exercise your talent which you particularly came to earth to use — your greatest gift which you most delight to use, in places and settings that God has caused to appeal to you the most, for those purposes that God most needs to have done in the world.[18] Each of us has a personal mission that derives from God's passion. It remains consistent through our lifetime, though it may be expressed in various ways and generally becomes increasingly present to us as we walk with God in the prophets' company. This passion may be clouded or even misdirected through personal sin, the sins of others against us, dysfunctionalities in our personality, and the resistance of fallen structures.

We can discover this by asking ourselves several questions: Where do I have a burden? (Not, Where is the greatest need?) What are the strengths, gifts, and talents God has given me? Where do I see the brokenness of the world? What are the desires of my heart? It is impossible to be in relationship with the living God and to be completely uncaring, to have no passion, no emotional solidarity with God, and no heart after God's heart.

18. Richard N. Bolles, *How to Find Your Mission in Life* (Berkeley: Ten Speed Press, 1991), pp. 13-14.

6

The Way of Wisdom

R. PAUL STEVENS

As we make our way through the Old Testament, we encounter prophecy that strikes with the incisiveness of a two-edged sword. But then, with the wisdom literature, we are invited to stop and look right at what is going on under our noses (in the Proverbs), to consider the mystery of God's ways when life doesn't make sense (in Job), to overhear with a God-perspective the tender and sensuous dialogue of a lover and his beloved in the intimacy of a passionate marriage (in Song of Songs), and to ask hard questions about what it all means (in Ecclesiastes). The wisdom books of the Old Testament include Proverbs, Job, the Song of Songs, Ecclesiastes, and some psalms.[1] This literature has a distinctive contribution to make to our spiritual journey. If the prophets deliver cannonballs of "Thus says the Lord," the wisdom books are more subtle, even subversive. They invite us to observe (in the Proverbs), to have faith that rebels (in Job), to address the meaning of our own yearning for intimacy (in the Song of Songs), and to ask probing

---

1. The part of the Hebrew Bible known as the Writings *(Kethubim)* includes the prophecy of Daniel, the historical books of Chronicles, Ezra, and Nehemiah, the poetry of Job, Psalms, and Proverbs, and the so-called "Five Scrolls" — the Song of Solomon, Ruth, Lamentations, Ecclesiastes, and Esther, these five being read at public festivals. The Song of Songs (or Solomon) was read at Passover, Lamentations at the anniversary of the destruction of the temple, Ecclesiastes at the Feast of Tabernacles, and Esther at the Feast of Purim recalling the deliverance of the Jews from genocide.

questions about the enigmas of life and the strange ways of God (in Ecclesiastes).[2] Wisdom is simply righteous living wrung out of life, the way we wring out a wet towel by squeezing it. What has this to do with spirituality? It is in the very thick of everyday life that God meets us and shapes our souls. So wisdom does not deal with philosophical abstractions. Wisdom invites us to think, to observe, and to question.

These books can be compared with houses. Proverbs is a seven-pillared house of wisdom (or as Derek Kidner suggests, the well-stocked home of the accomplished wife in Proverbs 31).[3] Job gives us a different picture. His home is devastated by storm and disease, flattened to the ground by a wind that kills all inside except Job who sits in the ashes scraping the puss off his sores and asking "Why?" The Song of Songs suggests a cedar country cottage. This book tells the story of a young maiden in love with a country shepherd. And the most desired place of their love union is her mother's simple house in a village away from the gaudy splendor of Solomon's court. Ecclesiastes, struggling with the emptiness of the human pursuit "under the sun," could be compared with a great mansion that is gripped in slow decay as window sashes and roofs leak, doors creak, and vines overgrow this once stately but now doomed edifice, a silent sentinel to the meaninglessness of human enterprise.

And finally Psalm 49, a wisdom psalm, can be compared with a tomb. Echoing the sentiment of Ecclesiastes, the psalmist says, "For all can see that wise men die; the foolish and the senseless alike perish and leave their wealth to others. Their tombs remain their houses forever. . . . But God will redeem my life from the grave; he will surely take me to himself" (Ps. 49:11, 15). "But God!" Karl Barth once said that this last "But" and the many other reversals in Scripture crystallize all the wisdom in the Bible and signal the good news of God, something that is just below the surface in all of the wisdom books.[4]

---

2. The wisdom psalms are not considered in this chapter.

3. Derek Kidner, *The Wisdom of Proverbs, Job & Ecclesiastes* (Downers Grove, Ill.: InterVarsity Press, 1985), p. 116.

4. G. S. Henry, "Ecclesiastes," in F. Davidson, A. M. Stibbs, and E. F. Kevan, eds., *The New Bible Commentary* (London: Inter-Varsity Fellowship, 1961), p. 545.

Observing the Spirituality of the Proverbs

It is tempting to entitle this section "The Spirituality of Solomon," to whom the collection is attributed (1:1). And there is little doubt that a substantial core of this fascinating book owes its origin to King Solomon.[5] At the zenith of his monarchy Solomon did embody wisdom, though as we shall see in the Song of Solomon, for all his wisdom he had a fatal flaw, a sexual Achilles' heel. Solomon did love the Lord (1 Kings 3:3), the essential root and source of wisdom. The "fear of the Lord is the beginning of wisdom" is a key theme of the Proverbs (1:7; 9:10), and wisdom literature generally. Such "fear" is a respectful affection for God that is rational, emotional, and practical. So wisdom involves the whole person. And Solomon prayed for that (1 Kings 3:9, 12), sought it from God (1 Kings 4:29), and expressed it in wise administration and diplomacy (1 Kings 3:16-28; 5:12). Solomon composed proverbs, songs, and hard sayings, often derived from his careful observation of nature (1 Kings 4:32; 10:1; 4:33).

In Hebrew a proverb literally means something compared, a simile. In Greek the word is translated "parable" and it seems that Jesus loved this book and adopted its method of teaching.[6] But the meaning of the word "proverb" was extended to include short, wise, pithy, and insightful sayings that invite reflection, that insinuate themselves into mind and heart and evoke faith in God that issues in living the way of holiness — for that is what the fear of the Lord is all about. The point of a proverb, as Jesus said about his own use of parables, is not to ram revelation down the throats of the readers and listeners, but to throw down an image and invite the onlookers to reflect. Those with ears to hear will hear. As Derek Kidner says, "we learn our lessons from them better by a flash of wit than by a roll of sermonic thunder."[7] A proverb is subversive. It sneaks into our

---

5. Other stated authors in the book are "The Wise," "Hezekiah's men," "Agur the son of Jakeh," and "The Mother of King Lemuel."

6. Jones and Walls note the echoes of Proverbs in the Gospels: those who seek the chief seats (Prov. 25:6-7), the parable of the wise and foolish men and their homes (Prov. 14:11), the rich fool (Prov. 27:1), and Jesus' statement that wisdom is justified of her children (Matt. 11:19). W. A. Rees Jones and Andrew F. Walls, "The Proverbs," in F. Davidson, A. M. Stibbs, and E. F. Kevan, eds., *The New Bible Commentary* (London: Inter-Varsity Fellowship, 1961), p. 517.

7. Kidner, *Wisdom*, p. 31.

lives unobtrusively, wearing jeans and a T-shirt, speaking the language of family, work, and marketplace. So what has this to do with spirituality?

Subversive Spirituality

First, *God speaks in and through everyday life.* The single sayings, clusters, and occasional extended paragraphs of Proverbs invite observations on almost every aspect of life. Look at what happens to the "simple" person who is open to every influence (1:22). Observe how the way of the adulteress leads right to the grave (2:16-19; 6:24-29; 7). Look at what people do with their money (11:24-25). Observe the effect of various table manners (23:6-8). Consider what happens when people really get into their work (13:4), and when they don't, like the sluggard (13:4). See how friendship thrives through praise and correction (27:1-21). Take a look at how business is done badly with bribes and swindling, and wisely, as money and wealth grow little by little (13:11). Consider that a good wife is a gift of God (19:14) and why you should not let your sexuality, like a precious spring of water, overflow in the streets (5:15-19). See how the wealthy think that their assets are a fortified city (10:15) but then consider how they only imagine that they are insurmountable (18:11). Look at what happens when parents do not "parent" and children grow up without discipline (30:17) — and when they do (17:6; 22:6). Listen to how people talk, what effect their words have (12:18), words that have the power of life and death (18:21). Consider what gossip does to relationships (11:13; 26:22). And finally consider the honor and dignity of a woman who is praised by husband and children (31).[8] God is not found at the periphery of our lives but in the living center.

Second, *wisdom spirituality insists that true piety cannot be enclosed in church services, evangelism, and prayer meetings.* In considering the well-worn proverb, "The fruit of the righteous is a tree of life, and he who wins souls is wise" (11:30), one must remember that "soul" is the whole hungry and expressive person, not the sacred center. So the verse means "the wise man by his example gains the lives of other men, so that

---

8. 30:10-31 is in the form of an acrostic with each verse beginning with one of the letters of the Hebrew alphabet. Taken alongside the adulteress and prostitute, this beautiful poem and the "teaching of the mother" exalt the dignity of womanhood.

his righteousness is a tree of life to others as well as to himself."[9] In Proverbs wisdom does not call out from the pulpit, the synagogue, the temple, the sanctuary, the theological college, or the retreat center. Wisdom calls out from the streets and public squares (1:20), from homes and places of business, palaces of kings and hovels of the poor, out in the fields and in the bustling marketplace. Life is a spiritual discipline.

Third, *the source and center of in-this-life spirituality is "the fear of the Lord"* (1:7; 9:10). In fact this concept meets us in all of the wisdom books: Proverbs 1:7; 9:10; Job 28:28; Psalm 111:10; Ecclesiastes 12:13; and possibly as an allusion in Song of Songs 8:6 — "love is as strong as death," the assumed context in which pure human love is expounded. The fear of the Lord is essentially the same as the knowledge of God — it is the kind of relationship we are meant to have with God and therefore the way we know God in the sense of intercourse and communion (Prov. 1:29). Further, "fear" is not a numinous dread but reverent awe. It is, at the same time, loaded with affection and comes close to being simply "love of God." It is profoundly moral, affecting every aspect of life individually and corporately. Such fear, says James Houston, "brings blessing to every sphere of life."[10]

To say, as Proverbs does, "the fear of the Lord is the beginning of wisdom" implies "both starting point and essence."[11] Without right relationship to God we cannot rightly relate to life, to neighbors, to family, to the community, to strangers, and to the earth. So, in Proverbs, wisdom requires diligent search (2:1-5). The fear of the Lord enables us to shun evil (3:7). More specifically Solomon says, "Through love and faithfulness [in Hebrew, covenant love and faithfulness] sin is atoned for; through the fear of the Lord a man avoids evil" (16:6; cf. 10:12). Therefore we are invited to bind around our necks covenant love and faithfulness (3:3-4). Wisdom, personified in Proverbs 8, is to be sought out, cherished as a dear friend (7:4), loved (4:6), and embraced as a spouse (4:8). But humility is needed. Wisdom is not the result of human effort but given by God (2:6), and God keeps in his will those who receive it (2:7-9). As Kidner notes, some of this language was destined to

---

9. Jones and Walls, "The Proverbs," pp. 528-29.

10. James Houston, *I Believe in the Creator* (Grand Rapids: Eerdmans, 1980), p. 189.

11. W. J. Cameron, "The Song of Solomon," in F. Davidson, A. M. Stibbs, and E. F. Kevan, eds., *The New Bible Commentary* (London: Inter-Varsity Fellowship, 1961), p. 518.

prepare the way for the New Testament picture of Christ as the "wisdom of God" (1 Cor. 1:24).[12]

But if Proverbs seems to present life in an overly simplistic way — if you follow the Lord you will prosper and thrive — the next book, Job, will say, "Yes — but!" This "but" also signals a reversal that brings a surprising and transforming perspective to spirituality.

Resistance — The Spirituality of Job

The book of Job starts with a duel between God and Satan over a fundamental question about spirituality. Satan is convinced that Job, who is obviously a righteous man, maintains his integrity only because God has profoundly blessed him with family, houses, cattle, public esteem, and friends. Take these away, Satan argues, and Job will curse God (1:11).

Dueling with God

God agrees to a test, really a duel, and thence this wonderful man, arguably a patriarch for the Gentiles long before there was law and temple, lost everything but his life. His three friends, Eliphaz, Bildad, and Zophar, came to comfort him in his distress. Most of the book is the monologue (so Job thought) between Job and God, and a dialogue between Job and his friends. The friends are impeccably orthodox; their speeches could be published in a respectable religious journal. They hammer away at one fundamental belief, namely that Job is suffering because he is a sinner and what he needs to do is to repent. Job knows he is a sinner (7:20). But he also knows that his suffering does not bear a cause-effect relationship with his sin. Deep inside he is convinced he is righteous (27:5-6) and approved by God — grasping the wonderful good news of justification by faith through grace long before Christ came. So he confronts God in prayer, charging God with using him for target practice (6:4; 7:20) and demanding that God "show up." In the process he stumbles on three gospel truths. First, if God were human he could have a day in court and get his case settled with God (9:32-33), an-

12. Kidner, *Wisdom*, p. 23.

ticipating the coming of the God-man. Second, Job has a witness, an advocate and intercessor in heaven pleading his case (16:19-20). Third, most breathtaking of all, he has a kinsman, a *goel* like Boaz was to Ruth, a living Redeemer, who will liberate him (19:23).

Meanwhile the God-talking friends hit Job when he is down, pounding away in judgment, joined in the end by the young man Elihu. Then God speaks in a storm (vv. 38-41). And instead of answering Job's questions, God asks a thousand questions of his own. And confronted with this awesome God, Job repents — not of the puny sins his friends pestered him with but of having too small a God.

Job never stops praying, seeking God, pleading with God, complaining to God, even being angry with God. More than anything he wants the fellowship of God, the presence of God (23:3; 29:4). And what he gets in the end is God. The deepest answer to his questions about the meaning of his life is simply God. So what does the book of Job have to do with the spiritual journey?

Journeying with Job

First, *faith is not for anything.* It is not for wealth and health, for personal happiness or personal fulfillment. Faith is for God. And the only evidence of faith is faith. That of course is the fundamental issue over which God and Satan engage in their duel. "Does Job fear God for nothing?" (1:9). At one point Job shouts, "Though he slay me, yet will I hope in him" (13:15), effectively demonstrating that his faith in God was not *for* anything but God (in spite of Satan's accusations).

Second, *life is a spiritual discipline.* The best context to grow in faith is through the warp and woof of everyday living. Job confronts God with the hard questions of his life, and this becomes the medium of real spiritual growth and a transforming encounter with God. Job brings to God his discouragement (3:3), his revulsion of food (6:7), the loss of real friendship (6:14), his experience of futility (7:3), his sleepless nights (7:4), the unjust accusations of his friends (13:4), the devastation of his household (16:7), the shattering of his plans and the desires of his heart (17:11), his physical reduction to "skin and bones" (19:20), and even the plight of the poor, the marginalized, and the oppressed (24). All this gets poured out to God. And through this Job comes to know God (and to see his life) in a much deeper way. Life becomes transparent, a lens through which he can look at God.

Third, *persistence in prayer is worthwhile.* Sometimes the phrase "the patience of Job" is bandied about as though it were Scripture. It isn't. What Scripture commends is not Job's patience but his perseverance. "You have heard of Job's perseverance and have seen what the Lord finally brought about" (James 5:11). Job is not compliant before his life situation, lying down and "taking it." Nor is he compliant before God — simply going along with God while secretly nursing a bitter grudge against God for not giving him the desires of his heart. No, Job sticks with it, worries over it like a dog with a bone, can't get it out of his mind, pesters God to death until, as an act of real submission (in contrast to compliance), he repents (42:6) — the very thing his friends had been trying to induce in him. But if he had complied with the friends' pressure to repent, he could never have entered freely of his own will into a deeper love and worship of God.

At the end of the book God speaks to Eliphaz and his two friends and tells them that he is angry with them because "you have not spoken of me what is right, *as my servant Job has*" (42:7, emphasis mine). How can this be? Can Job, the blustering prayer warrior who tells God off really have correct theology while his orthodox friends are condemned? The secret is this: Job talked *to* God. The friends talked *about* God. Therefore Job was an orthodox believer and the friends were heretics.

Compared with Job's gut-wrenching God-shouts, the prayers of most Christians, especially those spoken in public before a congregational audience, are anemic and bland, more like pabulum or cold mashed potatoes than a rich steak and vegetable dish. Better to be angry with God than to give God the silent treatment. There are, after all, no bad prayers. What God wants more than anything is our fellowship, and he can have that only if we pray, pray anything, pray anytime, pray anyhow. The book of Job helps us in being honest with God. The next of the wisdom books helps us be honest with ourselves.

Longing — The Spirituality of the Song of Songs

I have graciously forgotten the name of the church leader who once said to me, "Only a person with a dirty mind could read this book as anything other than an allegory of Christ's love for the church." And therein is the problem of the book. It exposes not only what God thinks of our bodily life, but what *we* think of our sensuality and sexuality. This book is an erotic love-song. It is a series of poems loosely connected, sometimes in a descriptive sequence (the lover seeks and finds the beloved and they consummate their love), sometimes as a drama, and sometimes, it seems, as a dream sequence (when the beloved loses her lover and tries to find him at night). The live center of the book is the saying of the beloved, "Let my lover come into his garden and taste its choice fruits" and the lover says, "I have come into my garden, my sister, my bride" (4:16–5:1). Here one meets a double entendre. Some of the lovemaking takes place in a private garden. But there is a second meaning. "Garden" is a euphemism for the female genitalia and her sexual charm generally.[13] The word "come" denotes sexual penetration.[14]

Make no mistake, however: this song is not about promiscuous sex. The young Shulammite woman is a "garden locked up" (i.e., a virgin) and a "sealed spring" (4:12). Her encounter with her lover is not an illicit affair but erotic love in a true marriage. She is his bride (4:12; 5:1) and friend (5:16). Nor is this simple copulation, a "sex act." Before the consummation there is anticipation of union, a lost and found drama, and a final affirmation.[15] And the woman in this case takes as much initiative as the man, indeed more, as there is one whole section (5:2–8:4) devoted primarily to her entreaty to her lover.[16] Here is no naïve maiden being seduced by an aggressive male but a fully mutual erotic love that will consummate a marriage. Commitment and covenant undergird the entire narrative. The Song is really an extended exposition of the first hymn of praise by a human being: Adam's "at last" in Genesis 2:23 when he discovers a partner that is suitable for him and becomes "one flesh" with her. The sensuality expressed in this book "goes

---

13. Other double entendres include some of the fruits mentioned — "apples" (2:5) and "mandrakes" (7:13) commonly thought to be aphrodisiacs, the "feet" (5:3) and "hand" for the male copulative organ, the hand coming into the latch (5:4).

14. See Gen. 38:8, 16; Ezek. 23:44.

15. This structure is called chiastic as it forms a pattern leading up to and away from the climax.

16. Of the 111 lines in the Hebrew 80 are the words of the girl. As Lloyd Carr says, "this is her book." G. Lloyd Carr, *The Song of Solomon,* Tyndale Commentaries (Leicester, England: Inter-Varsity Press, 1984), p. 130.

far beyond what any allegory or typology requires, and makes it, in Fuerst's words, 'beyond the bounds of credibility' that the book was intended to be understood that way."[17] But just how can one interpret this book?

This Hard-to-Interpret Book

Not surprisingly, the main problem has been its explicit sexual imagery. Some rabbis said that the book should not be read by people under forty years of age! The act of sexual union, while nuanced and expressed in metaphors and images, is repeatedly presented. It is an unashamedly physical book. Both lover and beloved are described from head to foot, emphasizing mutual delight in shape, size, perfumes, clothing, jewelry. Not surprisingly, celibate monks and priests have protected themselves from its eroticism by treating it all as an allegory. Bernard of Clairvaux spent his whole life expounding the book as a "spiritual" love-song and, when he died, had only reached the end of chapter two, bequeathing to his disciples the completion of the task. In the Middle Ages, it was the most commonly expounded book.[18] There are literally hundreds of commentaries and thousands of sermons, all taking the approach that each and every image has a "spiritual" and mystical significance in our relationship with God and nothing to do with our sexuality.[19] For example, the exclamation in 8:1, "If only you were to me like a brother. . . . Then, if I found you outside I would kiss you. . . . I would lead you and bring you to my mother's house," is taken to mean that "they render Christ good service who introduce Him to their family circle and freely

17. Carr, *The Song*, p. 114.

18. Examples of allegorizing are found in W. J. Cameron, "The Song of Solomon," in F. Davidson, A. M. Stibbs, and E. F. Kevan, eds., *The New Bible Commentary*. For example, 7:10 reads, "Come, my lover, let us go to the countryside, let us spend the night in the villages." "The words of the request have been taken allegorically to suggest the desire of the Church to go forth into the highways and hedges in self-denying quest of the lost and in company with the Son of Man, who came to seek and to save the lost" (p. 554).

19. A common medieval interpretation identified the beloved with the Virgin Mary whom the true worshiper should worship, and the phrase "You are fair, my love; there is no flaw in you" (4:7) was used to support the doctrine of the Immaculate Conception of the Virgin Mary. Carr, *The Song*, p. 26.

acknowledge Him in home life."[20] The allegorical interpretation taken by devout Jews in the first century and Christians since the time of Origen does express some truths. But it does not render the plain sense of the text.[21] The book needs to be taken in its "natural" or "literal" sense as a "series of poems which speak clearly and explicitly of the feelings, desires, concerns, hopes and fears of two young lovers — without any need to allegorize to escape the clear erotic elements present in the text."[22] But who are these two probably ordinary young people? Or are there three?

While the Song is entitled "Solomon's Song of Songs" (1:1) with the name "Solomon" occurring occasionally in the text, and while sometimes the lover is addressed as "king," the name Solomon may be used as a symbol of the class of society for which "the desire is the same as possession" — they get what they want.[23] Or, as is more probable, this is not merely the love-song composed *by* Solomon as he acquires yet one more woman for his vast harem of 700 wives and 300 concubines (1 Kings 10:1-13), wives that tragically led his heart astray from undivided devotion to God (1 Kings 11). This is a love song *about* Solomon.[24] It is a story in which there are three main characters: Solomon, about to acquire another wife; the Shulammite woman, a swarthy but beautiful country woman; and the Shulammite's true betrothed shepherd lover with whom she longs to be married and consummate their relationship. This last approach, expounded brilliantly by Calvin Seerveld and others, seems mandated by three texts in particular. First, there is a refrain throughout the story: "Daughters of Jerusalem, I charge you . . . do not arouse or awaken love until it so desires" (2:7; 3:5; 8:4), words probably spoken to the other women in the harem, as Shul pleads not to be awakened sexually for someone she does not desire (i.e., Solomon).

---

20. Cameron, "The Song of Solomon," p. 554.

21. For an excellent summary of how this book has been interpreted see Carr, *The Song*, pp. 21-36.

22. Carr, *The Song*, p. 34.

23. See Carr, *The Song*, p. 20.

24. Solomon's name appears in 1:1, 5; 3:9, 11; 8:7, 12. Carr notes that a basic question that must be asked if one assumes there are only two characters in the Song — Solomon and the young woman — is "why someone as notoriously lascivious as Solomon should appear in an account of pure holy love, or even of pure sexual love between a man and a woman" (p. 109).

Second, the lover says, "Sixty queens there may be, and eighty concubines, and virgins without number, but my dove, my perfect one, is unique" (probably a comparison being made early in Solomon's reign before his harem had reached its full size). Third, at the end the beloved says, "Solomon had a vineyard. . . . But my own vineyard is mine to give" (8:12), an obvious comparison between the king who gets what he wants and the maiden who gives what she wishes to her true love.[25]

As Calvin Seerveld notes, "It is this note critical of Solomon for which the readers must be prepared if they would also understand what they read in *The Greatest Song*. . . . Old king Solomon was a lascivious old king."[26] So what does this book, a book that does not mention the name of God, have to do with God-honoring spirituality?

Sexual Spirituality

First, *true spirituality is embodied*. This book tests whether we have a biblical view of the human person, whether we regard our bodies and sexual longings as "lower" selves, "flesh," a hindrance to true spirituality. This lie has been promoted throughout the ages by supposedly "spiritual" people and is philosophically founded on Neoplatonism, the two-

---

25. Following Seerveld, Ewald, and others who take this interpretive approach, the book should be outlined as follows:

1:1–2:7	The maiden recalls her beloved in the palace where Solomon promises to adorn her with jewels.
2:8–3:5	The maiden recollects a visit her beloved once paid her and a dream that followed it.
3:6–4:7	The maiden is again visited and praised by Solomon.
4:8–5:1	Unmoved, the maiden remembers the words of her beloved and anticipates their marriage day.
5:2–6:3	The maiden relates a dream and describes her beloved.
6:4–7:9	The maiden receives a further visit from Solomon, who makes a fresh attempt to win her affection.
7:10–8:3	The maiden, maintaining her loyalty to her absent lover, longs for his society.
8:4-14	The maiden returns home with her beloved and desires faithfulness (Cameron, "The Song of Solomon," p. 547).

26. The translation of 8:12 is Seerveld's. Calvin Seeveld, *The Greatest Song: In Critique of Solomon* (Toronto: Pennyasheet Press, 1963/67), p. 63.

story — upper and lower (spiritual and material) — view of life that is deeply rooted in Christian piety throughout the ages. In contrast, biblically we do not *have* bodies; we *are* bodies. Touch the body and you have touched the person. Living Christianly means living bodily. The soul is not the vital person surrounded by a bodily shell so that the body, shucked on death like an ugly cocoon, will allow the immortal soul to survive and thrive. That's the Greek idea (and one that is profoundly present in Christian thinking). When the lover speaks of the "one whom my soul loves" (1:7), his whole person is loving a whole person. The soul is the hungry person, not the inner and sacred person.[27] That's why biblical saints dance, eat, have parties, and make love — all to the glory of God.[28]

Second, *the heart of true spirituality is love, but love cannot be forced, manipulated, or compelled. And the beloved cannot be possessed.* Solomon tries to *make* love. But love must be evoked or it will be simply lust. So argues Seerveld: the Song was given to "teach the sex-saturated populace who had forgotten the Way of the Lord the meaning of faithfulness again and to capture the hearts of frustrated men and women by the telling beauty, joy, and freshness of human love that honored the Law of the Lord."[29] Our own lust-saturated culture desperately needs the message of true love contained in the Song.

Third, *full sexual expression within the marriage covenant is a form of worship of God and mutual ministry between husband and wife.* In the New Testament the Lord's Supper is the ritual of the covenant for those who belong to Jesus Christ. God communicates a spiritual grace through a material reality. Sexual intercourse is the ritual of the marriage covenant. Just as the bread and wine offer us spiritual nourishment, so in marriage sexual intercourse is an extension of and deepen-

27. The soul involves the desire of a lover for the beloved (Gen. 34:2-4); of a man for his favorite food (Micah 7:1) or possession (Deut. 14:26) always involving choice and willing (Deut. 21:14; Jer. 34:16).

28. Carr notes that the Hebrew word for "love," *'hb*, is translated in the LXX by *agape*. "In summary, *agape*, at least in the Old Testament, is not limited to self-giving, non-sensual 'love.' It is a word filled with all the Hebrew concepts of passion, sexual attraction, friendship, obedience, loyalty, duty, and commitment to the other person. *Agape*-love is not just for bloodless 'saints'; it is the expression of our full humanity and wholeness." P. 63.

29. Seerveld, *The Greatest Song*, p. 76.

ing of the ministry to each other that was begun when the vows were made publicly.

Fourth, *whether single or married, our sexual longing is written into us as a code that we were never meant to be alone.* We were created male and female in the image of God (Gen. 1:27). We are built for community, and our spirituality is not a solitary search for God. The Roman Catholic author Richard Rohr, himself single, insightfully explains:

> God seemingly had to take all kinds of risks in order that we would not miss the one thing necessary: we are called and even driven out of ourselves by an almost insatiable appetite so that we would never presume that we were self-sufficient. It is so important that we know that we are incomplete, needy, and essentially social that God had to create a life-force within us that would not be silenced.[30]

Finally, *our sexual longing is an invitation to faith and hungering for God.* For good reason many ancient religions deified sexuality. There are in our sexual longing experiences that correspond to our search for God: abandon to another, playfulness, ecstasy, going beyond oneself, polarity (rather than merger), and the hunger for union. Alan Ecclestone notes that the sexual experience prompts between human beings "features that are characteristic of prayer; a noticing, a paying attention, a form of address, a yearning to communicate at ever deeper levels of being, an attempt to reach certain communion with the other."[31] To say that our spirituality has nothing to do with our sexuality is to deny that God intends us to become increasingly fully human. But, as we shall now see, sometimes that hunger takes the form of asking hard questions about the meaning of life.

Questioning — The Spirituality of Ecclesiastes

The enigmatic book of Ecclesiastes, admittedly a collection of fragments not unlike Pascal's *Pensees*, contains question after question. Un-

---

30. Richard Rohr, "An Appetite for Wholeness," *Sojourners,* November 1982, pp. 30-32.

31. R. Wild, *Frontiers of the Spirit: A Christian View of Spirituality* (Toronto: Anglican Books Centre, 1981), p. 23.

like the book of Job, these are directed not to God, though God is not absent from the book, but rather to himself, or perhaps to an inquiring secularist. It is often noted that Ecclesiastes and Job both correct the apparent overly simplistic approach of Proverbs that proposes that the righteous way works and leads to success. Not that these two books reject the way of wisdom. Indeed, as in Ecclesiastes 10:18-19, the Preacher seems to say the same thing: "If a man is lazy, the rafters sag; if his hands are idle, the house leaks." But, and the "but" is what the book is about, the person who toils asks, "For whom am I toiling?" (4:8) and may see all his efforts lost in a single stroke (5:14). From the opening salvo of "Everything is meaningless" (1:2) or a "wisp of smoke," to the final coda "Meaningless! Meaningless!" that completes this vivid description of the inevitable decay of the human creature (12:1-7), the book shows that secular utopianism does not take sufficient account of evil and death, a matter of some contemporary relevance. In the modern world the fig leaf has slipped from the genitals to the subject of death itself, as if death were a "sleeping dog one could pass by on tiptoe."[32]

Encountering God in Life's Hard Questions

There are two ways of interpreting this book. Either Qoheleth, in translation called the Preacher or Professor, here explores his *own* deep questions about the meaning of life, or, as is sometimes argued, the Preacher addresses the questions of others. In this latter case it is an apologetic written for the hearing of the secularist who thinks he can do well enough without faith in God.[33] Either way, as a person questioning, or

---

32. G. S. Hendry, "Ecclesiastes," in F. Davidson, A. M. Stibbs, and E. F. Kevan, eds., *The New Bible Commentary* (London: Inter-Varsity Fellowship, 1961), p. 543.

33. This latter view, taken by both Derek Kidner and G. S. Hendry, is suggested by the meaning of *Qoheleth,* "the Preacher" (Ecclesiastes is the Greek equivalent of this). The word is derived from *qahal,* the public assembly. This may suggest that this is the kind of wisdom delivered by the speaker to those in the outer court of the assembly as distinguished from the "secret wisdom, a wisdom that has been hidden and that God destined for our glory before time began" (1 Cor. 2:7). While the name of Solomon is associated with this book it appears that this is either the convention of using a famous name as a suggested author or, as Jacques Ellul suggests, as a critique of Solomon (along the lines of Song of Songs). "Qoheleth mentions Solomon mainly to challenge him. His awe-

as a piece of apologetics for the questioner, the book constitutes a penetrating observation of life, leaving hardly a stone unturned. He explores "wisdom," meaning not the wisdom of God but the wisdom of the world (1:12-18; 2:24–3:15; 7) and concludes that the attempt to conceive of an ordered system of reality will prove to be a puff of smoke. Then he turns to pleasure and culture (2:1-23). The paradox of pleasure is that "the more you hunt for it, the less of it you find."[34] One must face "the morning after" and the nausea of satiety. Or, continues the Preacher, consider work and industry (2:17-23). For all their late-night efforts people will leave the fruits of their work to others, who will probably be fools. And it won't stop with late nights at the office. "Even at night his mind does not rest" (2:23). And for what? The workaholic ultimately discovers the meaninglessness of living for work.

And the same goes for money. If you love it you never have enough (5:10), and the rich person cannot sleep at night for worry (5:12). Even secularized religion is, in the end, meaningless. For what secularized religion does is to try to *use* God. There are lots of words but they are empty, and the worship of such vacuous chatter in the house of God is "the sacrifice of fools" (5:1). And finally there is death, the unmentionable (9:1-10). "Whatever your hand finds to do, do it with all your might, for in the grave, where you are going, there is neither working nor planning nor knowledge nor wisdom" (9:10). And what can we say to that?

First, *we should not shrink from asking the hard questions about what it is all for.* Some surveys have indicated that well-scrubbed Christians find life as meaningless as well-wishing pagans. "Only one life, t'will soon be past. Only what's done for Christ will last." The presupposition implicit in that poem has driven more than one generation into seminary and professional ministry or sacrificial volunteer work in the church on the assumption that only religious work lasts and has mean-

---

inspiring reign? Vanity, mist, a chasing after wind. The wise king pursued wisdom, but even he was found wanting. When he fell into the female trap, he proved he had found nothing. This whole passage [7:26-28] represents what Solomon might have said if he had been truly wise. But precisely because he could not say these things, we say them in his place. This thought is at the bottom of Qoheleth's words." Jacques Ellul, *Reason for Being: A Meditation on Ecclesiastes,* trans. Joyce Main Hanks (Grand Rapids: Eerdmans, 1990), p. 202.

34. Derek Kidner, *A Time to Mourn, and a Time to Dance: Ecclesiastes and the Way of the World* (Leicester, U.K.: Inter-Varsity Press, 1976), p. 31.

ing. It would be better for all to ask the hard questions, to really get into them in sufficient depth. If they did, with Qoheleth, they might agree that it is good to get into life rather than out of it, "to eat your food with gladness, and drink your wine with a joyful heart," "to do [whatever your hand finds to do] with all your might" (9:7-10), to find "satisfaction in all [your] toil" (3:13), recognizing that the present is the only time at our disposal (11:7-8) and life is "the gift of God" (3:13). Life is short but "life is sweet" (11:7).

Second, *there is risk in every human enterprise and we should learn to live responsibly and humbly with uncertainty.* "Cast your bread on the waters" (11:1) is probably not about giving money to the church but living with uncalculating charity, much like the words of Jesus in Luke 16:9. It is an image derived from the sea-borne corn trade. To send grain across the Mediterranean involves risk; and someone unwilling to lose in a venture will never do anything, just as someone always looking at the sky for perfect weather will neither plant nor reap. So the course of wisdom is not to put all your eggs in one basket but to divide the risk (11:2, 6). But there is more.

Third, *the wisdom of life is to discern the time, the* kairos, *the decisive moment when chronological time is fraught with eternity and significance.* "There is a time for everything" (3:1) is not merely saying that there are ebbs and flows in the endless shifting tides of time but rather that God elects different seasons and times. Our spiritual work is to discern the movement of God and the opportunity given to us day by day (8:5-6). This means not living by the clock or calendar but by the heart, a matter raised by Jesus himself (Luke 12:56).

Fourth, (as with Proverbs, Job, and the Song) *life itself is an invitation to seek and find God, or more accurately to be sought and found.* Qoheleth puts it this way, "God has made everything beautiful in its time. He has set eternity in the hearts of men" (3:11). Derek Kidner says of this, "time and all things temporal will disappoint us, who have eternity in our hearts."[35] This last note is one of the pregnant hints in the book that points beyond a merely secular approach to life "under the sun." So work, pleasure, government, wisdom, marriage, money, and family are evangelists to lead us to the God and Father of Christ, who is also the God of Qoheleth.

---

35. Kidner, *A Time to Mourn*, p. 98.

Fifth, *it is through the fear of God that life is meaningful.* Where the Proverbs begin — "the fear of the Lord is the beginning of wisdom" — Ecclesiastes ends: "Fear God and keep his commandments, for this is the whole duty of man. For God will bring every deed into judgment" (12:13-14). For this reason, death is not the final answer — judgment is; meeting with God is; the final evaluation by the Creator is; God is.[36] This enables us to laugh at despair and cynicism, to rejoice in our finitude and creatureliness (8:14-17), and to stand in awe of God (5:7) whose ways are mysterious, as mysterious as the way a fetus is formed in the womb (11:5). There is mystery in God. If God could be fit into our puny human minds, or limited to our experience of him, or contained in our theological description of his ways, he would be too small a God to worship. While Ecclesiastes hints at the fall of man (Gen. 3:16) it hints of hope, a hope more fully expressed by Paul in Romans 8:18-25: "For the creation was subjected to frustration, not by its own choice, but by the will of the one who subjected it, in hope that the creation itself will be liberated from its bondage to decay and brought into the glorious freedom of the children of God."

The Way of Wisdom

So the spiritual posture that wisdom books propose is essentially contemplative. Not contemplative in the sense of being cloistered and detached, but reflective about the meaning of life as it relates to the fear of God, and attending to God himself. It has been suggested that the difference between meditation and contemplation is this: While meditation is the discipline of turning our attention from the things of the world to the things of God (God's glory, purpose, will, and creation), contemplation is turning our attention from the "things" of God to at-

36. In contrast to the Song of Songs, the name of God is everywhere in Ecclesiastes. It is God who lays a burden on men (1:13; 3:10); satisfaction is from the hand of God (2:24); God gives wisdom, knowledge, and happiness (2:25); it is the gift of God (3:13; 5:19); God brings judgment (3:17; 12:14); God tests people (3:18); God is in heaven (5:2); God gives life (5:18); God keeps us occupied with gladness of heart (5:20); God made mankind upright (7:29); God gives us the days of our lives (8:15); who we are and what we do are in God's hands (9:1); God favors what we do (9:7); God is the maker of all things (11:5), the Creator (12:1); the spirit of man returns to God who made it (12:7).

tend to God himself. This contemplative posture, however, does not start with turning away from the world but rather looking under our own noses, into our own pocketbooks, brooding at the end of a work-day, speaking a word of love into the eyes of our spouse, and even in the darkest moments of misunderstanding and emotional or physical pain, refusing to give up the righteousness that we know we have only because we have been loved by and approved by the living God. So the fear of God — again in the sense of reverent and affectionate relationship — is not only the beginning of living wisely, it is the end.

Part Three

New Testament Spirituality

7

Partners in Fellowship

MICHAEL GREEN

If ever a word has been devalued, this is it. "The fellowship hour" after church turns out to be ten minutes worth of watery coffee which most of the congregation have skillfully evaded. "Where do you fellowship?" means "Where do you go for an occasional hour to hear the choir sing and the minister preach?" It all tends to be very superficial. We in the West know very little of sharing our lives in deep and costly fellowship. Our consumerism infects our religion. We even pick and choose our place of worship: there is often no lasting commitment to it. We know little of having our hearts deeply knit to others, not only because of our hedonism but also because of our independence. This determination to paddle our own canoe lies behind our entrepreneurial attitude to business and our take-it-or-leave-it attitude to the church. If we have a serious disagreement with the leadership, in England we opt out: in North America we go and found our own church. Consequently we know little of sharing the joys and sorrows, the strains and triumphs of our fellow Christians. We tend to live in our little box of a house, keeping ourselves pretty much to ourselves, watching our James Dobson tapes about the development of the nuclear family, and giving little consideration to the quality of life that can be found in the family of God.

It was not always thus in the Christian church, nor is it still in many parts of the Two-Thirds World, particularly in the great continent of Africa where they would never dream of putting their old folks in an

Old People's Home, or their orphaned or illegitimate children in a Children's Home.

Imagine the scene at the very start of the Christian movement. Here are twelve men in an upstairs room, celebrating the strangest of Passover meals: the lamb is not on the dish but at the head of the table! The meal, though mysterious, sad, and very special, marks the climax of three years' shared life on the road, through the countryside, in the boat. Years when they had laughed and cried, prayed and toiled together. That was Christian fellowship — so deep, so committed, that when one of them left it they forever remembered with ignominy the name of Judas.

Or come with me to one of the homes in Jerusalem in A.D. 33. It was a hotbed of love and sacrifice, of sharing and thoughtfulness. The nearest I have seen to the teaching and fellowship, the breaking of bread and prayers that marked these first Christians was a cell of the Christian counterculture in Toronto in the sixties, where nobody had any personal possessions, and love simply overflowed. Two people broke that Jerusalem fellowship in a surreptitious way. It would not have been noticed in today's church. Nobody would even have gone round to visit the two people in question. But they presented such a contrast to the quality of fellowship in that earliest church that the whole world now knows the shame of Ananias and Sapphira.

Or let us join a group sitting relaxed under a tree in the midday sun of Miletus, on the coast of Turkey. A weatherbeaten, hook-nosed, dark-eyed Jew with a wonderful smile and large, workworn hands is deep in conversation with a number of men who look at him with a mixture of awe and deepest admiration. "I have been with you three years," he says. "These hands have ministered to my needs and to those who were with me." And he commissions them to care for the flock of God over which the Holy Spirit had made them overseers. That is Christian fellowship.

Or let us share in the hospitality of a large country house at Colossae, in the glen of the Lycus valley. An aristocratic lady and her sunburned, distinguished-looking husband are entertaining a crowd of believers, many of them from their estate, in their roomy farmhouse. There has been wine by the fountain in the courtyard, dinner in one of the rooms overlooking it, and then they turn to welcome the guest of honor for the evening, Tychicus, who comes with news and letters from their dear imprisoned friend, Paul. He brings with him one of the slaves that all great estates had in those days, Onesimus. This man had robbed his master, run away, and landed up in prison with St. Paul, who led him to Christ and then sent him back to his old master in the company of Tychicus and a cover letter, the Epistle to Philemon. This was a tremendous risk to take. Torture and death awaited a runaway slave, if caught. But Onesimus is welcomed back with a hug by Philemon, his master. He had left in darkness and theft. He returns as a beloved brother in Christ. Only the Jesus fellowship made something like that possible. There was nothing to rival it anywhere in antiquity.

Of course, there were various different expressions of fellowship in the ancient world. Athens in the fifth century B.C. had almost invented it, with its *polis* and its democracy. But disenchantment set in, as it did with Jewish institutions. The ordinary people were excluded from meaningful relationships and from any exercise of real power. Increasingly, therefore, if you were a Jew in the ancient world, you resorted to one of the *haburoth,* the brotherhoods where you could enjoy some togetherness. If you were a Gentile, you would turn to one of the trade guilds or partnerships to prepare your funeral expenses: both were commonplace. Or you might turn to one of the mystery religions in which you tried to make some sense of your existence through participation in secret rituals of death and rebirth.

In one sense, then, Christian communities would cause no surprise. They were part of a growing movement towards voluntary associations in the ancient world. Often these unofficial associations were called *koinoniai,* fellowships, and the Romans were tolerant of them. But actually there was a qualitative difference in the fellowship of the Christians. Here were associations in which aristocrats and slaves, Roman citizens and provincials, Jews and Gentiles, rich and poor, men and women mixed without distinction and on equal terms. Here were societies that possessed a quality of care and love that amazed and attracted those who saw it. That is why, among other reasons, we find not only the New Testament writers but Ignatius, Clement, and Tertullian in the second and third centuries laying such store by unity. It was a harmony that demonstrated something of the unity-in-diversity of the God they worshiped. It was only a church that was manifestly united, where each member was free to share as the Holy Spirit moved him or her, that could convince the visiting observer that God was among them. There is, in fact, no doubt that many were convinced in this way. Tertullian, for example, notes the affection and purity that marked these Christian fel-

lowship groups, fittingly called "brethren" because of their common relationship to the heavenly Father.[1] Worship, fellowship, and feasting are
all carried out under the Father's eye. The lowly, the needy, the sick are
shown particular consideration. "One in mind and soul, we do not hesi-
tate to share our earthly goods with one another. All things are common
among us except our wives" — the very area, Tertullian unkindly
pointed out, where pagans were most willing to share. There was a great
deal of love flowing in these Christian meetings, and it was sustained by
"the sacred words with which we nourish faith, animate hope, make
confidence assured, confirm good habits, and administer rebukes and
censures."[2]

What was the secret of this remarkable fellowship? There are a
number of New Testament words that give us some insight into it, particularly *agape* and *philadelphia* (love and care for the brotherhood); but
perhaps the most significant word is *koinonia*, fellowship.[3]

Koinonia, fellowship, basically means "joint participation in," and
is not inherently a religious word. Like most important New Testament
words it is scandalously and intentionally secular. So you get it used of
being partners in business (Luke 5:10), or sharing in an enterprise (Phil.
4:15), and Paul uses it of his fellow workers (2 Cor. 8:23). But, with explosive force, the first and main meaning of fellowship erupts from the
pages of the New Testament.

Sharing in God

This is expressed in a number of ways in verses like Romans 15:27; 1 Corinthians 1:9; 2 Corinthians 13:13; Philippians 2:1; and 1 John 1:3. The
most breathtaking example in the New Testament is 2 Peter 1:4, where
the recipients are saluted as being *koinonoi*, participants, in the very nature of God himself!

1. Tertullian, *Apology*, 39.
2. Tertullian, *Apology*, 39.
3. Among the more useful studies of Christian fellowship are: A. R. George, *Communion with God in the New Testament* (London: Epworth, 1953); David Prior, *The Church
in the Home* (London: Marshall, Morgan & Scott, 1983); Edwin Judge, *The Social Pattern
of the Christian Groups in the First Century* (London: Inter-Varsity Press, 1960); Robert
Banks, *Paul's Idea of Community* (London: Paternoster, 1980).

This fellowship with Jesus and his heavenly Father, in which the earliest Christians exulted, can be looked at in two ways.

The way the words are used could mean that we share our lives with him. He is our friend, our brother with whom we can share our feelings and requests at any time of day or night. We can share our ordinary, humdrum lives with God himself!

But there is a deeper sense in which this *koinonia* can be construed. We share in his life. We share in his suffering (Rom. 8:17), in his death and resurrection (Rom. 6:8; Phil. 3:10). We are raised with him (Eph. 2:5-6). We will reign with him (2 Tim. 2:12). We will share his future glory (2 Thess. 2:14). Not only, then, does he share in *our* problems and difficulties; we have a share even now in *his* own risen life, with touches of its power and traces of its glory. So "When Christ who is our life shall appear, you too will appear with him in glory" (Col. 3:4). What a prospect!

Needless to say, fellowship with God is impaired by human wickedness and failure. It is spoiled (1 John 1:6) but not abrogated. When we are conscious of wrongdoing in our lives, we need to confess it and ask for pardon (1 John 1:9; 2:1).

We will find God *faithful* in forgiving — after all, we are in the family. We will also find him *just* in forgiving — after all, Christ took the accusing load of evil on our behalf on the cross. "We have an advocate with the Father, Jesus Christ the righteous." And the word used of Jesus in this verse, 1 John 2:1, is, significantly, *parakletos,* the word used of the Holy Spirit in the farewell discourses in St. John's Gospel. The Holy Spirit is the Father's paraclete with us, to plead the Father's cause in our hearts. And Jesus is our paraclete with the Father, to plead our cause in the courts of heaven! For he is the propitiation, *hilasmos,* that has dealt with our sins once and for all. By his presence he presents his completed task of sinbearing to the Father. What a God, who thus in perfect justice and incredible love allows us selfish mortals to have the inestimable privilege of fellowship with him!

But our fellowship is never from the alone to the Alone. It is jointly held with others. The Christian faith is so different from all self-improvement cults and the faiths that seek fulfillment or enlightenment "for myself alone." It is inescapably corporate. You cannot have fellowship with the Triune God who *is* fellowship without that fellowship spilling over to others in the same family.

Sharing with Believers

Paul referred to Christian life together as "the right hand of fellowship" (Gal. 2:9). He was referring to the reality behind the handshake. From the Day of Pentecost onwards the believers found themselves plunged into the apostles' fellowship (Acts 2:42). We do not choose our fellowship in the Christian family. The choice has been made for us. After all, we cannot choose our brothers and sisters! Significantly, *adelphoi* is a favorite term for Christians in the New Testament — brothers. The Spirit teaches us to cry "Abba, Father," but never in isolation. The One to whom we cry is *Our Father!* So fellowship in the New Testament means partnership both with God and with fellow Christians. And that double fellowship is perfectly expressed in the Eucharist. First Corinthians 10:16-17 sees the bread and wine as expressive of our relationship with Jesus and at the same time with our fellow Christians. Both the church and the sacred bread are described as "the body" in which we all share. Christianity is inescapably corporate.

That word "body" is very important in the self-understanding of the early Christians. We are one body in Christ (as Paul insists in Romans 12, Ephesians 4, and 1 Corinthians 12), and we are individually members of it. There is no room for superiority in that body, for we did not choose or merit our incorporation. Nor is there room for inferiority complexes, for God takes special care of the apparently less attractive parts. Least of all is there any excuse for absenteeism, for we are members one of another, and if one member suffers, all the members suffer hurt.

So sharing in God inexorably means sharing with others in his family. That is why the church is so important, frail and sinful though it is. It is the body of Christ, of which we are limbs. It is the flock of Christ in which we are sheep. It is the bride of Christ, which we help to constitute and adorn. That is how the New Testament church sees itself.

The church has three main aspects in the New Testament. It can mean, and often does, "the church in a town," comprising several such home associations (1 Thess. 1:1). It can also mean "the church worldwide" (Acts 9:31). The singular "church" and plural "churches" are used indifferently. The important qualifier is *tou theou* — of God. It is *God's* church.

The origin of the word *ekklesia*, or church, lies in the Greek city state where it was an assembly. But it is often used in the Greek translation of the Old Testament to render the Hebrew *qahal*, meaning God's congregation. Christians at worship are not just a fortuitous assembly but part of God's heritage down the ages, stretching back to Abraham. So unity within that heritage is very important. The people of God already, they must still strive to become that people more and more. One in the Spirit already (Eph. 4:3), they must strive towards it. It is the theme constantly repeated in the Bible: we are accepted by God because of his generosity alone. Then we must, by his power, become what he already sees us to be.

This has a powerful word to say to our casual denominationalism. There is no trace of denominations in the New Testament. They are part of the sin of the church. The temptation to sheer off into a Jewish Church, a Samaritan Church, a Gentile Church was seductive, to be sure. But they refused to fall for it. The early Christians went to enormous efforts to maintain their unity. And therein lay part of their strength. Even today we see something of the sort. When churches of widely different denominations sink their differences and pull together for a mission or some other joint enterprise in a city, there is great surprise and great impact on the whole community, and opportunities for the gospel are offered to them in their togetherness which none of them would have been accorded in their isolation. Fellowship with God must be matched by fellowship with other Christians.

Sharing Each Other's Experiences

Joys and Sorrows

Koinonia is used in a further sense in the New Testament: sharing in each other's joys and sorrows. First Corinthians 12:26 shows our intimate interdependence in the Christian body. Just as a family would rejoice when one member succeeds or grieve when one member fails, so it should be in the church.

Financial Needs

It means sharing in each other's financial needs. It was like that in the very earliest days when the Jerusalem Christians shared their all (Acts

4:34-35). It was like that in Antioch when the Christians heard of impending need for their brothers and sisters in Jerusalem (Acts 11:27-30). It was like that when Gentile churches wanted to make a collection for the Jewish Christians from whom the gospel had reached them (Rom. 15:26). The word used is *koinonia*, fellowship. The meaning extended far beyond sympathy: it meant sacrificial giving. Philippians 4:15 is a good example of the same thing: a project of giving and receiving is called *koinonia*, and the same holds good of Galatians 6:6 and Romans 12:13. Christians did not see this as some unwelcome tax: they longed to give and to have a share in this sort of fellowship, although it seemed beyond their means (2 Cor. 8:4). Paul explains it further in 2 Corinthians 9:13 (chapters 8 and 9 are full of teaching on the privilege of giving). Christians give to impoverished brethren out of obedience to the gospel: the recipients long for them and pray for them because of God's abundant generosity received through them. Thus joy and partnership abound, and it springs from God's inexpressible generosity to them all (2 Cor. 9:15).

If we were really to take this level of fellowship to heart, it would be very noticeable. I heard of two examples from Pakistan that illustrate it powerfully. After church, the pastor gathered the wage earners in the little church together and told them of a brother who had been sick for months and could not pay his rent. The men immediately agreed to pay it for him, poor though they were. Would that have happened in your church?

The other example shows how fellowship through giving does not have to flow from the richer to the poorer. It can go the other way. A poor Pakistani widow heard of a missionary family who were, for some weeks, unable to go outside because of anti-Western riots. "Maybe they need some provisions," she thought. And so she bought vegetables from the local market and traveled a few miles by bus to bring this gift to the missionary home. It was valued far more highly than the cost of the vegetables! If this sort of thing became the norm in our churches, society round about us would sit up and take notice. Not only would needs be met, but the bonds of gratitude and fellowship between church members would be greatly strengthened, and those who are not yet Christians would be profoundly attracted.

Suffering

Fellowship also means sharing in suffering — and the consolation God gives. Suffering is an inescapable part of being human, and Christians are invited to be willing for a costly sharing that at times will involve suffering. Second Corinthians 1:7 is a case in point. Paul has suffered greatly. He expects the Corinthian Christians to suffer too. But just as he has known the comfort of Jesus, aided by their prayers (vv. 5, 11), he anticipates the same consolation for them. St. Peter too gives us the same juxtaposition of suffering now and glory later, at the very outset of his letter (1:5). It is a challenge to endurance. "We shall sometimes be publicly exposed to abuse and affliction, and sometimes be *koinonoi* with those so treated" (Heb. 10:33). But the writer urges them not to throw away their confidence, which awaits a great reward. After all, they follow a crucified yet risen Lord. Their destiny, in both respects, is to share in his.

Commitment

Fellowship means sharing in an exclusive commitment. This sits ill with the happy-go-lucky Western world, so prone to wanting to have our cake and eat it. But there is a black-and-white aspect in Christianity that simply cannot be reduced to various shades of grey. The much misquoted 2 Corinthians 6:14-15 is stringent in this requirement. "Do not be mismated with unbelievers . . . what fellowship has light with darkness? . . . What has a believer in common with an unbeliever?" Tough talk indeed, and it is clear that Paul is intransigent on the need to safeguard Christian purity and distinctiveness of life. So firm was he, that he laid himself open to misinterpretation, as if he had been urging his followers to come out of the world altogether, and he had to correct this impression (1 Cor. 5:9-11). "But rather I wrote to you not to associate with any one who bears the name of brother if he is guilty of immorality or greed, or is an idolater, reviler, drunkard or robber — not even to eat with such a one."

Paul is anxious to maintain the freshness and purity of Christian living in all sorts of ways. Christians must not share in any enterprise that is sinful (Eph. 5:11; 1 Tim. 5:22; 2 John v. 11; Rev. 18:4), but in particular he dreads that those who take the sacred bread and wine of the Eucharist should enter into *koinonia*, partnership, with demonic forces (1 Cor. 10:18, 20). The idols to whom sacrifice was offered in antiquity may have been imaginary; but dark forces that were far from imaginary were given the opportunity, through idolatry, of invading the Christian's heart, and inducing civil war there. How powerfully this concern of the apostle's applies to the occult and to secret societies like the Freemasons. It applies also, Paul knows, to sexual immorality such as prostitution, when I "wrench away" the "limb of Christ" and make it the member of a prostitute (1 Cor. 6:15ff.). Commitment to Christ is exclusive of other total commitments: the Lord is jealous over his bride, the church, and every member of it.

Care

Fellowship means deep loving care for our brothers and sisters in the church. *Philadelphia*, love of the brethren, is a great New Testament word. In the ladder of virtues in 2 Peter 1:7 it is second only to *agape* itself, the undifferentiating, God-given love for all and sundry. The difference between the two is simply this: *philadelphia* is the heaven-sent family love for other members of the family, while *agape* is the outworking of God's own love for the unlovely. Love like this is beautiful when it marks the life of any church. It is chilling when it is absent. This attractive mutual love, springing from the heart, is the fruit of reconciliation with the heavenly Lover (Rom. 12:10; 1 Peter 1:22). New Testament writers take it almost for granted: it is, after all, taught and inspired by God himself (1 Thess. 4:9). But they are concerned that it should be constantly lived out in consistent Christian attitudes: "Let brotherly love continue" (Heb. 13:1).

Sharing God's Work

Koinonia is heavily tinged in the New Testament with the meaning of joint partnership in the work of the Lord (e.g., 2 Cor. 8:23; Phil. 1:5; Heb. 10:33). Paul's closest friends were those who shared the work with him, men like Titus, "my partner and fellow worker in your service" (2 Cor. 8:23). There is a profound spiritual truth that deep fellowship is almost a by-product of service. It is forged and bonded not by studying it and discussing it, but by joining together in service for God. I have spent some of my life in the smoke-filled rooms of the ecumenical movement, discussing Christian unity. But it is not achieved by talk, as is obvious from the state in which the World Council of Churches finds itself. I have spent some of my life in evangelistic enterprises and Christian social concerns with brother and sister Christians from widely different denominations, outlooks, and backgrounds. And it is here that I have found really deep fellowship. It came through service.

Many churches are flaccid because their members want the joy of fellowship without the sweat of service. It is not to be had. For fellowship means sharing in the work of God and, in particular, evangelism. Paul speaks very clearly about this in 1 Corinthians 9:22-23 where he discloses the flexibility and consistency, the courage and imagination, the motivation and persistence with which he spreads the good news of Jesus to Jew and Gentile alike. "I have become all things to all men, that I might by all means save some. I do it all for the sake of the gospel, that I may share in its blessings." Note that *koinonia,* "sharing" word again. You only really begin to taste the blessings of the gospel when you set out to give it away. Churches need to learn that. Theological seminaries need to learn that. Individual Christians need to learn that. And so do you and I.

I have the impression that Philemon knew the truth of that. Paul writes, in an obscure allusion in Philemon 6, "I pray that the sharing of your faith may promote the knowledge of all the good that is ours in Christ." But it emerges with notable clarity in Philippians 1:7: "I have you in my heart because you are partners in the same grace as I — both in my bonds and in the defense and confirmation of the gospel." The Christians at Philippi shared with Paul in his bonds by means of a gift of money and provisions that they sent him in prison. They shared in his defense and prosecution of the gospel by doing the same themselves. The gospel needs a cool head to explain it and defend it, to show its inner consistency and its relevance to every side of life. It is sad to see how low Christian apologetics have sunk during the past half century, and encouraging to see just the beginning of a fresh interest in this most important part of evangelism. But if the gospel needs a cool head, it also needs a warm heart to seek out people who need this wonderful news, and to love them into the kingdom of God, come rain or shine. When

Christians do that together, they engage in the work of rescue that is the supreme concern of the Holy Trinity, for the Father sent the Son to be the Savior of the world, and the Spirit baptized him for that task. And as they enter into this crucial aspect of the life of the Godhead, serving poor needy sinners, so they come to understand a vital dimension of fellowship. It is cooperating with God in his gracious work of rescue for a fallen world. If you and I long for a deeper fellowship, maybe we should involve ourselves more deliberately in ministry and mission.

Fellowship in the church of Jesus Christ is a many-splendored thing. It means sharing in the life of God himself. It means sharing with other believers. It means experiencing a wide range of the experiences of other Christians. It means sharing in God's work.

Perhaps the best way of experiencing these four main aspects of Christian fellowship is in the house group. There the horizontal and the vertical axes of fellowship intersect. We have fellowship with the Lord and with each other. And it comes about in three main ways.

First, there is the Godward side of it. We worship him in the house group as we praise and pray. We learn together from the scriptures and from the way these scriptures impact one another's lives as we reflect on them. This leads naturally into the second aspect of it, fellowship with one another.

For the house group is the natural place to share each other's joys and sorrows, and to enter into each other's experiences. In this way we not only get far closer to one another than we could in a month of Sundays simply by attending church, but we have the thrill of seeing and hearing of God at work in other lives. This level of sharing is impossible among folk who do not know each other well. People will only share intimate details of their lives with those they know to care, those they can trust. And how can this level of trust and caring be fostered? In a small, regular house group. Every church should encourage house groups. They are almost essential to a church's vitality and growth.

And of course such a group is a ready-forged unit to engage in ministry and mission in the neighborhood. It begins, naturally, with ministry to one another and moves out from there. A missionary writes of a small house group in the Muslim land where he works. One of the group, an old man, was due for major surgery. He and his wife were understandably nervous. So the group prayed with them and for them. After the operation they took turns in visiting the old man and providing meals for him. So although this old couple had no family to support them, they were lovingly supported by their Christian family, the members of their house group.

But a house group that does not look beyond itself soon becomes stale and unhealthy. Ministry and mission need to take place beyond the confines of the group. A warm, cohesive group like this can easily split for a while in order to invite some friends in, and do an inductive series of Bible studies on, say, passages in St. John's Gospel. Or it can be more ambitious, and hold a few evangelistic supper parties with an appropriate speaker and plenty of opportunity for discussion. For fellowship is not only with God and with other Christians. Its quality is enhanced, its purpose is fulfilled only when, like the God we serve, it reaches out beyond its comfort zone to those who are strangers to the divine love. No wonder the house group is an invaluable part and embodiment of true fellowship in every congregation. We each need to take seriously the need to belong to a house group. And we need to take no less seriously the outward thrust of such a group if we are to enjoy its greatest dimension of fellowship.

8

People of Prayer

R. PAUL STEVENS

Bible searching and searching prayer go hand in hand. What we receive in the Book's message we return to Him with interest in prayer.

Prayer is, for us, paradoxically, both a gift and a conquest, a grace and a duty.

P. T. FORSYTH

Prayer is difficult. A few giants of the faith say that prayer is as normal to them as breathing. But most of us find that prayer is like any other form of relational communion — it takes constant effort. One never feels that graduation from kindergarten has taken place. Karl Barth rightly concludes that Christian living can never "be anything but the work of beginners. . . ."[1] Prayer is not only difficult but, not surprisingly, it is largely unpracticed even today. The growing interest in spirituality seems focused on personal development rather than the conquest of God in prayer. We are a prayerless generation. Even preachers, whose business it is to pray, on the average pray only a few minutes each

---

1. Karl Barth, *The Christian Life — Dogmatics IV, 4 Lecture Fragments* (Grand Rapids: Eerdmans, 1981), p. 79.

day. Some have given up praying completely. What relief can be brought to this famine of the soul?

In this chapter we will look for answers in the prayer life of Jesus, the first disciples, the apostles Paul and John, and the author of Revelation. We do this intentionally. What we need to counter prayerlessness is not burdensome exhortations but a rediscovery of the source of Christian prayer. Prayer is communion, conversation, and spiritual conquest. This must be voluntary and mutual, just as satisfying lovemaking between a husband and wife cannot be compelled or reduced to a technique described in a manual. As we examine the prayers of Jesus, Paul, and John we will discover that the source of our prayerlessness is to be found in our inadequate grasp of the God with whom we commune. True prayer is not taught but evoked by the God who is Lover, Shepherd, Husband, Friend, Judge, Savior, Visitor, and Counselor. We are drawn to prayer by the seeking Father.

The Triune God not only invites us to pray but prays through us. "We do not know what we ought to pray for, but the Spirit himself intercedes for us with groans that words cannot express" (Rom. 8:26). Further, "Christ Jesus . . . is at the right hand of God and is also interceding for us" (Rom. 8:34). Speaking to how the Triune God helps us in prayer, Edwin Hui says:

> In this praying event, the person who prays has an unmistakably three-facets "experience" of the Triune God as she is being incorporated by the "Spirit" into the life of the "Son" towards the "Father." It is an experience of being caught in the Trinitarian life of God . . . of being invited into the conversation of God to God in and through the one who prays. In such a literally Godly prayer, and indeed in a truly Godly life of prayer, what else can a human person say other than "Amen"?[2]

So the good news is that God engages us in prayer. P. T. Forsyth says, "He who speaks to us also hears in us, because He opens our inward ear (Rom. viii.15; Gal. iv.6). And yet He is Another, who so fully lives in us as *to give us but the more fully to ourselves.* So our prayer is a soliloquy

---

2. "Experiencing the Trinity" (unpublished lecture, Regent College, Vancouver, B.C.).

with God, a monologue *a deux*."[3] We begin our inquiry by trying to "get inside" the spontaneous prayers of Jesus.

Praying Spontaneously

The most revealing statement by Jesus about his life of prayer is simply, "I and the Father are one" (John 10:30). Prayer for Jesus was not primarily a "discipline" but the daily meat and drink of fellowship with the Father. Like friendship, prayer is not *for* anything at all, not even for "answers." It is for the relationship, for communion. What we are speaking about is not the natural or instinctive turning to God in a crisis — good as this is — but turning in faith to God moment by moment with the actual details of our life, and so praying without ceasing. To do this we must know the character of the one to whom we pray. The primary contribution of Jesus to the life of personal prayer is just this: he reveals the Father. Jesus reveals a Father-God who is more willing to give than we are to ask, a God who invites us to come boldly, persistently, and honestly (Luke 11:1-13).

Equally important, Jesus reveals that what God wants from our prayers is not the substance *but the relationship* implied in our praying. So there are probably no "bad" prayers. If there are "bad" prayers, praying them is better than not praying at all. It is my hunch that praying even inadequate prayers places us in the spiritual posture where God can teach us how to pray better. We learn to pray by praying. So we have every reason to be spontaneous when we pray and not to worry what God or anyone else thinks about the form of our prayers. This deeper principle of spontaneity, involving the liberation of the person to relate authentically with God, is illustrated by the windows given to us in the Gospels on the spontaneous prayers of Jesus.

Enjoying God

There is the prayer of spontaneous joy. Jesus worshiped the Father in the Spirit at the return of the Seventy disciples from a successful mission.

---

3. Peter T. Forsyth, *The Soul of Prayer* (London: Independent Press, 1954), p. 15, emphasis mine.

At that time Jesus, full of joy through the Holy Spirit, said, "I praise you, Father, Lord of heaven and earth, because you have hidden these things from the wise and learned, and revealed them to little children. Yes, Father, for this was your good pleasure" (Luke 10:21).

Recognizing that the Father had not signaled the presence of his kingdom by employing the theologians and established religious leaders, but, rather, a motley collection of disciples, Jesus exulted in the wonder of God's ways. The text suggests, though it does not clearly say so, that Jesus may have spoken in a prayer language or in tongues on this occasion. He enjoyed the Father in the depths of his spirit. It was a joy that needed to be expressed.

In the Gospels Jesus is presented as nurturing his relationship with the Father by frequent, extended times of prayer on a mountain alone (Luke 6:12), in a solitary place (Mark 1:35), or in a private garden. On one such occasion Jesus invited his "inner circle" of disciples to be present. On the occasion of the Transfiguration, Peter, James, and John witnessed his majesty and joy in the Father while he prayed. We may speak of this as the *prayer of divine affirmation.*

Christians of the Orthodox persuasion especially prize icons of the Transfiguration because this prayer-event forms the essential paradigm of the spiritual life. As we commune with God we are transfigured (2 Cor. 3:18) just as Jesus was. Then, like the disciples, we are inspired to become, in a limited way, "eyewitnesses of his majesty" (2 Peter 1:16), so ministering out of who we are becoming in Christ and not merely delivering words we have heard. The liturgy for the feast of the Transfiguration contains some insightful words about the connection of the disciples' experience of Jesus and their own future ministry. Reflecting on the presence of Moses and Elijah who spoke with Jesus about the "departure [*exodus*], which he was about to bring to fulfillment at Jerusalem" (Luke 9:31), we are invited to pray:

> Having uncovered, O Saviour, a little of the light of Thy divinity to those who went up with Thee into the mountain, *Thou has made them lovers of Thy heavenly glory.* Therefore they cried in awe, 'It is good for us to be here.' . . . Thy disciples beheld Thy glory, O Christ our God, as far as they were able to do so that when they saw Thee crucified, *they might know Thy suffering was voluntary,* and might

proclaim unto the world that Thou art truly the Brightness of the Father.[4]

Trusting Submission

Transfiguration and crucifixion are closely linked. After Jesus completed the Last Supper he paused in the Garden of Gethsemane before his arrest, trial, and crucifixion (Matt. 26:36-46). This prayer, in the presence of the disciples, illustrates perfectly that the relationship of the Son to the Father was one of voluntary submission. Jesus addresses God each time as "My Father." The Aramaic "Abba" includes the idea of a child's familiar access to one's father, though it expresses a deeper respect and loyalty than is normally communicated by our use of "Daddy." The biblical basis of seeking God's will is the supremacy of our heavenly Father who knows better what we need than we do. So to pray, "thy will be done," as Jesus does here, is to decide not to ask God to embrace our will. Forsyth suggests, "Nothing would do more to cure us of a belief in our own wisdom than the granting of our eager prayers."[5]

In this matter Jesus models humility and true meekness, which is more God-honoring than it is self-depreciating. In the garden prayer Jesus freely expresses his own heart options to the Father, always affirming that his central desire is that the Father's will be done. He explores with the Father what drinking the cup of suffering might mean and asks if there is any way for the cup to be taken from him. There is struggle in this prayer, and only a misdirected reverence for the divinity of Jesus can ignore it. As Jacob discovered long before (Gen. 32:22-30), those who fight with God get blessed while those — like Esau — who do not care enough for the blessing of God to fight for it never know communion. Therefore the author of Hebrews later reflects that Jesus was superbly equipped to be our human and divine high priest because he was tempted at all points as we are (Heb. 5:7-10; 4:15) in moments like this. As Jesus prays he freely agrees with the Father's will. But he does so as a matter of submission rather than compliance.

---

4. John Baggley, *Doors of Perception: Icons and Their Spiritual Significance* (Crestwood, N.Y.: St. Vladimir's Seminary Press, 1988), p. 136, italics mine.

5. Forsyth, *The Soul*, p. 29.

Compliance in marriage and in prayer is a psychological adaptation to avoid pain. But there is always a sliver of resentment in the compliant person; there is no such sliver in the heart of Jesus. One reason is the remarkable candidness with which he explored the options of his own heart with the Father. Behind this deep spontaneity is the trustworthy Father who invites such a conversation around a will (his) that *could* be imposed, but is not.

Father, Forgive Them

The same freedom is revealed on the cross. "Jesus said, 'Father, forgive them, for they do not know what they are doing'" (Luke 23:34). This prayer reveals his mediatorial, saving work even for those who were instruments of his crucifixion. It also reveals his unsullied integrity. He had earlier taught that we should "pray for those who mistreat you" (Luke 6:28). It is hard to believe this prayer was premeditated. Taken with his spontaneous ministry to the repentant thief at his side (22:43), Jesus' prayerful responses to the violence of crucifixion are profoundly significant, especially as the next prayer indicates.

The cry of dereliction on the cross (Matt. 27:46) is also a window on the interior life of Jesus, now darkened by the full weight of our sin and alienation from the Father. He became "sin" for us that we might become in him the righteousness of God (2 Cor. 5:21). "My God, my God, why have you forsaken me?" is an obvious quotation from Psalm 22, the paradigmatic prayer of the innocent sufferer who finds his vindication and deliverance in God, even in face of death. Jesus turns to God in his darkest moment, speaking God's own word as a prayer, and, in Luke's account, commits his spirit to the Father as a final act of prayerful trust (Luke 23:46), a prayer that is echoed in the prayer of Stephen, the first Christian martyr (Acts 7:59). As with all true prayer there is paradox here as well. Luther is said to have exclaimed, "God forsaken by God! Who can understand this?"

These glimpses into the prayer life of Jesus are highly evocative. The God and Father of Jesus Christ is one to whom we can pour out all our thoughts and concerns, our joys and our sorrows, our ecstasy and our anger, knowing that a faithful God will sift out the wheat and, with a breath of kindness, blow the chaff away. God is Father, Shepherd,

Lover, Judge, and Savior waiting to vindicate us (Luke 18:14). The age-old question is: "If God is as good as you say, and knows what we need before we ask, then why should we need to ask?" The age-old answer is a deep one. What if God knows that what we need more than anything is himself? And what if our asking for things, pouring out our hearts about our needs and decisions, is God's chosen vehicle for giving us what we most deeply need — though we may not know it when we first ask for things?

Praying Corporately

Most of the prayers of Jesus recorded for us were solitary prayers. But solitary prayer is not really an individual activity. We are never alone when we pray *to* the Father *in the name* of Jesus *through* the Spirit. Solitude invites communion with God, in contrast to loneliness, even loneliness in prayer. Ironically, among the prayers of Jesus only the prayer of dereliction from the cross seems to be a lonely prayer. But even in this prayer — wrung from his priestly heart on our behalf as he takes our sin upon himself — Jesus has the joy of restored fellowship with the Father in view (Heb. 12:2). In contrast, Jesus warns against real loneliness in prayer in those who "parade" their prayers to impress their human listeners. These get their reward *now,* in contrast to those who pray in the closet (seemingly alone) but who get the implied greater reward, the presence and affirmation of God himself (Matt. 6:5-8). The first, like the Pharisee in the parable, may turn out to be praying either "with" himself or "to" himself (Luke 18:11) even though onlookers may be duly impressed. But corporate prayer includes both the Lord and other believers. True corporate prayer was encouraged by Jesus when he gave us the "Our Father" prayer, wrongly called "The Lord's Prayer" (Matt. 6:9-13; Luke 11:1-13). It is more accurately described as "The Disciples' Prayer."

The Disciples' Prayer

There are at least two remarkable features of the origin of this perfect prayer. One is that it originates from the disciples' observation of Jesus at prayer (Luke 11:1). The second is that this prayer arises as a response to the request of his disciples to be taught to pray as John the Baptist taught his disciples. Jesus responds to the request, "Teach us to pray" by saying, in effect, "Let us pray!" We learn to pray by praying, by *praying like this*, not merely by praying *this*.

In A. B. Bruce's classic examination of the Lord's training the disciples in prayer, Bruce notes that Jesus dealt in his training with the three "wants" that shut down our prayers: lacks in ideas, in words, and in faith. Jesus' prayer, he says, forms "the alphabet of all possible prayer. It embraces the elements of all spiritual desire, summed up in a few choice sentences, for the benefit of those who may not be able to bring their struggling aspirations to birth in articulate language."[6] If the Disciples' Prayer teaches us how to pray, the true Lord's Prayer teaches us why.

In John chapter seventeen we are permitted to overhear the actual prayers of Jesus. This is actually "The Lord's Prayer," though the Lutheran theologian David Chytraus (1531-1600) gave this prayer the title, "the high priestly prayer." The title "stuck" for good reasons.

The Lord's Prayer

In speaking of this magnificent prayer Milligan and Moulton describe some of the qualities: "No attempt to describe the prayer can give a just idea of its sublimity, its pathos, its touching yet exalted character, its tone at once of tenderness and triumphant expectation."[7] In passing we notice that, unlike the incident in John 11:41-42 where Jesus prays out loud for the edification of his disciples, the high priestly prayer originated not in the desire to give an example to his disciples but because *Jesus wanted and needed to pray*. This is all the more remarkable when one believes, as the authors of this book believe, that Jesus is both man and God. God praying to God! But if God is Father, Son, and Holy Spirit, dwelling in a family of covenant love, and if prayer is the way that one

---

6. A. B. Bruce, *The Training of the Twelve: Passages Out of the Gospels* (New York: A. C. Armstrong & Son, 1902), pp. 54-55.

7. Quoted in Leon Morris, *The Gospel According to John*, NICNT (Grand Rapids: Eerdmans, 1971), p. 716.

person communes with another person, then for Jesus to pray is divinely reasonable. Further, the Lord's Prayer shows us the social and relational nature of prayer. This prayer more than any demonstrates that we are least alone when we pray.

In each of the sections of this prayer Jesus begins with a statement (he speaks about someone) and then moves into a petition (he speaks on behalf of someone). This structure is significant. The Christian life moves from the indicative to the imperative, from what *is* to what *should* be. In communion with God we should move from certainties to concerns, from worship to petition.

In the first section (17:1-5) Jesus prays for himself. "Father, the time has come. Glorify your Son, that your Son may glorify you." Among the many remarkable dimensions of this prayer is the fact that Jesus prayed for himself *without a shred of selfishness.* Here is petition without self-centeredness.

In the second section (17:6-19) Jesus prays for the disciples. The disciples *belong* to God. "They were yours; you gave them to me" (17:6). In response to the statement of Jesus, "all you have is mine" (17:10), Luther is reported to have said, "This no creature can say with reference to God." As high priest Jesus prays that they will not be taken *out* of the world (17:15) but that they will be protected, while they are *in* the world, from the evil one.

In the final section (17:20-26) Jesus prays for all future disciples. Others will believe in Jesus through the message of the first disciples. Of all the things he could have prayed for the believers to follow in countless centuries, it is remarkable that his petition focuses on unity: "that all of them may be one, Father, just as you are in me and I am in you. May they also be in us so that the world may believe that you have sent me" (17:21). The deepest prayer of Jesus on the way to the cross, when his hour had come (12:23; 17:1), is that his disciples will experience Trinitarian unity.

Trinitarian unity is not "mashed potato" unity, as someone tried to describe it, in which the individual identities of believers are lost in a great social merger. Not so. Each is more himself by being in unity. God the Father, Son, and Holy Spirit, who invite us to join *their unity,* dwell in a complex fellowship in which each is for the other but all are for the One. The Orthodox theologian Tomas Spidlik notes that within Orthodox spirituality "the divine Trinity is the fundamental mystery of the

Christian faith." Spidlik says that "only the Christian revelation teaches the highest and most intense union as embracing that which in the finite realm divides and is a principle of division: personality."[8] In other words, God is one not in spite of being three but *because* he is three. Christian experience means being included in the unity of the Trinity, participating in the mutual love, order, and interdependence of the three persons of the Trinity. In this way John allows us to view discipleship to Jesus as a transcendent experience in prayer.

In the Synoptic Gospels (Matthew, Mark, and Luke) disciples of Jesus are presented as being with him and being sent out by him. In the days of his earthly ministry this involved having physical proximity with him, joining his company, observing his lifestyle, hearing his words, and sharing in the healings and controversies that surrounded him. But John presents discipleship as the privilege of being included in the life of the Father, the Son, and the Holy Spirit, not merely doing what Jesus asks or hearing what he says. Corporate prayer is prayer that takes us into the corporate life of God and, through the Lord's continuing high priestly intercession, invites us to discover our common life as disciples in him.

The Church's Prayers

As we turn briefly to the rest of the New Testament, we note both the communal *practice* of the first generation of disciples, and the communal *content* of the prayers. On the first, it appears that the Lord prayed in the Temple. We can assume this from Luke 18:10 and from his presence at festivals like the Passover where he would sing the Hallel (Mark 14:26). In the Acts of the Apostles the first disciples continued the Lord's practice by attending the Temple daily for prayer (Acts 2:46). We note also the extended prayer meeting in the "upper room" following the Lord's ascension. The disciples waited in prayer for the promised Holy Spirit. "They all joined together constantly in prayer, along with the women and Mary the mother of Jesus, and with his brothers" (1:14). It is a fascinating question to consider *what* they prayed for and *how*.

On the second, the communal content of their prayers, the early

---

8. Tomas Spidlik, *The Spirituality of the Christian East: A Systematic Handbook* (Kalamazoo, Mich.: Cistercian Publications, 1986), p. 45.

church undoubtedly used the Psalter as the prayer book of the church (Eph. 5:19; Col. 3:16). But the content of these corporate prayers (Acts 1:14, 24; 2:42, 47) is not revealed until we are given a compressed summary of the prayers offered when Peter and John were released from imprisonment by the Sanhedrin and returned to the waiting disciples. "They raised their voices together in prayer to God" (4:24). This prayer, reportedly uttered together and out loud, is a remarkable combination of Scripture, thanksgiving, and petition. I do not think it necessary to assume that this spontaneous prayer, obviously not in the Psalter and undoubtedly not composed in some written manual, was uttered simultaneously by the whole group in perfect unison with no premeditation. More likely we have a summary of prayers offered out loud by various people who, led by the Spirit, contributed to a symphony of prayer on a single theme.

The prayer starts as a typical Jewish prayer and then, quoting the second psalm, marvels at the paradoxical meaning now apparent to them, that whatever the enemies of Jesus do against Jesus and his followers can only *further* God's preordained purpose in Jesus. Herod, Pilate, the Gentiles, and the Jews all unwittingly serve God! So following Jesus' pattern of moving from certainty to petition, these believers now bring their requests. They *do not ask for protection,* or grace to accommodate to the command "not to speak or teach at all in the name of Jesus" (4:18). Rather they pray, "Now, Lord, consider their threats and enable your servants to speak your word with great boldness. Stretch out your hand to heal and perform miraculous signs and wonders through the name of your holy servant Jesus" (4:29-30). These early disciples asked that they might identify boldly with the continuing service of God's Suffering Servant. We know they were heard because of the physical shaking of the room, the manifest filling of the Spirit, and their being empowered to speak the word boldly. They asked what God wanted, and they received what they most deeply wanted. Such is the mystery of wills in prayer. Undoubtedly, the timid church today is not praying this way.

This case study in early church corporate prayer is a powerful illustration of the promise Jesus gave: "Again, I tell you that if two of you on earth agree about anything you ask for, it will be done for you by my Father in heaven. For where two or three come together in my name, there am I with them" (Matt. 18:19-20). Corporate prayer is not merely prayers said together in unison but prayers made together in which God himself through the Spirit orchestrates and harmonizes the various contributions made by individual members of the body of Christ. Corporate prayer takes us into the social life of God himself. In the light of this, much that passes for corporate prayer is promiscuous, not in the sexual sense but in its relational depth: it is idle verbal chatter in the context of superficial and sometimes anonymous relationships.

Christian unity, as we have seen in the high priestly prayer (John 17:23), is not something believers must achieve among themselves in order to get God's work done. It is the work God is doing among believers. Paul's prayers in Ephesians (1:3-23; 3:14-21) are passionate prayers for unity. He longs that the Ephesian Christians will know who they are in Christ *together.* Laced throughout the letter is Paul's sense of vocation, to be a steward of the mysterious and transcendent unity of Jew and Gentile in Christ (3:6), making a new humanity (2:15). In chapter four he starts with the "given" unity the Ephesians have in God the Father, Son, and Holy Spirit (4:3-6) and then prays that godly leadership will equip the church to attain "unity in the faith and in the knowledge of the Son of God" (4:13).

Paul's prayer for and exhortation to the Ephesians is not directed to a bouquet of individual believers, each needing edification and equipping, but rather they are directed to the body. So he prays that "Christ may dwell in your heart through faith" and "that you, being rooted and established in love, may have power, *together with all the saints,* to grasp how wide and long and high and deep is the love of Christ" (3:17-19). We read this prayer as a prayer addressed to God on behalf of our individual hearts, but Paul prayed that for the community. For Paul individual Christians, in the Western granular sense, do not exist. If we are in Christ at all, we are in Christ together, even if we come one by one. The believer cannot be filled with the fullness of God (3:19), be filled with the Spirit (5:18), or have the mind of Christ (1 Cor. 2:16) alone, but only together.

What makes prayer truly corporate is the divine Conductor orchestrating the praying community to find a common mind and life through the unifying process of their prayer. There is a divine synergy in this, not only because the whole of the believing community is more than the sum of the individual parts, but because when we pray together we are drawn into the prayers of our heavenly high priest (Heb. 4:14) and the Spirit's interpretive intercession (Rom. 8:26-27). So we are most Christ-like and most united when we are together in our prayers.

Until now we have been examining the prayers of Jesus, the early disciples, and the apostles to discover a New Testament spirituality of prayer. But now we must explore one final dimension of truly Christian prayer: it takes us to the last book of the New Testament.

Praying Imaginatively

The Apocalypse of John (the Revelation) ushers us into a world of dragons, beasts, angels, cosmic catastrophes, and martyrs chanting hymns. We are swept from one riveting vision to the next as we are transported from heaven to earth and back again, in an upstairs-downstairs drama. Bowls of judgment are poured out on the earth while cringing multitudes call on hills to cover them from the wrath of the Lamb. There is a final battle, a wonderful wedding supper, and an exquisite garden city. Understanding all this is complicated by the fact that apocalypse is a lost literary genre to the modern western Christian.

Apocalyptic Prayer

Apocalypse was to the first century what science fiction is to the twentieth. Imagine trying to explain science fiction to a first-century tentmaker in Ephesus, or apocalypse to a cab driver in Boston or Toronto. Comparisons may, however, be made. The Revelation of John can be compared with a dissolve-fade slide show (the Lion dissolves into a Lamb standing as though slain), a drama (organized in dramatic form with overlapping sequences of seven seals, trumpets, and bowls with the major pastoral messages offered at the moments of maximum dramatic intensity) or a symphony (it has more songs than all the rest of the New Testament). But none of these comparisons does justice to the unique form of literature that flourished between 200 B.C. and A.D. 100.

John uses apocalypse to help people to pray. He wants people to learn to pray and worship on the job, in the marketplace, at the trade-guild meeting, at the neighbor's house. So John presents a thoroughly "lay" spirituality, intended for ordinary Christians like the ones in Pergamum compelled to worship Caesar, and the Christian bronze workers in Thyatira struggling with the orgies and idol feasts of the pagan guilds to which they were forced to belong (Rev. 3:20). Lay spirituality must deal not only with the ecclesiastical life (Rev. 2–3) but with power, politics, economics, marketing, and social responsibilities in secular or religious society. This John does. The stillness he seeks is not quietude but the triumphant voice of God himself in Psalm 46:10, in the context of our conflict-ridden life in this world. God commands all the powers of evil: "Be still, and know that I am God." In this case stillness is discovered right in the center of life rather than at its circumference.

John accomplishes this by pulling back the curtain of "normal" perception to let us see a transcendent reality that is actually present in our everyday existence, to see *through* the eye, as Blake proposed, not merely with it. The Lamb has triumphed even though the Harlot appears to reign supreme. Heaven, for John, is not up there, or later, but bursting into the here and how. He shows us how the world looks to a person in the Spirit. Its "otherworldly" atmosphere is precisely what makes it so relevant when the church is facing persecution from a hostile culture or is being seduced by a friendly culture. It tells us that behind either hostility or seduction is a sinister personage called the Beast that is really Satan's puppet. Behind that is the plan and purpose of God, who is already overruling (13:7; 17:17) and will eventually be seen to rule everything (19:1). The Revelation is much more than a book of predictions. It provides our praying spirits with an imaginative vision of the realities that will evoke prayer and consistent living, realities associated with the second coming of Jesus.

The Praying Imagination

Revelation is to the second coming of Jesus what the Ignatian exercises and inner healing prayer are to the first coming of Jesus: they involve an imaginative presentation of the affective, emotional, and spiritual meaning of the appearance of Jesus in a way designed to evoke a deep and personal encounter with the Lord himself. This cannot be done without imagination. Indeed Cheryl Forbes says "we cannot have faith (belief in what is unseen) unless we have imagination; imagination is the vehicle through which faith is expressed."[9] Our prayers are often fitful

---

9. Cheryl Forbes, *Imagination: Embracing a Theology of Wonder* (Portland: Multnomah Press, 1986), p. 46.

and half-hearted because we cannot "see" the one to whom we pray, and we cannot envision what we are praying about.

A story is told about a kindergarten teacher who asked a boy what he was drawing. Without pausing to look up he said, "A picture of God." The teacher smiled and responded, "But nobody knows what God looks like." The boy carefully put down his crayon, looked her squarely in the eye, and declared, "After I am finished here they will." There is more than a half-truth in the child's boldness.

Since the Renaissance, the Industrial Revolution, and the advent of high-tech society, our lives have been de-imaged and stripped of imagination. This is tragic not only because of the aesthetic loss this entails for our personhood, but the loss more critically to our faith. Imagination relates to our essential dignity as made in the "image" of God (Gen. 1:27). We are a visual and social metaphor of God himself. Human beings are God's imagination incarnated, icons of God, just as Christ was his word incarnated. God expressed his glory in creation not primarily through propositions but through persons with imaginations. Mystery can be understood only through imagination. Jesus, who is God's perfect image, used metaphors and images to express the deepest truths about God, himself, and the kingdom. And John in Revelation uses imagination to invite prayerful participation in Christian hope and radical discipleship. S. S. Fiorenza suggests, "the strength of Revelation's language and images lies not in the theological argumentation or historical information but in their evocative power inviting imaginative participation."[10]

With marvelous reserve John describes the throne of God and the effects of God's presence without actually describing God, the indescribable, thereby enlarging our faith without seducing us into idolatry (4:1-5). "Come, Lord Jesus" (22:20) is the epicenter of prayer in this book, yet the prayer is evoked not by persuasion or doctrinal instruction but by an imaginative presentation of all the realities associated with the second coming of Jesus. The repeated exhortation, "He who has an ear, hear," is a call to converse with God imaginatively. John evokes prayer not by *telling* us to pray, but by appealing to our imaginations to grasp the transforming beauty of the Lord's final victory. He invites us to join

10. S. S. Fiorenza, *Invitation to the Book of Revelation* (Garden City, N.Y.: Doubleday & Co., 1981), p. 46.

the angels, the living creatures, the elders, and the believing multitude to shout, "Hallelujah! For our Lord God Almighty reigns" (19:6). Equally remarkable is the fact that Revelation empowers us to attend to God in prayer by envisioning a God who attends to us; God keeps a half-hour silence in heaven to receive the prayers of the saints (8:1-4). If that does not bring us to our knees then nothing in heaven or on earth can!

Praying spontaneously. Praying corporately. Praying imaginatively. Christian prayer is not tacking "in the name of Jesus" on the end. Rather, Christian prayer is evoked by the God and Father of Jesus Christ to come to him through Jesus, as we are equipped to do so by the unseen prayer-companion in our heart — the Spirit. True prayer, as James Houston says so clearly in *Transforming Friendship*, is simply friendship with God, communion — prayer for God's sake.

> Bernard of Clairvaux wrote that our natural inclination is to love for our own sake. When we first learn to love God, we still love him for our own sake. As we grow in friendship with God, we come to love him not just for ourselves alone, but also for God's sake. At last, we may reach the point where we love even ourselves for the sake of God.[11]

---

11. James Houston, *Transforming Friendship: A Guide to Prayer* (Oxford: Lion Books, 1989), pp. 195-96.

9

Committed to the Sacraments

MICHAEL GREEN

The Christian faith is the most earthly of all religions: after all, it is rooted in the Incarnation. Among other things, that supreme miracle insists that the physical matters a great deal. It matters so much to God that he expresses himself through it. He did so uniquely when Jesus took human flesh. But the same principle of divine life through physical means remains central to Christianity. That is why the faith of the New Testament is unashamedly sacramental.

A lot of confusion gathers around the term "sacrament." Some Christians are shy of it: others can speak of little else. Basic Christian usage is to see a sacrament as a physical token that expresses a spiritual reality: as the old Anglican Catechism put it, "an outward and visible sign of an inward and spiritual grace." It rightly goes on to say that Christians use this word "sacrament" of two ordinances "ordained by Christ himself, as a means whereby we receive the same [i.e., his grace] and a pledge to assure us thereof." The word derives from the Latin, where it was used of a soldier's oath of allegiance. All of this helps us to understand the normal Christian usage of the word.

Clearly the sacramental principle runs through the whole of life: a kiss, for example, or a handshake are "outward and visible signs" that should, and normally do, convey the "inward and spiritual grace" of love and friendship. But of course they may not do so — depending on the attitude of the donor and the recipient. It is like this with the two great sacraments Christ left us. Baptism and the Lord's Supper are outward and visible signs of the inward and spiritual grace of God that enables us to begin and to continue the Christian life. They are meant to be channels of his unseen but very real grace to us. And we can certainly rely on the attitude of the Donor. But that may prove ineffectual if on our side there is no response: if we grasp the hand, so to speak, but not the friendship proffered; if we accept the kiss but reject the love. The sacraments, then, like the Incarnation whose influence they continue, are not only pledges of God's lasting grace to us but should be, and normally are, channels of that love. Most Christians restrict the word to describe the two great outward actions with inner meaning which Jesus himself inaugurated, namely the Communion and baptism. Some denominations, rather unhelpfully, it seems to me, add five more which were not inaugurated by Christ and which are five among many other external acts with inward meanings. We will here therefore concentrate on baptism and the Lord's Supper.

Baptism

One Baptism — or Three?

There is one baptism (Eph. 4:5), but you'd never guess as much from the way Christians talk about it. For the Catholic, it was his baptism as an infant that brought him into the church and made him a Christian. For the Baptist, her baptism was by immersion, administered after profession of faith. For the Pentecostal, baptism was in or by the Holy Spirit, normally accompanied by the gift of tongues: this eclipses all else.

All three are saying something important. All three are stressing one aspect of what Christian baptism is.

The Catholic sees baptism as the gateway into the people of God. Just as you entered the old-covenant people of Israel by circumcision, so you enter the new people of God by baptism (Acts 2:40-41; Gal. 3:27-29). A noble view, strong on God's act of incorporation, but weak on response. If we think of it as the only strand in Christian initiation, it degenerates into magic.

The Baptist sees baptism as a seal on the profession of faith, and that is clearly the emphasis in Acts 16:31. The church is the company of believers. This view is strong on response, but very individualistic. It makes human commitment almost more significant than divine initiative. Moreover it is very cerebral: it gives little room for those too young or too handicapped to make a decisive response.

The Pentecostal sees it very differently. The church is not so much a historical continuum (which may well be apostate), nor a company of believers (which may mean little more than intellectual assent). No. Reception of the life-giving Spirit of God is the authentic mark of the church. Baptism with the Holy Spirit is the only baptism worth having (Rom. 8:9). Important though this emphasis undoubtedly is, it too is deficient. Cut off from historical continuity, it can be, and often is, very divisive. Cut off from any serious emphasis on the content of the faith, it can easily go off the rails in doctrine or morals. There is such a thing as church history. There is such a thing as Christian doctrine. The Spirit of God, the word of God, and the people of God need to walk hand in hand.

These different strands belong together. We find them all in Acts, where baptism is sometimes seen as the agency of salvation (Acts 2:38), sometimes as the seal on faith (16:31-33), and sometimes as the sovereign anointing of the Holy Spirit (10:44-48). All three strands are needed. For baptism is a big thing. The Catholics are right to see it as the objective mark of God's great rescue achieved on Calvary, to which we can make no contribution or addition. The Protestants are right to see in it our personal response to the grace of God, in repentance and faith. The Pentecostals are right to see baptism as the way whereby we are ushered into the world of the Spirit. Without that divine endowment, you can be baptized until you are blue in the face, you can profess the creed with unfailing zeal, and still be a stranger to the love of God. Baptism is as deep and broad as the salvation of which it is the sacrament.

What Can We Learn from the Baptism of John?

It caused an immense stir, and for a number of reasons. It was a mark of repentance. No pedigree, no good deeds could bring you into the coming kingdom of God: the only path lay through the baptismal waters of repentance. And that was very humbling.

Moreover it pointed ahead to the forgiveness of sins and the gift of the Spirit that Jesus, the Messiah, would bring.

It was also a very public and a very humiliating act. Never before had Jews been baptized: baptism was the initiation ceremony for Gentiles joining the people of God.

And finally, it was decisive. Either you went through the waters of God's judgment on sin symbolically in the Jordan, or else you would have to face it in stark reality later on. In all these ways, John's baptism, a landmark in Judaism, was a preview of the "main film," Christian baptism.

What Can We Learn from the Baptism of Jesus?

In his baptism Jesus identified with sinners, something that even John the Baptist found scandalous (Matt. 3:14ff.). It was, if you like, a dummy run for Calvary, when his cross was to be his baptism — in blood (Luke 12:50). We cannot enter with him into the unspeakable agonies of bearing the world's sin, but Christians can and should share in three other implications of his baptism.

It was an assurance of his sonship (Matt. 3:17 and parallels). So it is with the Christian, adopted into the family of God (Rom. 8:15-17).

It was an anointing by the Spirit (John 1:32; cf. Isa. 11:2). So it is for the Christian, because "Anyone who does not have the Spirit of Christ does not belong to him" (Rom. 8:9).

It was a commissioning for costly service. The voice from heaven at Jesus' baptism, "You are my Son; in you I am well pleased," was a combination of two significant Old Testament texts, the first from Psalm 2:7 and the second from Isaiah 42:1. Jesus, the Son of God, is also the Servant of God. Those Servant Songs in Isaiah, culminating in Isaiah 53, sketch out the path of ministry and suffering. And for the Christian, as for his Lord, ministry and suffering are inescapable: baptism points inexorably to that calling.

Christian baptism catches us up into the baptism of Jesus himself. This had three great dimensions to it. The baptism of repentance in the Jordan, the baptism of rescue on the cross, and the baptism of power in the Holy Spirit. And in my own baptism I see those same three realities. It calls me to repentance. It shows me where pardon is to be had. And it offers me the power of the Holy Spirit.

How Are We to Understand Christian Baptism?

In the light of these precedents of John and Jesus, how are we to understand Christian baptism? It is no optional extra, by the way. Jesus solemnly enjoined it upon us at the climax of his life on earth (Matt. 28:18-20).

1. *Christian baptism embodies God's challenge to repentance and faith.* It cannot be conducted without some expression of both. It says to us, "You are foul. You need washing. I can do that for you. But you must change your ways." It takes us to the heart of the gospel.

2. *Christian baptism offers us the blessings of the new covenant.* God approaches us in utterly unmerited grace. We respond in repentance and faith. And baptism signs over to us the blessings of the new covenant: forgiveness, sonship, servanthood, the Holy Spirit, the new birth, justification, and the promise of life after death.

3. *Christian baptism plunges us into the death and resurrection of Jesus.* We are brought to the point of death to the old life, which had no room for God, and the dawning of new life as the Holy Spirit enters our hearts. This dying and rising life is the essence of Christianity. It is what we are called to — and empowered for. It has a profound impact on the way we behave. So baptism is the gateway to a complete revolution in morals and lifestyle, even though we shall never achieve perfection in this life. It embodies our aim to live out the life of Christ in our own daily circumstances.

4. *Christian baptism initiates us into the worldwide church.* It is the adoption certificate into the family of God. It is the mark of belonging, the badge of membership. That may not always be obvious in traditionally Christian lands. But if your background is in Judaism or Islam, your baptism is crossing the Rubicon. It is the essential dividing line.

5. *Christian baptism commissions us to work for the kingdom of God.* It is God's commissioning service for his troops. For baptism is indeed a sign of the kingdom of God. It shows that we have surrendered to him as our king, and it is the uniform we wear as we go about the king's business.

6. *Christian baptism* does *something!* This New Testament emphasis is often overlooked by Protestants: we prefer to think it *symbolizes* something. But the New Testament uses some strongly instrumental language about baptism. It is through baptism that we enter the "name"

of the Trinity (Matt. 28:19) and thus are saved (1 Peter 3:21) or regenerated (John 3:5) or united with Christ in his death and resurrection (Rom. 6:3ff.; Col. 2:12), and incorporated into his body (1 Cor. 12:13). To be sure, several of these references mention the Holy Spirit (the divine agency) or faith (the human agency), but there is an undeniably instrumental flavor about the language used by the biblical writers. This should not surprise us. Justification, regeneration, incorporation into Christ, baptism — these are all different images of the way God makes us his own.

Baptism, then, is an "efficacious sign" of the new life. But of course it is not unconditionally efficacious, any more than a wedding ring is! It was not efficacious with Simon Magus (Acts 8:13, 21ff.) nor with some at Corinth (1 Cor. 10:1-6). But it is intended to bring about what it symbolizes. It is a palpable mark of belonging, like the wedding ring or the adoption certificate. Luther grasped this clearly. When he was tempted to doubt his own faith, he recalled the standing emblem of God's faithfulness marked upon him as an infant. He cried out in confidence *"Baptizatus sum,"* "I have been baptized," realizing that God's faithfulness was even more important than his faith.

How Was Baptism Administered?

Did the early Christians sprinkle candidates for baptism, or immerse them? We are not as well informed as we would like to be, but it is not a matter of supreme importance. They insisted on baptizing in water in the name of the Trinity, but the amount of water is nowhere specified. It is not a matter that should divide Christian brethren. Sometimes a river was at hand and they would doubtless immerse. Sometimes it would take place in a home, like that of the Philippian jailer, where immersion facilities would not exist. One of the early murals in the catacombs shows John the Baptist and Jesus standing waist-deep in the Jordan, and John *pouring* water over the head of Jesus: both methods have prizes!

But does not the word *baptizo* mean immerse? Not necessarily: it can mean wash (Luke 11:38). It could be argued that if a tiny piece of bread and a sip of wine enable us to enjoy God's grace in the Communion, it would not be incredible that a small amount of water may avail to seal God's grace to us in baptism. The early Christians seem to have been very relaxed about the mode of baptism. The very early *Didache* says "Baptise in the name of the Father and of the Son and of the Holy Spirit, in running water. But if thou hast not running water, baptise in other water. And if thou canst not in cold, then in warm. But if thou hast neither, pour water three times upon the head in the name of the Father and of the Son and of the Holy Spirit."[1]

Who Received Baptism?

Adult believers, certainly, and they are primary in any theological reflection about baptism. But it seems that children, wives, and slaves in the household were baptized also, when the head of the household professed faith. This, though not certain, is very probable and would not be in the least surprising to the first Christians. After all, children were sacramentally admitted to the Old Testament church (Gen. 17). Whole families of proselytes, including children and slaves, were baptized into the Jewish faith. Households were baptized in the New Testament itself (Acts 16:31, 33). The attitude of acceptance that Jesus displayed to tiny children would have helped (Mark 10:13-16). The baptism of infants was the virtually unchallenged practice of the early and medieval church. Moreover, it emphasizes the objectivity of the gospel: you have the mark of what Christ did for you at Calvary marked upon you, whether you choose to respond to it or not. And it emphasizes the initiative of God, reaching out to us before ever we think of reaching out to him. That is why most Christians baptize the children in their families. But it is a practice open to gross abuse if it does not take place in the context of faith. It is only intended for the children of believers, not to be an indiscriminate charm. It should not be administered without careful teaching of the obligations it calls for and the blessings it offers. And it requires personal reaffirmation on behalf of the candidate when he or she is confirmed.

On the other hand, the Baptist case is strong. It stresses that baptism is the Christian badge of belonging, not a social ceremony for the very young. It gives a clear, dateable time of commitment. It produces far less in the way of fallout than infant baptism does, and it is a powerful evangelistic occasion. My prayer is that Baptists and paedo-baptists

---

1. *Didache*, 7.1

may grow in mutual understanding of the strength of the other's position, and respect rather than criticize one another.

Can You Repeat Baptism?

No. It is as unrepeatable as justification or adoption, of which it is the sacrament. The early Christians were clear about this. There is a strange lust for rebaptism today. People very often feel that their baptism as an infant was deficient. There was too little faith around, too little water, too little feeling, too little chance for public confession of faith. The desire to "do it again, and do it properly" often springs from the modern cult of feelings. But strictly, it cannot be done again, any more than birth can. It is ever to be remembered but never to be repeated. Baptism may be reaffirmed. It may even be re-enacted: "If you are not already baptized, I baptize you. . . ." But it cannot be repeated.

What Is Baptism with the Holy Spirit?

There are seven references to baptism with the Holy Spirit in the New Testament. Six of these texts (Matt. 3:11; Mark 1:8; Luke 3:16; John 1:33; Acts 1:5; 11:15-16) draw the distinction between John the Baptist's baptism which was looking forward to Jesus, and the baptism Jesus would himself give "in" (or "with" or "by" — the Greek word can be translated in any of these ways) the Holy Spirit. All six point forward, then, to Christian initiation. It is precisely the same with the seventh, where Paul reminds the Corinthians, "charismatics" and "non-charismatics" alike, that they had all been baptized by one Spirit into the one body (1 Cor. 12:13). So all the New Testament references to this contentious phrase are initiatory. None points to a second and "more profound" experience. That is not for a moment to deny that such subsequent infillings may and do occur. Sometimes they are the most momentous spiritual experiences in our lives. But it does not help to call them baptism. It simply causes confusion. As we have seen, the Pentecostals are right about the importance of having the Spirit to come and flood your life: they are wrong to call that experience "baptism in the Holy Spirit" in contrast to "baptism in water." That is not how the Bible ever speaks of it.

Although there are not a great many references to baptism in the New Testament, it was clearly critically important to them as the sacrament of initiation. It sealed for them the unrepeatable incorporation into Christ. It pointed them to the dying and rising life that Christians are called to live. It joined them to brothers and sisters throughout the world. And it released in them the power of the Holy Spirit, so long as they claimed in faith the gift God so generously offered them.

The Eucharist

Baptism is the sacrament of Christian initiation; the Eucharist is the sacrament of Christian growth and development. Both are vital. The early Christians were well aware of this, and they valued the Communion highly. Here again we are often impoverished by our own tradition. The very names used for it in Scripture hint at the breadth of meanings in this most wonderful sacrament. The "Lord's Supper" takes us back to the Upper Room (1 Cor. 11:20). The "breaking of bread" (Acts 2:42) alludes to Jesus feeding the multitude. The "Holy Communion" indicates a joint "participation in the body and blood of Christ" (1 Cor. 10:16). The "Eucharist" speaks of blessing God for all that Jesus has done for us (1 Cor. 11:24; *Didache* 9.1). And the "Mass," though somewhat obscure in etymology, probably means dismissal of the congregation into the world for ministry and mission. Mass is not, however, a New Testament term, though the idea of sending out certainly is.

Imagine the Setting

Most early Communions did not take place in a church at all, but in a home. People begin to appear in the early evening with materials for a potluck supper. They are happy and relaxed: work is over. All are on a level here, men and women, Roman citizens and commoners, slaves and free. Oil lamps are lit. Couches are set. Feet are washed. They have a meal, reclining round a courtyard, or squashed into a room. They share news. Someone produces a musical instrument and they begin to sing. Indeed, they create new songs, snatches of which are to be found in the New Testament, like "Awake, sleeper, and arise from the dead: Christ shall give you life," or "Holy, holy, holy, Lord God Almighty, who was and is and is to come." Meanwhile someone has brought out the church box that contains their most precious Christian belongings: some sayings of Jesus, perhaps a letter from an apostle, or Communion vessels. The praise is heartfelt. Tongues might well follow. There could be prayer for a healing or a specific need of one of the members. Certainly prayer, the reading of an Old Testament scripture, the recitation of a story about Jesus, and some words of encouragement from members of the community, along with joyful singing, would all feature. And as the evening comes to an end, they would tell again the story of Jesus' passion, and break bread and drink wine in remembrance of him. Every scrap is finished. The prayer that Jesus taught them is recited. They move round and embrace one another with a holy kiss, and then go home. All very simple. No service books. No priests. No altars. Every eye is on the unseen Lord, the bread, the wine, and each other. And then — out into the night, spiritually refueled for the journey of the coming week.

What Is This Meal?

There have been many speculations. Some have seen it as a *haburah,* a special religious meal held by a group of friends. Others have sought to show that it derived from a *kiddush,* a Friday evening family gathering to prepare for the Sabbath. Others again have looked to pagan sources for this meal. None of this need detain us now. For the clue to understanding this meal lies in the Passover of the Old Testament, and 1 Corinthians 5:7 makes this very plain. "Christ our Passover has been sacrificed for us. Therefore let us keep the feast."

A Passover with a Difference

Joachim Jeremias persuasively demonstrated this Passover background to the Communion in his book, *The Eucharistic Words of Jesus;*[2] and all subsequent scholarship on the subject has been beholden to him. He

2. Joachim Jeremias, *The Eucharistic Words of Jesus* (London: SCM Press, 1970).

points out eleven elements in the account that substantiate this Passover background. For example, the Last Supper took place in Jerusalem; it extended into the night; it was a small intimate gathering; they reclined instead of sitting; a dish preceded the breaking of bread; wine, an essential at Passover, was drunk; the words of institution are an adaptation of Passover *haggadah;* Judas went out, ostensibly to give to the poor — a Passover custom; and so on. Jeremias piles up the evidence that the meal was an anticipated Passover. He then deals with ten objections. There are two that he does not handle. One is the absence of any mention of a lamb. Was this due to the compression of the account as Christians recited what was special about that Passover? Was it because they saw Jesus as the Passover lamb? We may never know. The other of Jeremias's omissions is an explanation of how the annual Passover celebration turned into the weekly (or even more frequent) Christian celebration. The frequency was probably due to the well-remembered fact that the Master had made a point of eating regularly with his disciples. They had a regular common meal (which turned in the early church into the *agape* meal). But all subsequent communal meals were impregnated with the meaning of this awesome night, repeated often, at his express command.

All the four accounts, despite their different nuances, are agreed that Jesus took bread, blessed and broke it, spoke interpretative words over it, and gave it to his disciples. There is no space to study in detail this meal that gave rise to the Holy Communion, but several factors are of great importance.

1. This was a complete meal, extended for a long time. Our accounts cover only the special Christian differentiae in this Passover meal; the bread and wine were only selections from a much fuller mealtime together.

2. The annual Jewish Passover was not a sacrifice but a memorial of the first Passover, which certainly was a sacrifice: the lambs of Israel died and their blood was painted on the door lintels to avert the angel of wrath. Equally, the Christian Eucharist is not a sacrifice, but is the memorial of that great sacrifice when the Lamb of God shed his blood to avert judgment on a sinful world.

3. The words "body" and "blood," clearly a pair, lead us back in Aramaic to the only pair that Jesus could have used: *bisra udema.* Both are sacrificial words. Each word denotes violent death. They point to his sacrificial death on the morrow.

4. By giving them the bread and the wine, he gives them a share in the benefits of his atoning sacrifice, just as the Israelites who ate the Passover lamb shared not in making the sacrifice but in enjoying its benefits — in their case, rescue from bondage and death in Egypt. This is how sacrificial language came to be applied to the Communion. Properly, the Eucharist is not a sacrifice. It is the memorial of his atoning sacrifice, and a means of enjoying its benefits.

5. The change in the *halakah* (explanatory word about the Passover) is truly amazing. Normally the president would (in obedience to Exod. 12:25; 13:8) take bread and say "This is the bread of affliction which your fathers ate in the wilderness." Imagine the electric atmosphere when Jesus, presiding, says "This is my body, given for you." In Aramaic it would have gone like this: "This — my body . . ." leaving it open whether representation or identity was intended — an issue that has divided Catholics from Protestants for centuries. Do this in *remembrance* of me! The word *anamnesis,* remembrance, does not mean mere mental recollection, as we Westerners would interpret it. To the Semitic mind it meant representation. The Jews were accustomed to say, at Passover, "This the Eternal did for me when I went out of Egypt." They saw the past as in some way made contemporary. Similarly Jesus seems to have intended his disciples at the Eucharist to see his death as in some way made contemporary, however many years ago it happened. Here in this service I see afresh before my very eyes what the Eternal did for me to bring me out of a bondage and a doom far worse than that which befell the Jews in Egypt. The broken bread and the poured-out wine not only dramatically reminded the early Christians of what Jesus did for them on the cross: it showed them that this historical event has present power and relevance. They could enter into the experience to which it referred, sharing in the benefits of his death and resurrection for them.

The blood is as significant as the bread. The Passover blood was originally applied to the houses of the Israelites, and brought salvation, rescue from the destroying angel who killed the firstborn of the Egyptians. That is why wine (to recall the blood) was an essential part of Passover. The benediction before the "cup of blessing" in the Passover specifically praises God for that deliverance from Egypt and the covenant he made with his people. The *hallel* of praise that followed had Psalm 116 as its core, a psalm that spoke of gratefully receiving the cup of salvation. So there were profound associations combined here: the blood, the covenant, the exodus, the vicariousness, the cup, and the appropriation.

6. The shocking language was intentional and was remembered. To eat human flesh and to drink blood was expressly forbidden in Judaism. We need to take seriously both the metaphorical and the realistic significance of this language. We feed on him in our hearts, really feed on him. But we do so by faith.

The Meaning of the Meal

Set as it is against the backcloth of the Passover, both historically and theologically, the depths of the Eucharist begin to become apparent.

1. The Passover had a *backward* orientation. The first Passover was a sacrifice. Indeed, it was the sacrifice that constituted Israel as a people. Succeeding Passovers were not sacrifices, though they might loosely be called such, and they had no expiatory significance. But they brought that original sacrifice powerfully before the worshiper. It is like that with the Communion. Not a sacrifice in itself, it is the representation of Christ's sacrifice, and we feast on the benefits he won for us through it.

2. The Passover had a *present* orientation. The first Passover had been a meal to strengthen the Israelites for their march from the land of bondage to the land of promise. This element was re-enacted annually. The theme of God's constant care and provision for them is prominent in the *haggadah* (the account of God's mighty rescue, recounted at the meal). The eating and drinking formed a sacred bond between the worshipers: one can see from Psalm 41:9 how heinous was the breaking of such table fellowship. It was the same with the Communion. It, too, has the effect of binding together all its participants into one (1 Cor. 10:17). Its fellowship, too, cannot be violated without the most heinous sin and disastrous consequences (1 Cor. 11:19, 20, 27-30). And it too strengthens pilgrims for the journey, for it feeds them with the body of Christ (1 Cor. 10:16), and he is the nourishment and sustenance of all Christian lives (John 6:51).

3. The Passover had a *future* orientation. It prefigured the ultimate feast of salvation as well as being the memorial of deliverance from Egypt. Passover would be the night when Messiah would come. "On this night they were saved, and on this night they will be saved," mused

the rabbis. This forward look is integral to the Christian Passover, the Eucharist. In Luke's account (22:7-23) it is stressed almost to the exclusion of all else. It is also there in Matthew and Mark, and in the allusive language about the "true" bread and vine in the Gospel of John. It is notable in 1 Corinthians 11:26, and the cry *Maranatha* ("Our Lord, come" 1 Cor. 16:22) was used at the Eucharist, as we learn from the *Didache* (10.4). The passage is worth quoting, since it shows something of the fervor of early Christians as they shared in the Communion.

> Remember, Lord, thy church to deliver it from all evil and to make it perfect in thy love; and gather it together in its holiness from the four winds to thy kingdom which thou hast prepared for it. For thine is the power and the glory for ever. Let grace come, and let this world pass away. Hosannah to the God of David. If any man be holy, let him come! If any man be not, let him repent. Maranatha, Amen.

Just as the Passover was the pledge of the coming of the Messiah, so the Eucharist is the pledge of his return, and of the Messianic banquet towards which every Communion points.

No wonder this is the central meal for Christians, the service important beyond all others: it is the archetypal symbol of our redemption, past, present, and future. We will grow deeper and deeper in its appreciation until we taste it new in the kingdom of God. Our Master knew what he was doing when he left just two sacraments to his church — baptism and the Eucharist. Both are incandescent with all the colors of salvation's rainbow. The one points to its once-for-allness, and its need to govern the dying and rising life of Christians. The other calls and empowers for persistence on the journey, as pilgrims climb the upward path. It lifts our eyes to the Lord, our Bread and Vine, and it points us towards God's wedding banquet when Christ will marry his bride the church forever, and there will be no more sorrow, no more crying, no more death. We shall see his face and share his likeness.

10

Aware of the Struggle

R. PAUL STEVENS

Only he who understands that sin is inexplicable knows what it is.

EMIL BRUNNER

The Stevens and the Zimmermans were driving through downtown Nairobi, Kenya, on July 8, 1990. A people's movement was taking place at that time. Thousands of people were bringing pressure on the government to allow more than one political party. But the real reason for the riots, which had begun the day before, was the fact that one-third of the people of the city, where the average age is seventeen, were unemployed. We were about to lead in an urban church seminar in Nairobi, and had come to bring a measure of redemption to the city. We did not expect the riot to last into the second day. But as we turned into a roundabout, and then into a one-way street, we were attacked by about fifty people with rocks and clubs who attempted to turn the car over and set it on fire. Through an amazing deliverance, I was able to do a U-turn in a single-lane street and get the car going in the opposite direction while the rioters caught up with the vehicle. One large stone was hurled through the window and grazed my neck, smashing the windshield. If it had been a centimeter to the left I would have been knocked unconscious and our escape would have been impossible.

The real reason for the rage was not black and white, but rich and poor. We were driving a car, and were therefore obviously rich. Many of the rioters were members of the church and, as part of their "fulfilling righteousness," were expressing their outrage about an unjust system against the symbols of that injustice, two rich couples who ironically had come to bring redemption to the city. As it "happened," our home church was praying for us at the very time of this encounter. Two years previous to this event one of the members of the church had a vision of one of the couples escaping from an African city, and prayed against this for two years. What was going on there? An encounter with fallen human nature? Unjust and unredeemed social, economic, and political structures? Direct harassment by Satan? Did angels — unseen by us — surround our car? Did God answer our sister's intercessory prayer for us offered over two years?

A few misguided teachers claim that becoming a Christian solves all your problems and makes you effortlessly happy and trouble free until you enter the final bliss of heaven. But they are lying. Following Jesus is a victorious battle, not a victorious life. And beware of anyone who can tell you there is a simple explanation for the struggle. They are probably wrong. Indeed there are so many confusing messages around the struggle that the gift of discernment may be one of the most important gifts needed in the church today.

Some people maintain that you can gain sinless perfection and a totally victorious life. Charles Spurgeon once heard a person at a conference claim that he had entered that blessed state. Spurgeon said nothing at the time. But the next day at breakfast a pitcher of milk was poured over the speaker to test his doctrine, which was shown, quite definitely, to be false! The reality is that the most godly saints still struggle. In fact we fight a multi-front battle: the world, the flesh, and the devil, as the Prayer Book defines it. And for this multi-front battle the New Testament offers a multi-front victory. First, there is the world.

The World: The Trouble Outside

A Canadian commercial artist works for a prominent advertising firm that keeps careful control over the kind of clients it accepts. While the senior partners in the firm are not Christians, they are moral men and women and do not wish to become involved in advertising products that are harmful to human life or to use advertising methods that are, in their view, overtly manipulative, appealing to drives that would swamp any rational decision-making. A Christian working for this firm has particularly enjoyed doing the advertising for a chain of stores over the years, and he has won several awards for his imaginative representation of new products. But the chain branched out into some new investments that are known to be linked with highly questionable products. It is rumored in the office that there is mafia money behind the company now, in spite of the high level of public acceptance of the firm's products. In order to keep this essential client the artist will have to advertise products he believes are destructive to the moral fabric of society. But, as his boss says, "In our society you are no longer dealing with a single customer but with multinational networks in all shades and colors. The only way to stay in the business world is to work in the system and don't ask too many questions about where the money is coming from." What is going on here?

The Trouble with the World

Whether working in a large corporation or a small business, work takes believers into a society where it is difficult to live by kingdom principles. They do not feel in control of the circumstances of their work, surrounded as they are by structures, powers, authorities, influences, and systems that compel them to lower their standards or seduce them to compromise. The problem is deeper than the personal sin of their superiors or workmates, or even of "the flesh." Indeed Paul says "our struggle is *not* against flesh and blood" (Eph. 6:12). There is something more than the mere sum of all the sinful attitudes and actions of people. It involves a system. Jesus taught that the world cannot receive the Spirit (John 14:17), hates Jesus, and hates believers (15:18). Believers have been chosen "out of" the world (15:19) and are not "of" the world (17:14) even though they must live "in" the world (17:15). "In this world," Jesus says, "you will have trouble" (16:33).

The trouble is multifaceted and comes to us through unjust or unloving structures, systems of business and finance, principles of conformity, social patterns, customs and traditions that marginalize the life of faith or positively oppose it, and the ever-present influence of the media. A friend of mine who teaches marketing in a university wrote a scholarly article proving that the advertising world appeals to the seven deadly sins: wrath, lust, avarice, gluttony, sloth, envy, and pride. Studies have shown that the average North American is exposed to fourteen hundred advertisements each day: fourteen hundred messages, by and large, from "the other side." The complexity of life in an increasingly neopagan society is so confusing that some misguided people feel that the only safe haven is to work for the church or a Christian organization. What they find — to their extreme disappointment — is more of the same, though often more cleverly disguised. There is no easy escape. But the Bible provides an indispensable framework for understanding our trouble and dealing with it.

God So Loved the World

Scripture uses "world" to describe the created order about which God could say, "it is very good" (Gen. 1:31). But there was more than mere matter involved in making the world. God's creative activity involved placing humankind in a structured universe that included time (seven days), space (a sanctuary garden), relationships (covenant marriage and family), authorities and structures (the tree of knowledge), and other creatures (animals and the serpent). Imagine a world without marriage, family, government, and without national borders (Acts 17:26)! All of these are designed by God for our protection and for meaningful life.

What are called in Scripture "principalities," "powers," "virtues," "dominions," "thrones," and "names" (Rom. 8:38; 1 Cor. 15:25; Eph. 1:21; 3:10; 6:12; Col. 1:16; 2:10, 15) are words used to describe the structured and ordered way that God has created the world. These terms imply government, human authorities, national structures, family and tribal structures, priorities within relationships of peers, and angelic realms. Far from being the result of "the fall," these powers are part of God's *good* creation. They are not innately evil. They are made by Christ and for Christ! Paul claims that through Christ "all things were created: things in heaven and on earth, visible and invisible, whether thrones or powers or rulers or authorities; all things were created by him and for him" (Col. 1:15). Hendrikus Berkhof describes this brilliantly as the invisible background of creation, "the dikes with which God encircles His good creation, to keep it in His fellowship and protect it from chaos."[1]

These good gifts of God (Col. 1:15) were intended to form a framework in which we serve God. But they have now, through the sin of humankind and the civil war that took place in the universe (Jude 6), become broken, hostile, resistant to God's rule, and intransigent. Some of these powers have taken on a life of their own, making idolatrous claims on human beings: government, religion, culture, "isms," and the demonic, being symbolized by the "names" and "titles" (Eph. 1:21) that dominate the news. Scripture speaks of the predicament of the "principalities and powers" in various ways. Sometimes we are told to regard these pretentious, tyrannical powers as "weak and miserable principles" that make god-like claims even though they are "no gods" (Gal. 4:8-9). In Ephesians, Paul says that our struggle is not against human problems — flesh and blood — but against "the spiritual forces of evil in the heavenly realms," suggesting that the devil himself has co-opted these powers, or "colonized" them for his own ends (Eph. 6:10-13). It is impossible for human beings to function in this world without encountering these habitual, fallen patterns, which will be experienced in competition, in compelling forces of conformity, and, in its worst form, in direct satanic attack through witchcraft and satanism.

Some Christian authors treat the New Testament witness to the powers *only* as structures of our worldly life having no relationship with the devil or fallen angels. Other authors concentrate exclusively on warfare with the demonic. But the Christian in the world must deal with *both*. And Scripture witnesses to the complexity of systemic evil: structures, spiritual hosts, and the last enemy, death (1 Cor. 15:24-27) — all arenas of spiritual warfare. But the Christian is not powerless in this spiritual warfare because Christ has already won the victory over the powers.

The Powerless Powers

Oscar Cullmann compares the powers to chained beasts, kicking themselves to death. Between the resurrection of Jesus and the second com-

---

1. Hendrikus Berkhof, *Christ and the Powers,* trans. John Howard Yoder (Kitchener, Ont.: Herald Press, 1962/77), p. 29.

ing they are tied to a rope, still free to evince their demonic character but nevertheless bound. This is certainly the perspective of the last book of the Bible (Rev. 18–19). Christ's relation to the powers is crucial for lay spirituality. Christ was voluntarily "victimized" by the powers when he submitted to a human crucifixion. The seeming victory of the powers was symbolized by the three-language title over his cross: Latin for government, Greek for culture, and Hebrew for religion. But ironically, Christ's death put the principalities and powers in their place as instruments, subject to God's sovereignty. His cross was a victory not only over the sin of humankind but over the powers. Christ's crucifixion was a political act and a cosmic victory. He "disarmed" the powers, "made a public spectacle of them," thereby showing how illusionary their pretensions were, and "triumphed over them" (Col. 2:15). Speaking to this, Berkhof says, "Whenever (the cross) is preached, the unmasking and disarming of the Powers takes place."[2] Without the eye of faith, these powers still seem almost omnipotent. But to the eye of faith they are vanquished even though they continue to press their claims and therefore complicate even the Christian's life in this world.

The first and most effective strategy against the false claims of the powers is proclaiming the gospel. Our duty is not to bring the powers to *our* knees: this is Christ's task. Our duty is to arm ourselves with Christ (Eph. 6:10-18) and to declare his cross. However much we attempt to "Christianize" the powers, we must not bypass preaching the gospel and calling people to embrace the reign of Christ through repentance and faith. And this task is not the exclusive duty of the church pastor but the vocation of the whole people of God to witness.

Some of these powers deserve the loyal submission of Christians (Rom. 13:1). Some of them should be Christianized by the involvement of Christians and the church in creational tasks: subjecting the resources of the world in education, politics, and culture to serve humankind as defined by God's intention. Some powers will be shown to be unmasked by the martyrdom of faithful believers (Rev. 12:11). But Christians and the church must be under no illusion. As Markus Barth says,

> The power of filling, subjugating, and dominating "all things," including these powers, is reserved to God and Christ alone. But the

2. Berkhof, *Christ and the Powers*, p. 39.

function of demonstrating God's dominion and love is entrusted to the church. She is appointed and equipped to be a public exponent of grace and unity . . . the beginning of a new heaven and a new earth.[3]

The Power of Public Discipleship

Christ's complete victory over the principalities and powers, over Satan, sin, and death, assures us that there is nowhere in the universe so demonized that a Christian might not be called to serve there. We fight a war that is already won. Therefore as far as now possible Christians should Christianize the powers, to "peace" the powers through involvement in education, commerce, government, the arts, and social action, all the while knowing that the task of subjugating the powers is reserved for Christ alone (Eph. 1:10; Phil. 2:10-11). We work on the problems of pollution, food distribution, injustice, genetic engineering, and the proliferation of violence and weaponry, knowing that this work is ministry and holy. In the short run this work may seem unsuccessful, but in the long run this work will be gloriously successful because we are cooperating with what Christ is doing to renew all creation. In this we must live with heavenly-mindedness knowing that Christ said "all power is given to me in heaven and on earth" (Matt. 28:18). While the beast is master here for a moment (Rev. 13:1-18), all dimensions of social unity will be restored according to God's design in the end. And in the New Jerusalem the "principalities and powers" will provide structure for our common life and work (Rev. 21:24).

So we have seen that our struggle in the world is not merely the sum of the effect of all the sinful human beings in the world. We deal with systemic evil, and systemic evil calls for spiritual warfare, a ministry for which we are gloriously provisioned. But we still must come to terms with ourselves, with our own tendencies toward evil, with our "flesh." Words attributed to G. K. Chesterton are *also* incisively accurate: "What is wrong with the world? I am wrong with the world!"

---

3. Markus Barth, *Ephesians,* The Anchor Bible (Garden City, N.Y.: Doubleday and Co., 1974), vol. 1, p. 365.

Flesh: The Battle Within

A pastor who loves preaching finds that when he stands up to preach his eyes connect with a particularly attractive woman in the congregation. He feels she reciprocates with an equal intensity. Something mysterious is happening between them. While he preaches eloquently, and convincingly, there is something electric going on between him and this woman. Both are married to other spouses, and he knows that he should not even be entertaining fantasies about another woman, but the woman frequently appears in his dreams and they have an affair of the eyes each Sunday. His secretary has just told him that she is coming this afternoon for marriage counseling. What is going on here?

In fact Christians struggle until the day they die. And part of that struggle *is* with flesh and blood, with human nature as it has become through sin. The word "flesh" *(sarx)* is a complex word in Paul's writing and we must attempt a short explanation.

The Flesh against the Spirit

First, we must note that Paul sometimes uses *sarx* merely to denote what is human about us. Once we regarded Christ "from a human point of view" (2 Cor. 5:16; 1:17). "By human standards" not many of the Corinthians were wise and educated (1 Cor. 1:26). Sometimes "flesh" simply refers to one's bodily life (Rom. 2:28), which is normally good or at least neutral. Paul was converted from the Greek view of the body as a hindrance, to the biblical view that believers can glorify God *with* and *in* their bodies. Our ultimate future is not to be holy souls floating around eternity but to be resurrected persons experiencing complete, personal, bodily, and human life in the presence of God and his people in a new heaven *and a new earth* (Rev. 21–22). So "flesh" is not always pitted against life in Christ, or the Spirit.

On this point it is remarkable that the works of the flesh Paul lists in Galatians 5:17 are largely non-physical: impurity, idolatry, witchcraft, hatred, discord, jealousy, fits of rage, selfish ambition, dissensions, factions, and envy. These are often psychological, spiritual, and relational. The war going on inside is not mainly between our physical body and our human spirits, but between something else that "desires what is contrary to the Spirit" (5:16). It is true that four of the listed works of the flesh — sexual immorality, debauchery, drunkenness, and orgies — involve the physical body. But the root of these destructive activities is to be found in our minds and in what Scripture calls the heart. Sexual problems are not primarily physical problems.

While many modern translations use the words "human nature" to translate *sarx,* this word must not be understood to mean we have *two parts* to our personhood, one good and one bad, one higher and one lower, one given to God and the other given to sin. No, it is our whole person — body, soul, and spirit — that struggles to live under the reign of Christ and in the Spirit. So the sexual sins listed in the "works of the flesh" are personal sins, and arise not from an irrepressible instinct in our bodies but from something wrong in our persons. "Idolatry" and "sorcery" involve the secret tampering with the powers of evil through drugs or witchcraft. "Enmity," "strife," "fits of anger," "selfishness," "dissensions," "party spirit," and "envy" are relational sins — persons out of sync with others, seeking their own advantage or cherishing pain when someone else is honored. Even "drunkenness" and "carousing" are, in the end, not exclusively physical problems, because they both involve giving one's consciousness to a chemical, a profoundly personal matter. So the works of the flesh are not to be located in our physical drives and appetites but in the fundamental orientation of our lives.

This brings us to the special way Paul sometimes uses "flesh" in his letters, in Romans 7:18 ("I know that nothing good lives in me, that is, in my sinful nature — *sarx*") and Galatians 5:16-17 ("For the sinful nature — *sarx* — desires what is contrary to the Spirit"). "Flesh" stands for human nature as it has become through sin. It is life lived as though Christ had not come, died, and been raised. It is life outside and against the Spirit. "Flesh" describes — but does not ultimately account for — the oft-repeated situation where a person knows what to do but feels helpless to do it (Rom. 7:18). There is a great range of interpretations of Paul's striking and troubling confession in Romans 7:15 — "For what I want to do I do not do, but what I hate I do." They include on one extreme the view that Paul is speaking of his pre-Christian state, and on the other extreme, that he is confessing his present experience of struggle as an apostle (and is therefore an exponent of our own struggle). The debate on this text will probably never be concluded. But James Stewart offers a helpful pastoral comment in these words: "It is safe for a Christian like Paul — it is not safe for everybody — to explain his failings by the watchword, 'Not I, but indwelling sin. . . .' A true saint may say it in a moment of passion, but a sinner had better not make it a principle."[4] It is my view that this is precisely the emphasis Paul brings in Galatians 5:16-26.

The Spirit against the Flesh

Seldom noted in Paul's correspondence — sometimes because of the translation — is the fact that Paul's most common use of "Spirit" and "Spiritual" involves the use (in the English) of a capital "S." The war within is not between a lower nature (flesh) and a higher nature (spirit), but between the flesh and Spirit, between human nature as a whole organized against God's purposes and thus turned inward, and, on the other hand, God's presence and power. Paul's point in saying that "flesh and Spirit are in conflict with each other, so that you do not do what you want" (Gal. 5:17) is not to underline that a war rages within, a war over which the believer is helpless, unable to live for God wholeheartedly. The passage is spoken to people who are already "in the Spirit." They have received Christ. They have found justification not by works of the law but by faith in Jesus. They are reminded by Paul that they began their Christian life not by human effort but by believing what they heard about Jesus and receiving the Spirit (3:2-3). Having begun with the Spirit they *still* cannot attain the goal of the Christian life by performance, religious or otherwise. The gospel not only takes us to heaven; it also equips us to live triumphantly now! It is faith and Spirit all the way.

So Christians are under obligation to live according to the Spirit and not to gratify the desires of the flesh (5:16). "Flesh" in this context is not merely human nature, but human life lived outside of the reality of Christ's having come. Living "according to the flesh" and living "according to the Spirit" are not two factions warring inside the beleaguered and troubled Christian. They are two ways of living that are completely inconsistent and are incompatible. Paul does not deny that people who have begun to follow Jesus may live "according to the flesh." What he denies is that they *must*.

4. James S. Stewart, *A Faith to Proclaim* (London: Hodder and Stoughton, 1953), p. 77.

Gordon Fee notes that the burden of the passage is not that the believer is helpless before the volcanic forces of flesh within. Fee argues forcefully that we cannot interpret Galatians 5 in the light of Romans 7. We must find out what Paul is saying to the Galatians. And what Paul insists to these misguided believers is that the Spirit has brought them to life. Therefore walking in the Spirit *precludes* making provision for walking in the flesh and gratifying the desires of their former way of life. "Spirit people cannot do whatever they like. Freedom is not freedom for the flesh; it is freedom for the Spirit, so that they serve one another in love."[5]

The possibility of a Christian giving in to sin from time to time remains. The flesh has been crucified with the cross of Christ but a Christian might still live according to the flesh, as though he or she had not been redeemed, adopted, forgiven, and indwelt by God's own Spirit. *But it is inconsistent so to do.* The fact that we continue to struggle makes it imperative not only to understand the nature of the conflict but also to learn how to deal with it. So we must now ask how to walk in the Spirit and not gratify the desires of the flesh.

Walking in the Spirit

What Paul teaches in Galatians is how to live victoriously in the thick of battle. He starts with the fruit of the Spirit and gives an *ad hoc* list of benefits from being in Christ, some aspects of the fruit being experiential (such as joy), some attitudinal (such as patience), and some behavioral (such as self-control). What is remarkable about this list is that Paul does not regulate the Christian life by a series of rules and behavioral requirements. For the Christian there can be no law (Gal. 5:23) to regulate food, clothing, religious practices, entertainment, and recreation. Human commandments have no value at all. What Paul proposes, rather, is letting the Spirit bear his own fruit in our lives. The contrast of *works* of the flesh, and *fruit* of the Spirit — actually a seven-fold fruit — is often noted. Works must be accomplished; fruit comes with very little effort

---

5. Gordon D. Fee, "The Spirit Against the Flesh: Another Look at Pauline Ethics" (unpublished lecture at New Orleans Baptist Theological Seminary, November 7, 1991), p. 17.

from ourselves when there is the irruption of life within. Ironically the first and foremost strategy for refusing to live by the flesh is indirect: to turn from concentrating on the flesh to concentrating on the Spirit.

In a shocking, anonymous article entitled "The War Within: An Anatomy of Lust" an American spiritual director revealed his long-standing struggle with pornography and voyeurism. He admitted that lust is fully pleasurable and has its own compelling rewards. He despaired that time after time when he repented in prayer, and cried out to God to take away his desire, nothing changed. Then he chanced on a line from François Mauriac, that there is only one reason to seek purity. Mauriac said that purity is the condition for a higher love — for a possession superior to all possessions: God himself. Whereas all the negative arguments against lust had failed, and guilt had provided no power to change, "here," this Christian leader discovered, "was a description of what I was missing by continuing to harbor lust: I was limiting my own intimacy with God."[6]

Fruit-bearing is also the context for Paul's second strategy, a strategy that is also positively motivated. Crucifying the flesh is not first and foremost a negative work. It is like repentance. C. S. Lewis once remarked that repentance "is not something God demands of you before he will take you back and which He could let you off if He chose; it is simply a description of what going back is like."[7] Paul's repeated exhortations in Galatians should be understood this way. He says, "Those who belong to Jesus Christ have crucified the sinful nature with its passions and desires" (5:24). "After beginning with the Spirit, are you now trying to attain your goal by human effort?" (2:3). "May I never boast except in the cross of our Lord Jesus Christ, through which the world has been crucified to me, and I to the world" (6:14). These statements are not appeals to self-crucifixion, mortification of one's bodily life, or self-hatred as though these negative "good" works could accomplish anything more than positive "good" works. Paul appeals for a full and continuous agreement with God's judgment on our autonomous, self-justifying life. It is worthy of death; it puts God to death, murdering him in our hearts. John Stott reminds us that a cruci-

6. Anonymous, "The War Within: An Anatomy of Lust," *Leadership* (Fall 1982): 43.

7. Quoted in Anonymous, "The War Within," p. 43.

fixion is pitiless (and we should not treat the flesh as respectable), pain-ful (even though the pleasures of the flesh are fleeting), and decisive (as suggested by the aorist tense in the Greek — fully accomplished).[8] Here, as everywhere in the Christian life, we move from the indicative (what exists) to the imperative (what ought to be done). Jesus *has* died for us and the flesh *has* been substantially overcome; therefore we should maintain a crucified perspective on the flesh. But mortification is less than half of living a victorious battle.

Once again Paul offers good news. We do not have to live defeated lives. "So I say, live by the Spirit, and you will not gratify the desires of the sinful nature" (5:16). "But if you are led by the Spirit, you are not un-der law" (5:18). "Since we live by the Spirit, let us keep in step with the Spirit" (5:25). Here again we move from the indicative to the imperative. We *are* children of God and by the Spirit call God "Father" (Rom. 8:14). We *are* led by the Spirit (an image used to describe a farmer leading cat-tle, or soldiers escorting a prisoner to court). We have a continuous, gentle pressure towards goodness. Because the Spirit leads, we *do* the walking. Two words for walking are used — the ordinary word for "walk" and *stoikeo,* which means to draw people up in a line, or to line oneself up with the Spirit's initiatives.[9] Both suggest an action on our part but it is an action that is responsive to the constant and creative ini-tiative of the Spirit in our lives. In contrast to "sowing to the flesh" which results in destruction, "sowing to the Spirit" results in reaping eternal life (Gal. 6:7-8).

Negatively, walking according to the Spirit means *not* setting the mind on the things of the flesh (Rom. 8:5) or doing the deeds of the flesh (Gal. 5:19-21). We put these desires and deeds to death by the Spirit (Rom. 8:13; Gal. 5:16-18, 24-26). This involves repudiating our boasting in human achievement, human wisdom, or human law-keeping as ways of achieving righteousness. Positively, walking according to the Spirit implies that the Christian "keeps in line" (Gal. 5:25) with what the Spirit is already doing. We set our mind on the things of the Spirit (Rom. 8:5), allow the Spirit to produce his character fruit (Gal. 5:19-21; Rom. 12–14), and receive the Spirit's power for works of holiness (Rom. 12:9-21; cf.

---

8. John R. W. Stott, *The Message of Galatians* (London: Inter-Varsity Press, 1968), pp. 150-51.

9. Stott, *The Message,* pp. 152-53.

Isa. 58). Until Christ comes again and fully consummates his kingdom on earth and introduces a new heaven and a new earth, we will never cease to experience tension and struggle. But we need not live defeated lives. As surely as Christ has come, as surely as Christ has died and has risen, we are now living in the age of the Spirit. And we *can* live by the Spirit. Indeed we *will*. New Testament "spirituality" is Spirit-uality. So Paul says, if translated literally, "live by the Spirit, *and you will not gratify the desires of the flesh*" (Gal. 5:16). But there is more to living victoriously than overcoming the flesh.

The Devil: The Invisible War

A Christian oral surgeon went through the trauma of having three patients die in one year through a series of strange accidents. In each case the anesthetist, not the surgeon, was directly responsible for the patient's life. But the presiding surgeon was held responsible. In one case the patient died of an undiagnosed heart problem while having a routine oral procedure under general anesthetic. In a second, faulty equipment was to blame. Each autopsy showed that the oral surgeon had performed his procedure with professional competence. But a specialist's business depends entirely on the goodwill of referring physicians and this broke down when the media got hold of the story. This surgeon's story was covered in tabloid newspapers and in local radio stations, and his "record" as a surgeon became a matter of public conversation. While the accrediting body for oral surgeons investigated and found that he was not at fault, and while his friends were convinced that it was an almost incredible sequence of accidents, none of his former medical friends felt free to refer their patients to him. He became less and less employed until he finally had to leave the country and start over somewhere else. As a family the experience forced them to go deeper with God as they struggled against public opinion and tried to ignore the media people hiding at the end of their driveway trying to make something more of the story. But the doctor whose career was being destroyed could not help wonder if this was not a direct attack by Satan. What was going on here?

Know the Enemy

We come now to a further dimension of the struggle. But we have difficulty even understanding this one! *Western society has largely rejected the spiritual interpretation of life.* Even the church turns to social analysis to find out what is going on, and leaves out the spiritual realities behind and within the visible and present. Years ago James Stewart traced the intellectual history of this demise of our biblical framework in these brilliant words:

> St. Paul's "principalities and powers" — the "spirit forces of evil" whose malignant grip upon the souls of men called forth "a second Adam to the fight and to the rescue" — are now known, we are told, to have been mere apocalyptic imagination. To this result Newton, Darwin and Freud certainly contributed. For Newton's work left no room for an irrational principle in nature; and the devil is essentially irrational, teleologically indefinable — as St. John marks by his significant use of *anomia* and St. Paul by the phrase "the mystery of iniquity" (1 John 3:4). . . . Darwin's picture of the biological struggle for existence was hailed as radically superseding the Biblical picture of the cosmic struggle between the demons and the kingdom of the Lord. Finally, Freud banished the powers of darkness from their last stronghold, the soul, by successfully dissolving them into psychological complexes, neuroses, and the like: so that the good fight of faith becomes simply a matter of inner individual adjustment.[10]

The ultimate enemy is a malevolent spiritual being who is totally opposed to God and God's purposes. He is called by various names: the prince of this world (John 14:30), the devil (Matt. 4:1), the great red dragon (Rev. 12:3, 9), the ancient serpent (12:9), Satan (12:9), and the accuser (12:10). His strategy is *derision* through making clergy and the Christian church look stupid, *destruction* by harassing believers and robbing them of joy (Rev. 12:9), *diversion* into sensualism, secularism, relativism, and bitterness (2 Cor. 11:3), *division* by splitting God's family, often starting with gossip (James 3:14), and *deception* through getting people to depend on human leaders (Gal. 4:17) or through seducing believers into accepting a compromised lifestyle (1 Peter 5:8). I will leave to

10. Stewart, *A Faith,* pp. 76-77.

the next chapter the specific ministry of exorcism and will restrict myself here to other aspects of spiritual warfare.

Don the Spiritual Armor through Prayer

Paul uses an elaborate metaphor for arming ourselves in Ephesians 6:10-18 by using the pieces of armor worn by a Roman soldier. Perhaps he was chained to one as he wrote this. The belt of truth means living with integrity. The breastplate of righteousness involves having right relations with God and living righteously. The "go" of the gospel implies that we are ready and "on the way" to share the gospel — there is more than *defense* here! The shield of faith deflects the enemy's attacks, and the helmet of salvation brings assurance to our minds that we belong to a God who will never divorce us. The sword of the Spirit is the Word of God, read, obeyed, and spoken. All these are ways of "putting on Christ": Christ's righteousness, Christ's message, Christ's faith, Christ's finished work on the cross, and Christ's word. All of these are put on by prayer: prayer on all occasions and all kinds of prayer (6:18).

Living a life of prayer and constantly putting on Jesus protects us from threats we cannot see. Sometimes we do not even know how we have been protected until long after a threat. Earlier I mentioned our deliverance in Nairobi. We did not see angels around the car, but I believe they were there. God has an invisible host of angels at his disposal. A year ago a student at Regent College received a letter from a friend in England. She had been walking across a campus by herself when a seedy and threatening man appeared in front walking alone. She put on the armor, crying to the Lord, "Please help me." When she got safely home and turned on the television, the local police were asking for help in identifying the very man she had seen on the campus, a man who had already molested several people. She immediately presented herself and identified the person.

"Why then," she asked the man, "did you not touch me?"

"I would not have dared," he said. "There were two strong men with you, one on the right and one on the left."

Doing spiritual warfare involves direct confrontation with the demonic — a subject to which we will shortly turn. But more commonly it involves putting on Jesus day by day and living the gospel. A crucial dimension of this is forgiving those who have hurt us. And even forgiving ourselves.

Practice Forgiveness and Intercession

Forgiveness plunders hell and sends Satan's hordes screaming for cover. It brings peace to the soul, and makes peace between people. It secures freedom from the past, opens up a new future, and permits people to live heartily in the present. It is the most significant healing of the soul, the most profound victory in the cosmic battle. When we forgive we do several things: *remember* that we ourselves have been forgiven by God and therefore empower ourselves to forgive others; *forget* the first meaning of offenses against us and regard them now, like the wounds in the body of Jesus after the resurrection, as the means of faith for others; *cancel* the debt others owe us and refuse to offer an easy repayment schedule or a trade-off; *prize* the value of the relationship even more than the behavior that hurt; *create* a new future (John 8:11) unencumbered by the sin. Lewis Smedes says that "our only escape from history's cruel unfairness, our only passage to the future's creative possibilities, is the miracle of forgiveness."[11]

Paul ends his magnificent metaphor of donning the armor with this simple request: "pray also for me" (Eph. 6:19). Karl Barth once said that "to clasp the hands in prayer is the beginning of an uprising against the disorder of the world."[12] It is also the beginning of an uprising against the disorder we see in others and in ourselves. Intercessory prayer, of which Ephesians 1:15-23 and 3:14-21 are stunning examples, is hard work. It is hard to hold people in our hearts and then to take them to God in our praying hearts. But calculated from the perspective of the New Jerusalem some very important things happen when we pray for others. First, we get God's mind about the person or the situation we are holding before God. Second, we piggyback on the Spirit's intercession since our prayers, even the most eloquent ones, are mere groans and babblings in

---

11. Lewis Smedes, "Forgiveness: The Power to Change the Past," *Christianity Today* 27, no. 1 (7 January 1983), p. 26.

12. Quoted in Kenneth Leech, *True Prayer: An Invitation to Christian Spirituality* (San Francisco: Harper & Row, 1980), p. 68.

comparison to the eloquence of the Spirit (Rom. 8:26). Third, in some mysterious way that offends the secular mindset we get in touch with persons on a deeper level than we might otherwise. Bonhoeffer explains that direct relationships between people are impossible. But Jesus as our mediator puts his hand on each and brings both together. So the most direct way to our brother is indirect — through Christ. Finally, something happens when we pray for people. Pascal said that "prayer is God's way of providing man with the dignity of causality."[13] P. T. Forsyth agrees that the earth is shaken daily by the prayers of the saints. "The real power of prayer in history is not a fusillade of praying units of whom Christ is the chief, but it is the corporate action of a Savior-Intercessor and His community, a volume and energy of prayer organized in a Holy Spirit and in the Church the Spirit creates."[14]

Doing spiritual warfare may well start with praying for ourselves. Our colleague and friend Dr. James Houston offers a prayer for the struggle:

> So we cry out to the father: lead me through all the evil tendencies of my heart. Help me to overcome the temptations of my temperament. Change inside me the evil tendencies of my own personality as it relates to other people. Protect me from the temptations of my own age group in the phases of life: passionate when young, cynical when middle-aged, self-pitying when old and lonely. Save me from the temptations of our culture, the modern world in which we live. For in all these realms, and above all to my sinful heart, I am seducible.[15]

The world, the flesh, and the devil — each is fought differently. We deal with the world through nonconformity with the world and conformity with the will of God (Rom. 12:2). We deal with the flesh by mortification (identifying with Christ's crucifixion) and aspiration (breathing in the Spirit). We deal with the devil by resisting and fleeing (James 4:7;

---

13. Blaise Pascal, *Pensées* (New York: The Modern Library, 1941), p. 166.

14. Quoted in Eugene Peterson, *Reversed Thunder: The Revelation of John and the Praying Imagination* (San Francisco: Harper & Row, 1988), p. 87.

15. James Houston, "Lead Us through the Temptation: A Meditation on the Lord's Prayer" (unpublished notes from the Ministry and Spirituality course, Regent College, Vancouver, B.C., 1990).

Rev. 12:11). It is a multi-front battle: the world, the flesh, and the devil. And our Lord meets us at each of these fronts: *transfiguring* us from within (Rom. 12:2) so we can transform the world rather than be conformed as we penetrate the world in our work and mission; *bearing Spirit fruit* through us (Gal. 5:22, 25) as we determine to walk in the Spirit and regard the flesh as crucified; and *overcoming the evil one*, the devil (Rev. 12:10) as we put on Christ's armor through all kinds of prayer (Eph. 6:13-18). During one of our many trips to Kenya I was traveling with a pastor in a remote rural area. I am always anxious to learn from African Christians because, by and large, they really believe in God, really believe in angels and the devil, and really believe that Christ can empower us to live triumphantly. They have a biblical worldview.

"Do you cast out demons as part of your ministry?" I asked naïvely.

"No, never!" was his surprising answer. And then he added, "Only Jesus does!"

11

Healing and Deliverance

MICHAEL GREEN

Divine Healing

Examples of healing are everywhere apparent in society. Healing through conventional medicine is the most common, and where would we be without it? But sometimes healing occurs through alternative medicine, such as acupuncture, and sometimes without medical means at all. In this context I want to look at divine healing, for there is no question that Jesus and his disciples saw this as an important part of their spiritual lives, and an evidence of the break-in of the kingdom of God. The healings, so notable in the ministry of Jesus, are continued in the Acts of the Apostles (e.g., 3:1ff.; 9:18; 14:8ff.; 20:9-10; 28:8 etc.). They are alluded to in the Epistles (e.g., 2 Cor. 12:12; 1 Cor. 12:9, 30; James 5:16). And despite the claims of dispensationalists that healing, along with other remarkable gifts of the Holy Spirit, ceased at the end of the apostolic age, this is demonstrably false if we are to credit the testimony of the Fathers who were well aware of divine healings from time to time in their midst, and who expected them. Here are some examples: they have been conveniently collected by John Wimber as Appendix A of his book *Power Evangelism*.[1] John Woolmer's *Healing and Deliverance* is more complete!

---

1. John Wimber, *Power Evangelism* (London: Hodder and Stoughton, 1985); and John Woolmer, *Healing and Deliverance* (London: Monarch, 1999).

Justin has much to say on the subject both in his *First* and *Second Apology*. He speaks of "many of our Christian men exorcising demoniacs in the name of Jesus Christ, who was crucified under Pontius Pilate. They have healed, and do heal . . ." (*2 Apol.* 6). Irenaeus, one of the greatest second-century leaders, remarks, "Some certainly and truly drive out devils, so that those who have thus been cleansed from evil spirits frequently join themselves to the church. Others heal the sick by laying their hands upon then, and they are made whole" (*Adv. Haer.* 2.32). Tertullian is no less explicit on the subject, giving examples of deliverance from evil spirits and naming some distinguished personages (such as Severus, the father of Antoninus Pius) who were healed of various diseases as Christians prayed for them (*Apol.* 23). Bishop Ambrose of Milan bears testimony to the Father bestowing "the grace of healing . . . and the gift of tongues." But it is his celebrated and learned follower, Augustine, who is most confident in writing about divine intervention to heal and to set people free from dark forces. "It is sometimes objected," says Augustine in *The City of God* (22.28), "that the miracles, which Christians claimed to have occurred, no longer happen. . . . The truth is that even today miracles are being wrought in the name of Christ, sometimes through his sacraments and sometimes through the intercession of the relics of his saints." And lest anyone should regard that as pious generalization, Augustine gives a whole catena of examples from his own experience: the healing of a blind man, a rectal fistula, paralysis and a hernia, gout; along with the liberation from demons for a young girl in Hippo, for some of Augustine's neighbors, and for a demonized boy whose eye was ripped out under demonic frenzy and was left "hanging by a tiny vein, as by a root." The eye was restored. He concludes, "It is a simple fact that there is no lack of miracles even in our day. And the God who works the miracles we read of in the Scriptures uses any means and manner he chooses." And to that claim the church throughout the ages has to say Amen, even though in the more rationalistic periods of its history these manifestations of divine power have been much rarer than in periods of vital faith.

Of course, we all know many examples of devoted believers who are not healed, despite prayer, the laying on of hands, and an attitude of deep faith. We are face to face with a deep mystery, and no slick generalizations about healing will avail. It is both cruel and naïve to attribute this failure to experience physical healing to prayerlessness or lack of faith. Suffering and death remain the ultimate mysteries that we must all face and to which there is no final solution within the bounds of this mortal life. However, the Bible does have a good deal to say on this subject of healing, and it was clearly something the early Christians expected to see in their midst.

God's Will for Humankind

The Genesis account makes it plain that God made humankind perfect, the man and the woman together. He put them in a garden. There is no hint that suffering and death were part of his purpose for them. On the contrary, it is made very clear that suffering, disease, sin, and death are all part of that disastrous fall from pristine innocence and obedience. And that same chapter, Genesis 3, where we dimly discern some of the ravages wrought by human rebellion, shows us God himself stepping in as Savior. He covers their nakedness with skins — the earliest hint of sacrifice in the Bible and the earliest suggestion of the cost of redemption. And, consonant with that early picture, throughout the Old Testament we see God's concern for the whole man: there is nothing ethereal and "spiritual" about "salvation" or "wholeness." It is embarrassingly physical. It means rescue from death (e.g., Ps. 6:4, 5), crippling fear (Ps. 107:13), sickness (Isa. 38:20), and trouble of many kinds (e.g., Jer. 30:7). It means rescue from enemies (e.g., 1 Sam. 14:23), often brought about by a "Savior" whom God specially raises up, such as Samson and Gideon: sometimes by divine intervention alone. But always we see God at work seeking to remove anything that inhibits and threatens the well-being of his covenant people. That is the basic meaning of the root *yasha'*, to save, or heal. It aims for the restoration of the whole person.

And Jesus underlined that understanding.

The Healings of Jesus

There is a studied ambiguity in the use of the word "save" in the Gospels. It means both to heal and to rescue in a deeper sense. This is very apparent from the story of the paralytic in Mark 2:1-12 and in verses like Mark 5:34; 10:52. Faith is a gateway to physical healing: it also brings spiritual restoration with God, the deeper meaning of "salvation." The biblical writers know nothing of our post-Enlightenment dichotomy between the sacred and the secular, the physical and the spiritual. The word "save" is most frequently applied by the Gospel writers to the healing miracles of Jesus. Thus "as many as touched were saved" (Mark 6:56 Gk.). Blind Bartimaeus was "saved" by believing in Jesus (Mark 10:52). So were the Samaritan leper (Luke 17:19), the man with a withered hand (Mark 3:3-4), and a host of others. Normally, but by no means always, Jesus is said to have healed *in response to faith.* "Your faith has saved you" is a constant refrain (e.g., Mark 9:23; 11:24; Luke 8:50). Equally, those healings were deliberately *messianic.* They were bound up with the person of Jesus the Messiah, and the irruption of the kingdom of God under his leadership and in his person. It is by the words of Jesus, by the person of Jesus, by the total mission of Jesus, that men and women were saved or healed (John 5:34; 10:9; 12:47). This is nowhere more powerfully brought before us than in the story of Jesus and Zacchaeus. In Luke 19:5-6 we are told that Jesus came to Zacchaeus's house: in verse 9 that salvation had come to his house. The two are identical.

Healing Continued . . .

Jesus intended his healing ministry to be continued by his followers. This is very evident from the mission charge to his disciples where "he gave them power and authority over all demons and to cure diseases, and he sent them out to preach the kingdom of God and to heal" (Luke 9:1-2). Again in the charge to the Seventy, Jesus says, "Heal the sick . . . and say to them 'The kingdom of God has come near to you'" (Luke 10:9).

The early Christians clearly regarded this as part of their mandate. The kingdom of God, they were persuaded, was not a matter of mere talk, but of power (1 Cor. 4:20). It is prominent in the Acts, as early as chapter 3 and as late as chapter 28. The Epistle of James expects God to raise a brother up in response to prayer (5:14ff.). And so it has continued, in the second and third centuries, as we have seen above, and up to the present day.

Come with me in imagination to a quadrangle of an ancient Oxford college. In a room off that quad lay a young man on his bed. He had been there for weeks with serious trouble in his back. He read James 5:14ff., and in obedience he called together the Christian leaders in his college and me, his parish priest. We prayed for him earnestly, laid hands upon him, and then invited him to get up and walk. He did — right round the quadrangle several times, with evident joy. We hastened away to get him his first decent meal in weeks!

Or come to a hospital ward, where I had been summoned to visit an old woman in our congregation who was dying. She momentarily regained consciousness as I prayed over her, but the medical staff were clear that she would be dead in an hour or two. That evening I returned to find her not only well on the way to recovery, but a changed personality: gone was the sharpness and complaining attitude for which she had been known, and a new gentleness and growing Christ-likeness began to bloom in her as she lived on for a few more years.

I think of a situation in Malawi. It was a clergy conference, and at the end a clergyman asked me to pray for his leg. It was clearly nonfunctional, and my faith was far from confident! I invited two others to come and pray with me, and we poured out our hearts to God in prayer as we laid loving hands on this man's leg. He then bounded to his feet and started to dance round the church, while we tried to urge caution — to no avail!

Or imagine the scene in an intensive care unit of a hospital. A twenty-one-year-old girl had been knocked down by a bus and had serious internal head injuries. The prognosis was death or, as an outside chance, survival as a cabbage. My colleague and I asked for admission to go and pray over her. It was granted. As we arrived she seemed to recognize us for a moment from the depths of the coma in which she had been for four days, since the accident. As we began to pray in tongues the nurses moved away, mystified, and the restlessness of the patient abruptly abated. After a while we had a conviction that God would heal her completely. We left. That was about 4:00 P.M. That girl was sitting up and having breakfast next morning (having eaten nothing, of course, since the accident). She was up at lunch. She was back in the ward in a day, and home a few days later. And now she is a missionary overseas! Her healing was the talk of the hospital, from consultants to porters. It was a marvelous exhibition of divine power, confounding human prognostication.

However, we know it is not always like that.

Failures in Healing

Stories such as I have just mentioned, all from my personal experience, are a glorious indication of the Lord's power to heal. But that is only half the story. And so it has been from the first days after the ascension of Jesus. For the healings brought about by the disciples were not of the same quality as those of their Master, although they were continuing his gracious work. For one thing, Jesus had no failure rate, and no reversions afterwards. All Christian healers experience both. For another, his healings seem to have been complete and instantaneous, apart from two recorded incidents where there was a short delay and renewed ministry before the cure was complete. Healings by the church are not like that, unfortunately. Often there is delay. Often there is failure.

Why is it that we so often experience failure when we pray for healing? The problem is not new. Even the apostle Paul had to say, "Trophimus I left ill at Miletus" (2 Tim. 4:20). He had to record unanswered prayer in his own situation, as he begged the Lord to remove some affliction which he called a "thorn in his flesh" (2 Cor. 12:8ff.). All in vain. His prayer was not answered in the affirmative — though the Lord provided his strength, the strength that is brought to fruition in human weakness, to enable him to face the situation. And that is often the case today.

Francis MacNutt in *Healing*[2] and John Wimber in *Power Healing*[3] face this issue head-on, and with great honesty. Both of them have been much used in a ministry of healing. Their writing on the subject comes from deep reflection and much experience, and is full of wisdom. Failure to secure healing is not because God is indifferent to the ailments of our bodies. And it is not always because of unconfessed sin or inadequate faith. No. To make that claim is to add insult to injury and heap gratuitous agony on the person who is already suffering greatly (though sometimes it may be the case, and if so needs to be exposed). But four major reasons stand out in my mind as obstacles to the healing grace of God.

First, it will often be the case that we do not have because we do not ask (James 4:2). Many churches and pastors seem not to believe that

2. Francis MacNutt, *Healing* (London: Hodder and Stoughton, 1989), chapter 18, "Eleven Reasons Why People Are Not Healed."

3. John Wimber, *Power Healing* (London: Hodder and Stoughton, 1986); chapter 8, "Not everyone is healed."

God heals today, and it nowhere figures in their teaching and church life.

Second, we have a great outside adversary, so the scriptures teach. Satan is involved in sickness. Think of the hunchbacked woman in the Gospels (Luke 13:16): Satan had bowed down that back of hers for years. Think of Paul's thorn in the flesh — it was a messenger of Satan to buffet him. I remember an illness of mine that vanished when friends came in, sensed the presence of evil, and challenged Satan to release his grip and go. We often fail to allow for this possible demonic dimension to suffering.

Third, we must always remember that Jesus was divine, and we are not. There is indeed continuity between his ministry of healing and ours. It is afforded by the Holy Spirit. But there is also a discontinuity: it is afforded by the ascension.

Fourth, there are three *tenses* to salvation, as it is set out in the scriptures. There is a sense in which salvation has already been achieved and appropriated. There is a sense in which we experience it constantly. And there is a sense in which it is still to come — and these are the references that predominate in the biblical teaching on the subject. Salvation and healing are always imperfect in this life. Think of it this way. It is not the will of God that we should experience disease and suffering, just as it is not his will that we should sin. However, in this mortal life he tolerates both, though he desires neither. If we are to get a balanced view of the situation, we must return to the scriptural insight that our present condition is neither what it was originally when God made the world, nor what it will be finally, when we go to share his home in heaven. To put it in a Pauline way, we remain "in this age" and are subject to its attacks and weaknesses, even while we enjoy some of the invasive and health-giving powers of "the age to come." One day we will be immersed fully in the "age to come." For now, we taste occasional fruits from it to assure us it is real and to incite our appetite for it.

The Christian Attitude

Christians who, like the first disciples, believe in divine healing, might usefully keep the following reflections in mind as they approach particular cases of illness and disease.

First, God is the supreme source of healing, and he plans whole-ness *(soteria)* for his children. We shall experience many a taste of that wholeness as we go through life, but it will only be complete after our fi-nal deliverance from disease and death. Then, and not till then, will wholeness be complete.

Second, it is important to remember that God is the healer. Some-times he heals through the natural recuperative powers of the body, sometimes through medicine, sometimes without. Exodus 15:26 re-minds us, "I am the Lord, your healer." It is not better if healing comes through prayer than through medicine; neither is it worse. God is sover-eign to use whatever way he chooses — or to withhold healing if he sees it to be in our best ultimate interest. The important thing, when we get sick, is to learn to turn to the Lord before we turn to anyone else, and surrender the whole problem into his hands. This will then free us up to see either medication or Christian ministry as his possible avenue of healing.

Third, following on from this, we need to search our hearts before God when sickness strikes. There may be something he longs to teach us through the experience. Confession of sin and openness to whatever he may send is called for, even if it be the final healing of all mortal ills in death. Only thus can God bless us as he longs to. Only thus can we be confident that our prayers for healing are according to his will, rather than ours. We must never forget that God is sovereign. Our prayers are not to twist his arm, but to cooperate in his purposes. And we can come to him in confidence, assured that not even death can rob us of complete wholeness at the last. We need to come in faith to the God who is well able to heal. We need to seek and accept his purpose and his timing. We need to have our sins forgiven and put away. We need to be open to gifts of healing, from whatever source they come.

Finally, it is worth reflecting that healing is of different kinds. We are so infatuated with our pleasures and our bodies that we seek physi-cal healing above all else. But it is not the ultimate good. Heaven, not health, is our goal. And a lot of sickness is not physical in origin or na-ture. Much is related to conflict between body and mind, the conscious and the unconscious, home and work, the individual and society; con-flict within the family, conflict between our ambitions and our achieve-ments. When the tension in any of these areas becomes intolerable, we get sick, and need healing. The Lord expects his body, the church, to be one of the agencies in human healing. Healing of frustration and disintegration by coming to Christ. Healing of anxiety by trusting Christ. Healing of painful memories by the touch of Christ. Healing of animosities by the reconciliation Christ brings. Healing of fear by the presence of Christ. These are palpable areas of human need to which Christ is profoundly relevant here and now in this life. The ultimate healing lies beyond the grave.

Deliverance

We come to a dark and controversial area of spirituality which was very familiar to the early Christians, as it is to believers in many parts of the Two Thirds World, but of which I, along with millions of Western Christians, was utterly ignorant until I was brought face to face with it — in one of the most sophisticated cities of the world. Many Christians deride the whole idea of the demonic. Others see demons under every bush. What does Scripture say?

1. *There is a supreme anti-God force* known in the Bible as Satan, the devil, the prince of this world, the prince of the power of the air, Beelzebul, the liar, the slanderer, the murderer — and other names. He is taken with great seriousness by the biblical writers. It seems to me that there are at least seven considerations which point strongly to the existence of this anti-God force: considerations of philosophy, theology, the environment, the occult, personal experience of temptation, the uniform testimony of Scripture, and the clear teaching of Jesus. I have filled out these headings in chapter 1 of *I Believe in Satan's Downfall*,[4] and I shall not rehearse them further now. I find it significant that Jesus himself has more to say about the devil than any other teacher in the whole of Scripture (e.g., Matt. 4:1-11; Matt. 6:13; 12:22-45; Mark 3:22-26; Mark 4:15; John 12:31; 14:30 etc.). It is only possible to evade the force of this testimony by having recourse to the theories of accommodation or kenosis, neither of which can withstand rigorous examination. If Jesus was clear and unambiguous about the awesome reality of Satan, that should be good enough for the Christian disciple.

4. Michael Green, *I Believe in Satan's Downfall* (London: Hodder and Stoughton, 1988).

Scripture is restrained in its treatment of the devil. But it does indicate that Satan is a fallen angel whose arrogant pride led to his being cast out of heaven (Ezek. 26–28; Isa. 14; Luke 10:18; Rev. 12). The book of Job makes it very plain that Satan is not equal and opposite to God: he remains God's devil, with comparative freedom, but at the end of a long chain. His aim is to spoil God's world: in society by war, in the home by broken relationships, in the body by disease, and in the soul by sin. Powerful though he is, his destiny is destruction (Rev. 20:10). In the meantime he wages unceasing war against all that is good — and supremely against God.

2. *Satan has demonic allies.* And these allies afflict human beings. Once again the scriptures are clear that God is the source not only of human but of angelic life. There are angelic beings in God's world, and they figure greatly in the Bible. Some of them joined Satan's insurrection against God, shared in his fall, and became his allies and agents against God (Rev. 12:7-9; 2 Peter 2:4; Jude v. 6). These spiritual forces of darkness assail human beings. There appears to be a wide variation in the extent of the grip they gain, though the common distinction between "oppression" and "possession" has no basis whatsoever in Scripture where the word most commonly used is *daimonizesthai,* to be demonized, i.e., affected by a demon. It would appear that these demonic beings may have knowledge (Mark 1:24; Acts 19:15), emotions (Mark 1:24; James 2:19), speech, and willpower (Matt. 12:44) — yet they are constantly referred to in the neuter gender in Greek. If all this seems bizarre to us, it could be because we have been imprisoned within a rationalistic post-Enlightenment worldview that discounts the supernatural — at the same time as millions of our citizens are involved in the fascinating, dangerous, and real world of the occult! It is at least worth examining the biblical alternative.

3. *Jesus came to set people free.* He came to destroy the works of the devil (1 John 3:8). He came to free the captives (Luke 4:18). There are many general statements in the Gospels about Jesus liberating demonized people (e.g., Mark 1:32-34; 1:39; Luke 4:41; 6:18). Demonic activity may underlie some diseases: blindness, dumbness (Matt. 12:22), epilepsy (Matt. 17:14-17), mental illness (Luke 8:27), and physical illness too (Luke 13:11ff.) *may* be thus caused, but the Bible never suggests that this is normally the case. It never suggests that *all* illness is caused by demonic activity. In fact it makes a careful distinction between healing dis-

eases and casting out demons (Luke 13:32). In Luke 4:40ff. we have a general picture of Jesus' liberating work, and find that whereas he often laid hands on the sick and healed them, he did not lay hands on the demonized (that might express solidarity with the demons), but rebuked them and cast them out. Demons are expelled. Diseases are healed. The distinction is clear. Jesus came to destroy both aspects of the work of the devil, and we find him doing it throughout the Gospels.

In addition to these general references, there are seven accounts of Jesus liberating individuals from demonic grip (Matt. 9:32; Mark 1:21-28; 3:22-27; 5:1-20; 7:24-30; 9:14-29; Luke 13:10-17). Three of these, the Gerasene demoniac, the epileptic boy, and the Beelzebul controversy, appear in all three Synoptic Gospels.

Certain significant principles emerge.

First, Jesus did not go around seeking confrontation with the demonic: people brought the patients to him.

Second, Jesus seems normally to have cast the demons out with a word of command (Mark 9:25) and not to have entered into parley with them; indeed, he often forbade them to speak (Mark 1:34). The only exception to this refusal to discuss with them is the case of the Gerasene demoniac.

Third, there was considerable variety in Jesus' very direct approach to demons. Sometimes he "muzzled" them (Luke 4:35), sometimes he "bound" them (Matt. 12:29) and sometimes he had to repeat his command (see Mark 5:8; and the Greek of Luke 11:14).

Sometimes he seems to have made a point of forbidding the evil spirit ever to return (Mark 9:25). He was well aware of the danger of reinfestation (Matt. 12:43-44). And in his forthright approach to the problem, he always addressed the demon, not the person.

Only once do we find him exorcising at a distance (Matt. 15:28). It happened to be a situation of exceptional faith and persistent, single-minded request.

Of course, the cross was the supreme exorcism. It was here that Satan and his demonic allies suffered rout. Matthew 8:16-17 is a significant hint of this; but the clearest expression of it comes in Colossians 2:15. "He disarmed the principalities and powers and made a public example of them, triumphing over them in it (i.e., the cross)."

4. *Jesus empowered and commissioned his followers to continue his work of liberation.* We find this is true of the Twelve in Luke 9:1, and of

the Seventy in Luke 10:17. It continued in the apostolic church (Mark 16:17; Acts 16:16-18; 19:11-17), and it was a major strand in the advance of their successors. One of the early second-century writers, Justin Martyr, for example, can make a claim like this:

> Many of our Christian men have exorcised in the name of Jesus Christ, who was crucified under Pontius Pilate, numberless demoniacs throughout the world, and in your city. When all other exorcists and specialists in incantations and drugs have failed, they have healed them and still do heal, rendering the demons impotent and driving them out.[5]

It has always been part of the practice of the church to seek deliverance from demonic infestation both of places and people. It is a very delicate area of ministry, because it is so easy to go wrong. To diagnose demonic interference when there is none can raise in the person concerned all manner of fears. It should be the last resort, not the first, in Christian ministry. Nevertheless this work of liberation is a proper part of the all-round ministry of the church, and therefore I propose to address some of the practical issues that will confront us as they did the first Christians.

Practical Issues

1. *Is there an increase in demonic activity these days?* There certainly is. It was a deliberate feature both in Hitler's Germany and Stalin's Russia. There is a massive preoccupation with the occult in our generation, leading often to ritual Satanic worship. There are reasons for this growth: the emptiness of materialism, the religious instinct of humanity, and the deadness of the church to the issues of the Spirit. There is also a hunger for thrills and significance in a society where the individual seems to matter less and less, along with a desire for power over other people and group coherence in a crumbling society.

2. *What is the purpose of occult involvement?* It is threefold, to correspond with the three main divisions of occult activity. Magic, be it white or black, seeks to control the spirit world. It is all about power. Fortune

5. Justin Martyr, 2 *Apol.* 6.

telling, whether by palmistry, tarot, clairvoyance, or horoscopes, seeks to penetrate the future. It is all about knowledge. Spiritism, through ouija, trances, séances, and mediums, seeks to break through to the world beyond. It is all about contact with the dead.

3. *Is there anything wrong with it?* There is. It is expressly forbidden in the Bible. Deuteronomy 18:9ff. forbids the children of Israel to be cajoled by their pagan neighbors into any of these three divisions of the occult. It was a capital offense (Exod. 22:18). In the New Testament the prohibition is no less stringent (e.g., 1 Cor. 10:20-21) and the Satanic origin of the occult is clearly exposed (Rev. 16:12ff.). Why this hard line? Because you are submitting yourself, in the occult, to a power that is not from God and may well be in active revolt against him. What is more, it betrays a lust for knowledge we are not supposed to have, along with an illicit power over people. It seeks to break the barrier of death which is God-given. It is dangerous and can become destructive, as it was to King Saul and Manasseh. Worst of all, involvement in the occult is hateful to God because it is direct disobedience: "Rebellion is like the sin of witchcraft" (1 Sam. 15:23).

4. *Is occult involvement the only way in which demonic infestation comes?* No, but it is the main way. It also seems that deliberate, persistent sin may sometimes allow powers beyond ourselves to force an entrance. Sexual sins and involvement in nature-worship or the worship of false gods may render people vulnerable. Sometimes the possession of a charm or decoration offered to heathen gods can have this effect, as can a curse and even trouble in the family tree.

5. *Can Christians be thus infected?* Indeed they can. The conviction that this is unthinkable springs from the unbiblical distinction of "oppression" and "possession," coupled with the conviction that if Christ's Spirit possess you, an evil spirit obviously cannot. If you look at it in "possession" terms, that argument holds good. But that is not what *daimonizomai* means in the New Testament, as we have seen. There is no reason why believers should not be influenced by dark forces: they are in fact a prime target, as the prince of the apostles found just after a moment of high spiritual insight! (Matt. 16:23). Sometimes there has been prior demonic influence in a life that becomes Christian: and unless it is dealt with at the time of initiation it may well lie low and cause trouble for years to come, like neglected clumps of weeds in an otherwise lovely garden.

6. *How should Christians approach this matter?* In general we need to appreciate that the critical victory over all the forces of evil has been won — by Jesus on the cross. That is the key to the understanding of all history: the Lamb once slain is in the midst of the throne of God (Rev. 5:1-12). In Satan we confront a defeated foe (Rev. 12:7-11).

The specifics are laid out in the famous passage on spiritual battle in Ephesians 6. We are to stand firm (v. 14) in an attitude of determined rejection of any strand of evil in our own lives. We must approach this ministry with no compromise, no defeatism, and no fear. We then need to take and don the whole armor of God (v. 13), claiming the Lord's protection. We need to pray and to get others to support us in prayer (v. 18). And we need to watch, to have our wits very much about us as we minister (v. 18).

7. *How are we to discern forces of active evil?* Discernment is a gift (1 Cor. 12:10) and it is a great help if someone in the little group ministering possesses this gift. Some indicators are: abnormal aggression and strength, preternatural knowledge, violent reaction against the name of Jesus, or when confronted by a cross, the Communion, the Bible, or entry into a church. Any involvement with the occult, Christian Science, Transcendental Meditation, and all animistic religions may alert us to the possibility of demonic presence, as may a series of suicides among close relations, or spiritism in a previous generation (often a grandmother). Unnatural bondage to sexual perversion, or other compulsive habits, unsought blasphemy, and uncontrollable mockery of God are also characteristics that should arouse our suspicion, as may strange behavior — the fluttering of eyelids, changes in voice and laughter, compulsive inability to pray, and the grip of a nameless fear.

These characteristics are not exhaustive, nor do they necessarily denote demonic grip. Some are found in conjunction with mental illness; some with people who have never learnt what it is to "crucify the flesh." It is extremely unwise to jump to hasty conclusions in ministry of this sort. But evil spirits like to remain hidden. They are normally driven to manifest themselves most in lively charismatic worship, at the Holy Communion, or in the presence of several deeply committed Christians. Often the person concerned will display that love-hate response to Jesus shown by the Gerasene demoniac. They are very much torn in two, and we need to help them find freedom. If we do make a mistaken diagnosis it need not be disastrous, particularly if we have established easy relationships. Explain that you are not clear whether or not dark forces are present, but will challenge them in case they are. The result will be obvious. One further word: if someone claims to de demonized — take leave to doubt it.

8. *How can we prepare for a time of deliverance ministry?* Quite simply. We need to go with at least one other person who is experienced in this work. It is important to operate only with the goodwill of those who are over you in the Lord: the forces of evil seem to be very aware of levels of authority and will not leave if we have not submitted ourselves to those in authority over us. Prayer is of course vital. And it is good to have a group of people praying in the background while ministry is actually being carried on. It is helpful to take with you oil for anointing when the job is done, elements for an informal Communion if appropriate, and a cross — all emblems of the victory of Jesus in whose name you go. Incidentally, it is important not to be rushed, and never to use a larger ministry when a smaller one will do.

9. *The ministry of deliverance.* There is no set way: it is interesting to notice the variety in Jesus' approach to different demonized people. But we should begin by setting fears at rest and getting the person relaxed and keen to cooperate. That will save much time and trouble. Be matter-of-fact about the job of liberation to be done: I find it helpful to allude to it as a very normal part of pastoral ministry.

Explanations over, it is time to move into a time of honest confession, with detailed renunciation of every form of activity through which the grip of the demonic might have entered. This should be followed by absolution, and encouraging verses from Scripture. I have found that fear and resentment are two of the most common blockages on the road to freedom. I often ask, "Is there someone you cannot forgive?" That has to be dealt with before proceeding.

Together we claim the armor of Christ, and then quietly but firmly command the evil thing to go, in the name of the Trinity and with explicit mention of the blood of Christ shed upon the cross. "Resist the devil," we are told, "and he will flee from you" (James 4:7). Command it to leave and never return. It may go immediately. It may temporize with strange voices emerging from the person, offering defiance, swearing it will never leave, insulting you, or whining not to be cast out. The insistent command to leave must then be repeated. Verses of Scripture may come to the mind of one of those ministering: that can help. So of course does praise (often in song), repeated recourse to prayer, the use of the gift of tongues, or perhaps of holy water (which I have found to be very effective) or some representation of the cross. We need to be prepared for anything, and to watch very closely to see what appears to be happening. Violence, deceit, a cynical smile, mockery, vomiting, animal behavior — any of these things may happen.

I find it most helpful to ask the persons concerned how they are feeling as we proceed. They always know when there is more work to be done, and they know when they are free. If you can get the persons concerned to call upon the Lord themselves for deliverance, that is best of all. They then see themselves as partners in the ministry, not just objects of it. I have not found it necessary to name the evil influences, though it is often obvious what they are and they sometimes name themselves. When they do, it is an advantage: there is power in knowing the name. It may take some time before freedom comes. It is important not to hurry, but to wait on God for his illumination while the ministry is going on. God may guide by a conviction, or a picture coming into the mind of someone ministering. His Spirit will lead you, as you trust him. If there is no progress in an hour or so, claim Christ's power to bind whatever evil force is there, and set another time for renewed ministry, after the person has had a time to reflect on the possible cause of the blockage, and you have had time for prayer and perhaps advice from those more experienced. Avoid a long, protracted session that is exhausting for all and deeply disappointing if it does not end in success.

The persons concerned always know when the thing has gone, and there are usually tears of joy and relief. Afterwards they need love, food, and rest. It may well feel as exhausting as an operation, and rest is essential. Make sure that tender loving care is continued.

A final word to those engaging in this ministry. Do not get hooked on it. It is so dramatic that it can easily become unhealthily addictive. I find it wise not to do it at all except among people to whom I am ministering in other ways.

Conclusion

If all this sounds like Alice in Wonderland to the reader, I can sympathize. It sounded like that to me. Unfortunately I have discovered that it is painfully real. The church has known this down the ages. It is only in this century that Christians in the West have ceased to expect deliverance for the demonized. The consequences of this failure of ours are great. People thus affected go to doctors, who cannot help them, or into mental hospitals that are not appropriate for their condition. Only Christ can set them free, by his life-giving Spirit. And the church is charged by her Lord not to fail people by neglecting this ministry of liberation.

Renewal, spiritual warfare, expectancy, and the power of God. These are our weapons. And remember Luke 10:19-20, "I give you authority . . . over all the power of the enemy. . . . Nevertheless do not rejoice in this, that the spirits are subject to you; but rejoice that your names are written in heaven."

12

Children of Hope

R. PAUL STEVENS

The only ultimate disaster that can befall us, I have come to real-ize, is to feel ourselves to be at home here on earth.

MALCOLM MUGGERIDGE

The Christians who did the most for the present world were just those who thought most about the next. . . . It is since Christians have largely ceased to think of the other world that they have be-come so ineffective in this. Aim at heaven and you will get earth thrown in; aim at earth and you will get neither.

C. S. LEWIS

C had Walsh once said that orthodox theology has not abandoned eschatology (the study of the End). Rather, theology has em-balmed it! Too often it has been embalmed in elaborate charts on the Revelation or in books claiming to provide a schedule for the presumed timing of events leading up to the new heaven and the new earth. These books feed on a deep human anxiety that the world and our work within it, have no meaningful result and, to quote T. S. Eliot, the world will end not with a bang but a whimper. So popular writers like Hal Lindsey make a fortune on claiming that this is the terminal generation.

176

The Theology of Hope

It is not surprising that the popularity of theologies that promise an instant evacuation come at precisely the moment in history when there is so much despair about the future. There was once a time when secular "prophets" preached a glorious future while Christian prophets preached hell-fire and brimstone (though I cannot honestly say I have heard such a sermon). But today, while secular "prophets" preach doom, Christians have the privilege of announcing both the hope of glory and a glorious hope. It is this which is the focus of the chapter.

Defining Eschatology and Futurology

We must start by defining our terms. Eschatology can be defined as the study of the End *(eschaton)*. Trying to understand the teaching of the New Testament about the End is like an early explorer of the Rocky Mountains or the Alps. Coming from the east and not having a detailed map, the explorer would see multiple ranges and peaks without knowing how deep are the valleys between. In the same way, the New Testament reveals six "peaks" about the End without giving us a detailed map of their order, or the distance between them. These are the second coming of Jesus, the resurrection of the body, judgment, eternal life, the full realization of the kingdom of God, and the new heaven and the new earth.

When we speak of these six eschatological dimensions we are not using the word "hope" as we do in normal conversation, as, for example, when we say "I hope to see you sometime in the future." Unlike human wishful thinking, *this* hope is as certain as Christ's first coming, as certain as God himself. So the New Testament speaks of Christ as our hope (1 Tim. 1:1); it affirms that "Christ in you, [is] the hope of glory" (Col. 1:27); it says that the calling of every Christian is to one hope (Eph. 4:4); it insists that to live without God means "to have no hope" (Eph. 2:12; 1 Thess. 4:13). This is eschatology. Futurology is related but very different.

Futurology is a term that describes how we are to live on planet earth until the end. Futurologies range from future bright to future night, and everything in between. There are a few secular futurists that hold out the promise of a limitless, unpollutable world in which everyone will be middle class, well fed, and well entertained. Marxism held out the hope of a classless society in which justice and prosperity would be evenly and universally distributed. Future bright proponents believe that human beings can bring in utopia. But most futurists today forecast the exact opposite: a future night. They envision a gloomy end through the final depletion of the world's resources, a deadly irradiation of the race through the gaping hole in the ozone layer, or the insane detonation of the world's nuclear stockpiles by people who have never signed nuclear disarmament treaties. Reflecting on the evening newscast, someone said, "Who can absorb any more bad news?" The question strikes a deep chord within us.

A sixty-four-year-old man in Britain being prodded by his sons about his failing powers told them to wait until they were his age and see how fit they'd be. There was silence, after which one son said, "None of us is going to get to sixty-four and we all know that." One obvious result of this short-circuited future is the proliferation of an instant gratification culture. People try to squeeze every pleasure they can out of the moment because there may not be another one. If there is no certain tomorrow, and if today is all one has, then it makes sense. Even Christians seem to be caught up in this, which is a certain indication that eschatology has been embalmed. As we will see, a person's futurology is dependent on whether that person has an eschatological hope, or on the kind of eschatology one believes.

Relating Eschatology and Futurology

The relating of eschatology and futurology is critical. When Christians are profoundly influenced by short-term future thinking and, if they forget the glorious prospect of fulfillment in the new heaven and the new earth, they try to get "the best of both worlds" by squeezing everything they can out of this life while they wait — albeit without any real hope — for the next. Sometimes our spontaneous remarks betray the inner reality. A church warden was once asked what he thought would happen to him when he would die. "I will immediately depart into everlasting felicity," he replied, but then continued along this line, "but I wish you wouldn't ask me about such unpleasant subjects!" The spirituality of hope had not permeated his soul. Some Christian couples are not sure they should conceive children and bring them into this kind of world, or whether they should keep the children they have conceived. Young Christians worry about whether there will be jobs upon graduation, and whether their marriages — if they marry at all — will last. It is hardly surprising that such world-weariness drives many young people to consider that the only thing worth doing in the world in these last days is to go into the professional ministry.

In contrast, followers of Jesus in the early church could not wait for the future to happen. They felt the pressure of the future as a positive pressure. They developed a futurology that related to the certain hope of their eschatology. They welcomed the future. They wanted not only to live in the light of the End, but to hasten the coming of the Lord Jesus. They believed that the second coming was such a positive goal for themselves and for God's creation, that their whole view of the future was shaped by that eschatological perspective. Peter said, "You ought to live holy and godly lives as you look forward to the day of the Lord and speed its coming" (2 Peter 3:11-12). The Roman Empire was, at the time, not too different from our own society. It was in rampant decay. There was widespread homosexuality; families were fragmented; marriage was despised; each man had a mistress for pleasure and a wife for domestic purposes. Slavery and poverty abounded. To become a Christian meant joining a radical and despised sect, to be persecuted at any moment, to experience losing one's job, or to suffer social rejection. Nevertheless, these Christians lived *in hope.*

The apostle Paul modeled a person living for the End in an unhurried way. He spent fourteen years preparing to become a missionary and when he was finally commissioned to his "worldwide" mission to the Gentiles, he spent forty or more hours each week making tents by hand as part of his service to God while he knew all along that thousands were still unreached. Nevertheless he never indicated that he was wasting his time or wasting his life, even when he was shuffled from prison to prison. To live this way one must have a futurology formed around a biblical eschatology.

Some Christians have an eschatology with *no* futurology. They believe that Christ will come tonight, or tomorrow at the latest. So there is nothing to do in this world except put on the white clothes and prepare for the coming of the Lord. Other Christians have an eschatology with a *limited* futurology. Like Hal Lindsey they believe this is the terminal generation and we have, at best, a short time to wait. Needless to say, this results in an otherworldly perspective in which work on the problems of ecology, or unjust food distribution in the world, seem to be pointless exercises. Preparing for a life of service to God as an educator, a scientist, a craftsperson, or a business person seems secondary to the imperative of preaching God's word, preferably in so-called full-time Christian work. Obviously everyone cannot live this way, especially if the End does not come soon.

It is often argued that this was exactly the perspective of both Jesus and Paul, namely that they did not believe in a future beyond their own generation. Careful biblical scholarship, however, shows that both Jesus and Paul spoke of the certainty and the character of the End of human history but said almost nothing about the timing. While they were *ready* for the End to come at any moment they did not predicate their actions or even their ethics on the certainty that the End *must* come soon. Our way of life in this world, they would argue, must be influenced by the possible shortness of time, but the real reason for our living in this world differently from the thoroughgoing secularist is the fact that the kingdom has come and will come fully one day. So, capturing the emphasis of both Jesus and Paul, Luther is reported to have said, "If I knew that tomorrow the world would perish, I would still plant a little apple tree in my back garden."[1]

The New Testament encourages an eschatology with a *long-term* futurology. Believers are to be ready for the Lord to come back at any moment, but they are also to be ready to work in this world for another thousand years if necessary. Like the wise women in the parable of the wise and foolish virgins (Matt. 25:1-13) they are ready *now* but are prepared, if necessary, for a long wait. Possibly for a long, long wait. The long wait is not a futile wait. Waiting is not inactivity. Rather the beautiful prospect of the End is a powerful motivation to do everything in this life with faith, hope, and love. With great wisdom the theologian Jürgen Moltmann explains that eschatology feeds our faith and transformed living now.

---

1. This dictum is ascribed to Martin Luther but it is an apocryphon. It may stem from a grenadier of Frederick II of Prussia. Quoted by Markus Barth, *Ephesians, Translation and Commentary on Chapters 4–6,* vol. 34A, The Anchor Bible (Garden City, N.Y.: Doubleday, 1981), p. 517.

Eschatology is the most pastoral of all theological perspectives showing how the ending impinges on the present in such ways that the truth of the gospel is verified in life "in the middle." It shows us that believers are not set "at the high noon of life," but at the dawn of a new day at the point where night and day, things passing and things to come, grapple with each other.[2]

On the Deck of a Sinking Ship

A vivid example of this is given in Acts 27:13-44 when Paul is being carried on a reeling ship that is foundering in a storm. Though a prisoner on the ship he became its master by assuming a pastoral and prophetic ministry to the captain, the crew, the other prisoners, and even his traveling companion, Dr. Luke, whose presence is signaled by the use of "we" (27:18). First, Paul had a long-range plan for his life — in his case, to evangelize the whole Roman Empire. It did not matter whether he did this in chains and he did not allow any negative present circumstance to overshadow his ultimate purpose for life in this world. Second, Paul expressed courage. "So keep up your courage, men, for I have faith in God that it will happen just as he told me" (27:25). This was not merely whistling in the dark or pumping oneself up. Paul was confident that God's purposes would not be thwarted and that all things would work for the good of those who love God (and even for those who do not!). Therefore he was able to tell them the hard facts that they must run aground on some island, but he did so with hope.

Third, Paul did the thing at hand as though he had an assured future. Though none of them had eaten for days, so sick, weary, and hopeless were they, Paul "took some bread and gave thanks to God in front of them all. Then he broke it and began to eat" (27:35). He made a eucharistic drama out of a normal meal and ministered to the practical needs of his fellow shipmates. Finally, Paul revealed that his hope was nurtured through his personal communion with God. "Last night an angel of the God whose I am and whom I serve stood beside me and said, 'Do not be afraid, Paul. You must stand trial before Caesar; and God has graciously

2. Jürgen Moltmann, *Theology of Hope: On the Ground and the Implications of a Christian Eschatology*, trans. James W. Leitch (New York: Harper & Row, 1967), p. 31.

given you the lives of all who sail with you'" (27:23-24). The modern Christian standing on the deck of a civilization foundering in the storms of a postmodern world can live by, and proclaim, the same hope.

The Spirituality of Hope

The centerpiece of Christian hope is the second coming of Jesus Christ, a truth mentioned 318 times in Scripture. But the emphasis in the New Testament is always on readiness and longing rather than on calculating *when.* Jesus himself admonished his followers to watch for him, not to watch the calendar (Acts 1:6-7; Luke 12:36; Phil. 3:20; Heb. 9:28). The second coming of Jesus will be the personal and final visit of the groom to receive the bride, the church (Rev. 21:2). But each of the other five "peaks" in the panorama of Christian hope points to a Christ-centered reality.

Our future bodily existence has been guaranteed and demonstrated by the resurrection of Jesus bodily as the first fruits of the grave. Resurrection is conformity to Christ bodily. Final judgment will not be an impersonal court-scene before an austere judge. Jesus is both judge and friend. Eternal life is life lived with Christ in the new age. Christ can properly be called, as he was by Irenaeus, the *autobasileia* — the kingdom of God in person — since he embodied the rule of God as king and the servant of his people. The New Testament suggests that the full coming of the kingdom will be like the first coming of Jesus *and even more!* The new heaven and the new earth, the sixth "peak," is characterized not only by the renewal of creation but by the fact that the Lamb (Jesus) is in the center (Rev. 21:23; 22:3). What does this imagery mean?

The Second Coming

The second coming of Jesus will be personal (Rev. 22:7), literal (Acts 1:10-11), glorious (2 Thess. 1:7-9), and unexpected (1 Thess. 5:2-3). This precious promise guarantees that our faith will become sight, and our partial and inadequate experience of Christ in this life will become consummated. Scripture does not use the metaphor of marriage for the Christian's relationship with Jesus in this life. That is reserved for the final wedding supper of the Lamb, so powerfully expressed in the last book of the Bible (Rev. 19:6-9). Rather, the term "betrothal" — which in the ancient world was presexual marriage, a more binding covenant than modern engagement — was the term Paul used to describe our present relationship with Christ (2 Cor. 11:2). His coming again means a full marriage experience with the Lord! At the moment we can hardly say we know God at all. Indeed even Paul corrects himself and indicates that it is more proper to speak of God's *knowing us* (Gal. 4:9). In spite of the impressive claims of some people to experience what they call "spiritual marriage" with God in this life, we cannot expect a full and final mystical experience of Jesus until he comes again, or unless we die first. But we can live hopefully with our betrothal experience because the marriage is absolutely certain.

The Resurrection of the Body

The resurrection of the body (1 Cor. 15:12-58) promises that our future in Christ is not to become disembodied spirits floating around in heaven, but completely whole people, more whole than we ever were in this life with our "psychological body." When my daughter was an intern in the only hospital in our city which at that time received AIDS patients, she would sit on the beds of these modern lepers and, touching them, tell them about the resurrection of the body. What a glorious hope! Our hope is to be invested with a "spiritual body" (1 Cor. 15:44) which has both continuity with our present bodies and discontinuity because it will be transfigured. Resurrection is the end of incarnation. But far from merely projecting a sensuous and materialistic heavenly future, as is proposed in some religions, Christian hope looks forward to a life in full and final conformity to the likeness of God's Son, *even with regard to our bodies.* So the resurrection of Jesus is not only the visible proof that it can happen. More important, his resurrection is the first stage of our final assumption of the image of Christ. If the body is *for the Lord,* as Paul argues, then we must glorify God *now* in our bodily life, including in such mundane things as eating and such sensitive things as sexual activity. One can only imagine how shocking this was to the "superspiritual" Corinthians who did not care what they did with their bodies. Equally shocking would be Paul's assertion that the truly spiritual person would be one with a resurrection body.

Last Judgment

Judgment is a theme hardly mentioned today even by Christian preachers. In contrast the psalmist longed for the judgment of God (Ps. 67:1-4; 96:10-13). The reason is that the psalmist lived in a topsy-turvy world in which he did not have justice now and he knew that God's judgment would mean restoration of justice and the vindication of the downtrodden. *We* imagine that we have justice in the world — at least a measure of it — and fear that the judgment of God will upset out apple carts. But without judgment and the accountability it brings, life in this world does not make sense. There is no final reckoning for the unjust suffering we experience, and no final reward for faithfulness (Heb. 9:27-28).

The unique perspective of the Christian faith is that our judge is the same person as our Savior-friend (Rom. 2:16; Acts 17:30-31; 2 Cor. 5:10; John 5:22), who has provided a covering for all our sins. Christians are not free from evaluation; but they are free from condemnation. Therefore question 52 of the Heidelberg Catechism asks: "What comfort hast thou by the coming again of Christ to judge the quick and the dead?" The answer is this: "that in all my miseries and persecutions I look with my head erect for the very same, who before yielded Himself unto the judgment of God for me and took away all malediction from me, to come as Judge from heaven." This dimension of our future gives us hope because *God* will judge and restore all things. It is also a warning. If God is the final judge we should refrain from judging others now (James 4:11-12). There is also an invitation. God is withholding his final judgment to give the maximum possibility of repentance to his creatures. We should settle the issue now before we go to court.

Eternal Life

Eternal life is simply life in the new age. As we discovered in the chapter "Aware of the Struggle," the Christian person lives in the overlap of the ages. This can be represented graphically by the following:[3]

3. Oscar Cullmann, *Christ and Time: The Primitive Christian Conception of Time and History,* trans. F. V. Filson (London: SCM Press, 1951), p. 84.

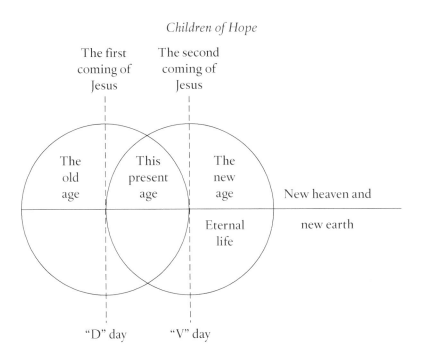

The first coming of Jesus

The second coming of Jesus

The old age

This present age

The new age

New heaven and new earth

Eternal life

"D" day   "V" day

Oscar Cullmann has helpfully used terms from the Second World War to explain the realities of living in the overlap of the ages. D-Day was "departure day," when the Allied forces invaded Enemy-occupied soil — so it is a brilliant analogy. It carried with it the certainty of final victory as the bridgehead at Caen was established, and the ensuing struggle made that fact increasingly plain, despite reverses that followed in the war. V-Day would come — and it did many months later! The first coming of Jesus, his death and resurrection, were D-Day. Sin and Satan were overcome and the principalities and powers that claim to dominate us were unmasked and disarmed (Col. 2:13-15). A bridgehead was established. Victory is in sight.

So we are invited to live in the overlap of the ages in the light of the new age inaugurated by Christ. The powers of the age to come are substantially available now. So eternal life breaks into our present existence. As the poet Browning said, "Earth's crammed with heaven." There *are* reverses in the battle now. And like the Allies in Europe we face a foe that is substantially defeated but refuses to admit it. But V-Day is coming. One day, we will enter fully and finally into eternal life. It is not merely everlasting life, but life that has the quality of eternity — life *in* Christ.

Kingdom of God

The kingdom of God, the fifth peak in the panorama of hope, is more than a realm. It is not a piece of territory. It is the rule of God as King and the response of his subjects. It is much more than the church. The church is an outcrop of the kingdom. But there is more. There is the full influence of the regal claims of Jesus in such areas as education, family life, politics, and culture. Like iron filings lining up under the influence of a magnet, both nonhuman and human life is lining up under the influence of Christ as King. The hope of the full realization of the kingdom of God is a powerful motivating reality in the Christian life. We already have the first fruits of the kingdom (Matt. 12:28; 21:31; 23:13), and Jesus himself embodied both the rule of God as king and the response of God's people as subjects. But when Jesus comes again the kingdom will come fully. All human systems and even the environment will be transformed into the perfect rule of God (1 Cor. 15:24). That kingdom will be truly international with Jews and Gentiles, indeed all kinds of people, sitting together at the great banquet of God (Luke 13:29). So our primary relationship in this life is not with the church but with the kingdom. Nor is our primary relationship with this passing age but with a world without end. So we are delivered both from false hope and false pessimism: false hope that our puny efforts in this life to make changes will accomplish the irruption of the kingdom; and false despair that our seemingly fruitless efforts in work and ministry have no eternal consequence. Anticipating these realities Paul said, "Let nothing move you. Always give yourselves fully to the work of the Lord, because you know that your labor in the Lord is not in vain" (1 Cor. 15:58).

New Heaven and New Earth

Place is part of our Christian hope. Our ultimate future is not to be immortal souls floating in a shapeless vacuum but to dwell in the place that Jesus has prepared for us. Nor is the future hope of the Christian merely "heaven." Our future is not dematerialized. We dare not drop "earth" from a "new heaven and a new earth," the subject of the last vision of the Bible (Rev. 21–22). It is a place with shape, structure, and exquisite beauty. This garden city fulfills both God's creativity — as suggested by the jewels — and humankind's creativity — as suggested by the description of kings of the earth bringing their splendor into the city (Rev. 21:24-26). It is also a place where creation and people experience full and final healing (22:2). So Christian hope envisions the renewal by Christ (Eph. 1:22) of the entire creation. In this final vision, the Lamb is in the center of the new creation. Lesslie Newbigin summarizes this hope magnificently.

> The gospel is vastly more than an offer to men who care to accept it of a meaning for their personal lives. It is the declaration of God's cosmic purpose by which the whole public history of mankind is sustained and overruled, and by which men without exception will be judged. . . . It is the invitation to be fellow workers with God in the fulfilment of that purpose through the atoning work of Christ and through the witness of the Holy Spirit. It calls men to commitment to a worldwide mission more daring and more far-reaching than Marxism. And it has — what Marxism lacks — a faith regarding the final consummation of God's purpose in the power of which it is possible to find meaning for world history which does not make personal history meaningless, and meaning for personal history which does not make world history meaningless.[4]

What a glorious future! To make a final rendezvous with Christ. To become like Christ in our resurrection bodies. To be evaluated and rewarded by Christ. To participate in Christ's eternal life. To experience the consummation of the kingdom of Christ. To live with Christ in a renewed creation. To see his face! How far these thoughts are from the instant-gratification, this-worldly Christian culture of today is well illustrated by merely quoting Paul's extraordinary confession in 1 Corinthians 15:19: "If for this life only we have hope in Christ we are to be pitied more than all men." Most people today would say that if in the next life only we had hope in Christ we are to be pitied. Fortunately, Christian hope is both for this life and the next. It is a hope to be lived now.

---

4. Lesslie Newbigin, *Honest Religion for Secular Man* (Philadelphia: Westminster Press, 1966), p. 46.

Living in Hope

But how can these convictions influence our lives? What will it mean to live in hope?

First, Christian hope *calls for a life of radical discipleship.* Paul's letters are full of exhortations that arise from the glorious future of believers. We are called to live soberly and righteously (Titus 2:12-13), with patience (James 5:7-8), with sincerity (Phil. 1:10), showing brotherly love (1 Thess. 3:12). "May he strengthen your hearts so that you will be blameless and holy in the presence of our God and Father when our Lord Jesus comes with all his holy ones" (3:13). Our characters should express our ultimate fellowship with Jesus, ready not only in longing but in life. The last book of the New Testament is especially eloquent on this subject.

In the Revelation you either worship Jesus by laying down your life, or you destroy yourself by worshiping the Beast. So while John transmits the heavenly call to "come out of (Babylon), my people, so that you will not share in her sins" (Rev. 18:4), these people must be rescued while *in* Babylon. For until they are martyred there is nowhere else they can serve God. John invites his friends to find God in the center of life, not at its circumference. In the Apocalypse (the word means "revelation" or "disclosure") of John there is no room for nominal Christianity. While the Revelation has more color than any other book of the New Testament — jasper, carnelian, emerald, sapphire — discipleship is presented in stark black and white. Eugene Peterson says, "Apocalypse is arson — it secretly sets a fire in the imagination that boils the fat out of an obese culture-religion and renders a clear gospel love, a pure gospel hope, a purged gospel faith."[5]

Second, *our work in this world has meaning.* Obviously the work of witness and the ministry of God's Word has great relevance when history is moving towards its final rendezvous and human beings are destined to meet their Maker. Though the verse is a little obscure, 2 Peter 3:12 hints that in some way beyond our complete understanding and certainly beyond our control, we may nevertheless have some part of "speeding" the coming of the Lord, presumably by our work of witness and by the worldwide mission of the church. This first application of

5. Eugene H. Peterson, "The Apocalyptic Pastor," *The Reformed Journal* 38, no. 2 (May 1988): 17.

Christian hope — to the work of "the" ministry — is so obvious that it hardly needs further comment. Less obvious, however, is the connection between Christian hope and projects of social justice and compassion. The Earl of Shaftesbury, one of Britain's most famous Christian reformers, wrote, "I do not think that in the last forty years I have lived one conscious hour that was not influenced by the thought of the Lord's return." It is literally true that those who have been of most earthly use have been the most heavenly minded. To those who naïvely charge that Christianity has never done the world any good we point to the first three centuries of Christians, who were eagerly waiting for the Lord to come back, but left us with a splendid record of social action: rescuing abandoned and aborted babies, burying the dead at great personal risk during plagues, caring for prisoners and the shipwrecked, and being leaders in providing women with status and dignity.

Even less obvious is the connection between the panorama of Christian hope and ordinary daily work: cleaning house, selling cars, teaching school, collecting taxes, building homes, and governing a nation. Paul obviously faced this problem in Thessalonica where some believers, convinced that time had run out and that nothing was worth doing in the world, stopped work completely and sponged on the others. It is in this context that Paul says, "If a man will not work, he shall not eat" (2 Thess. 3:10). His reason is not only that Christian love requires persons to provide for themselves if possible, but the fact that even ordinary work done for Jesus is never in vain (1 Cor. 15:58). Humankind was made to make God's world work (Gen. 1:28-30) and to take care of the world (2:5). Adam and Eve were priests of creation, a creation that one day will be transfigured. In some way beyond our understanding even the contributions we have made to life in this world, if done in faith, hope, and love (1 Cor. 13:13; 1 Thess. 1:3), will outlast the world, and may even have a place in the new earth, while many so-called Christian activities may go up in smoke on the Day and be burned with the hay and stubble (1 Cor. 3:10-15). So even the most mundane activities take on meaning when the travail of history and the groaning of creation has a worthy end.

Third, Christian hope invites us *to live the metaphors and symbols of the Christian life.* The word "symbol" derives from a Greek word that means "to throw, or put together." In contrast the word "diabolical" suggests "to tear apart." Obviously one of the most symbolic books of the Bible is the last. By using symbols, John intends to get his readers connected with another level of understanding and meaning: the spiritual and the divine. He is cultivating kingdom-consciousness, another worldview that would empower us to live triumphantly in this world even when we appear to be losing battles. John does this through symbols. The Lamb, Dragon, Harlot, Babylon, pregnant woman, witness, and martyr are like the symbolic language of Orthodox icons. Speaking of the symbolism of the icons, John Baggley says, "The icons are not simply illustrations of Biblical themes or stories; rather they are an embodiment of a long tradition of meditation on these themes and incidents and their significance for man's soul. . . ."[6] Similarly, John's Apocalypse is the fruit of inspired meditation on hundreds of symbolic Old Testament ideas, words, places, and people in the light of Christ's first and second coming. John Swete suggests that Revelation is a "Christian rereading of the whole Jewish heritage."[7] But John's interest in a metaphorical interpretation of the Old Testament is pastoral, not intellectual.

This pastoral interest is especially apparent in his choice of the central metaphor of the spiritual life in the Revelation: the martyr. After the first three chapters all the Christians we meet in vision after vision are martyrs. The Greek word "witness" *(martyr)* is invested with its second meaning: the Christian is simply one who loses his life in order to find another life in Jesus. It is irrelevant whether one does this on the installment plan, stage by stage, in face of direct opposition and indirect seduction, or in one extravagant act. The challenge of living this metaphor is simply this: either overcome with Jesus, or be overcome by the Red Dragon, Beast, Harlot, and Babylon. Overcomers are not supersaints but simply Christians. John's apocalyptic approach dissolves nominalism in the furnace of transformation. But how can one live the martyr metaphor?

A Celtic text — an Irish homily of the seventh century — takes up the idea that martyrdom was the normal spiritual outlook of the early Christians and expresses some of the options in a society less hostile though more seductive: Red martyrdom consists in death for Jesus' sake. Green martyrdom consists of fasting and labor through which the

6. John Baggley, *Doors of Perception: Icons and Their Spiritual Significance* (Crestwood, N.Y.: St. Vladimir's Seminary Press, 1988), p. 52.

7. John Swete, *Revelation,* New Testament Commentaries (Philadelphia: Trinity Press International, 1990), p. 40.

believer flees from his evil desires and lives a life of repentance. White martyrdom consists of abandoning everything one loves for the sake of God.[8] Eugene Peterson shows that by cultivating the praying imagination, John helps us *see* enough to live the martyr metaphor whether red, green, or white: "The contribution of the Revelation to the work of witness is not instruction, telling us how to make a coherent apology of the faith, but imagination, strengthening the spirit with images that keep us 'steadfast, immovable, always abounding in the work of the Lord' (1 Cor. 15:58). Instruction in witness is important, but courage is critical, for it takes place in the pitched battle."[9]

Fourth, Christian hope invites us *to worship God in the complexity of life in the world.* Martyr-candidates are invited to look into heaven (Rev. 4:1) and to join the concentric circles of heavenly creatures enthralled by the glory of God. Before they encounter eschatological drama, they are invited to worship the God who is both creator and redeemer. In the last two chapters, when Christ makes all things new, John sees an endless environment of worship in which the highest privilege is to see God's face (22:4). God is beautiful. So worship is the dominating atmosphere of the Revelation. Every chapter directs us Godward instead of towards the pretentious and false worship of the Emperor. John's business as a pastor is to keep his people dealing with God, and worship does this better than anything.

Indeed, in this book *everyone* worships. Unless we worship God, we shall inevitably worship the Evil Trinity: the Beast, the Harlot, and the False Prophet, joining those who choose to be sent to hell singing pseudo-hymns: "Who is like the beast?" According to John it is impossible not to worship. Behind this choice for John's parishioners is the imperial cult that had worship centers located in each of the seven cities/towns in Asia where churches had been planted. To worship Christ or Caesar amounts to choosing between the Lamb and the Harlot.

Faced with the temptations of idolatry and apostasy, we must worship God (22:9). The best time and place to do this is in the thick of life, not simply in our leisure time. Eugene Peterson sums up the crucial role of worship in facing the challenges of everyday life in these words:

8. J. Ryan, *Irish Monasticism* (London, 1931), p. 197.

9. Eugene Peterson, *Reversed Thunder: The Revelation of John and the Praying Imagination* (San Francisco: Harper & Row, 1988), p. 112.

Failure in worship consigns us to a life of spasms and jerks, at the mercy of every advertisement, every seduction, every siren. Without worship we live manipulated and manipulating lives. We move in either frightened panic or deluded lethargy as we are, in turn, alarmed by specters and soothed by placebos.[10]

Finally, *we will live with kingdom-consciousness.* As we have already seen, evidences of hopelessness are not restricted to those without faith in Jesus. Among Christians one finds both short- and long-range despair about the world (with a prayer for a speedy evacuation) as well as pathetic need to squeeze everything one can get out of this life (as if there were no other life and no other world). John invites a different approach.

In the Revelation we are invited to live with an open heaven. If we "see" heaven, we will see earth the way it really is. Kingdom-consciousness is another way of speaking of this: living hopefully within the tension of the "here" and "not-yet-but-coming" kingdom of Jesus. This heavenly-mindedness is conspicuously lacking in Western Christianity today. Kingdom-consciousness delivers us from false messianism (that our work, social action, ministry, and compassionate efforts will save society), and from false pessimism (that our work in this world has to be successful and "religious" to be meaningful). Like all contemplatives, Christians who live by this hope will seem a little bit irrelevant to the worldlings around.

So we have a glorious hope. We will see Christ face to face. We will live with him forever. We will participate in a renewed creation with Jesus at the center. We will live in the ultimate community of the people of God in a perfect environment. We ourselves will be transformed into his likeness bodily and spiritually. "Dear friends, now we are children of God, and what we will be has not yet been made known. But we know that when he appears, we shall be like him, for we shall see him as he is" (1 John 3:2). Today, the greatest need is not to proclaim faith, or even love, but *hope.*

So we pray "Come, Lord Jesus!" (Rev. 22:20). But this prayer offered in the thick of life's duties, joys, and disappointments is not a request to be evacuated from this life. Rather it is a commitment to be faithful to Christ unto death with the opportunities given to us to live and work for him in this world until he introduces us to a better world by his coming again.

10. Peterson, *Reversed Thunder,* p. 60.

13

Ambassadors of Love

MICHAEL GREEN

A s we look at the spirituality of the first Christians, one quality stands out above all others. They were ambassadors of love. Love is the life of God himself. The Holy Trinity is a relationship of constant self-giving in love, love that has overflowed upon the world God made and all the people in it.

Many Loves

There are many nuances to that much-misused word, love. The Greek language is full of them. The ancient world knew all about *storge*, family love: the love that binds together parents and children, and siblings in a family. They were deeply committed to *philia*, the bond that unites friends. They specialized in celebrating *eros*, sexual love. But the first Christians found none of these words satisfactory in describing the love of God. Instead, they made use of a very rare word; only occasionally had it been used before. It is the word *agape*. And they filled it with a profound and most unusual meaning. All other types of love are determined by the supposed worthiness of the ones you love, be they a relation, a lover, or a friend. You love them because you feel that in some way they merit it. It is utterly different with the New Testament word for

God's love, *agape.* His love springs from the generous heart of the great Lover, not from any worthiness in the recipient.

The Love of God

That is the sort of love exhibited in John 3:16, the most famous verse in the Bible. God did not *like* the world, or think it was attractive. No, he loved it, and was prepared to make the ultimate sacrifice for it. That is the sort of love that was fleshed-out in the life of Jesus. It is there in all he did and all he said. He is God's *agapetos,* love child, and *agape* characterizes his lifestyle. Naturally therefore he enjoined his disciples: "A new commandment I give to you, that you love one another; even as I have loved you, that you also love one another. By this all men will know that you are my disciples, if you have love for one another" (John 13:34-35). Again and again this command rings out: "This I command you, to love one another" (John 15:17). In one sense, of course, this is an underlining of his own summary of the whole Old Testament law: "You shall love the Lord your God with all your heart, and with all your soul, and with all your mind. This is the great and first commandment. And the second is like it. You shall love your neighbor as yourself. On these two commandments depend all the law and the prophets" (Matt. 22:37-40). But it was not simply this double duty of man that fired the teaching of Jesus. For God is love. "Beloved, let us love one another; for love is of God, and he who loves is born of God and knows God. He who does not love does not know God; for God is love" (1 John 4:7-8). That is the kernel of the matter. God is love, and if we mirror that love we show our parentage. If we do not love, that shows our parentage, too. It demonstrates that despite our protestations we know nothing of the God we claim to worship.

Love is the key to Christian discipleship. Love is also its measuring rod. Such love is very demanding. It is undiscriminating, like the rain that falls "upon the just and the unjust" with utter impartiality (Matt. 5:45-46). The falling of the rain is not in the least determined by the recipient: neither must our love be. When Christians love like that, people sit up and take notice. It is so unusual. So otherworldly. That is why Mother Teresa has made such in impact on this materialistic, selfish modern world. Though we do not love like that, we know the authentic article when we see it, and we know it comes from God.

Love in the Gospels

That is why Jesus encouraged his followers to love their neighbors as themselves, even to love their enemies (Luke 6:27). And that is what he himself did. He practiced what he preached — perfectly. His love was always flowing, to the women, the beggars, the lepers, the tax collectors, the religious hierarchy, the prostitutes, the rich young ruler, the Samaritans, Judas, and the men who nailed him to the cross. Was there ever such love? Surely not. In Jesus we have the supreme demonstration of what God is like. God is the Father who loves the prodigal. He is the wealthy party-giver who loves the street-people. He loves the disciples who failed to understand him. He loves their leader when he denies him. All he wants to know of Peter after his fall is summed up in that thrice-repeated question, "Do you love me . . . do you love me . . . do you love me?" Love is the acid test of Christian discipleship. The path for the followers is the same path the Master trod. We must love one another as he has loved us. Thirty-four times in St. John's Gospel alone this *agape* word is stressed. It is the flower of Christianity.

Love in the Acts

Curiously enough the word is absent from Acts. And yet we have the most wonderful examples of love brought before us in that exciting book. Think of the love that shared homes and possessions, that sold and shared out the proceeds of their property, that gave great encouragement to one another (2:43-47; 4:32-37). Think of the fellowship meals between Jews and Gentiles, once they had been reconciled to God through Jesus. Think of the love that burst from the page as Paul said farewell to his friends (20:36-38; 21:5, etc.). Love is the language of heaven. And it marks the citizens of heaven as with an indelible stamp. It is the ultimate badge of belonging. It is the essence of a truly Christian spirituality.

Love in 1 John

Love takes us to the very heart of God. All human love, however deficient and twisted, gives us some pale reflection of the love that makes

195

the world go round, the love that marks the character of God. This is made very plain in 1 John. Love is personal (4:8). Love is searching (5:3). Love is generous (3:1). Love is sacrificial (4:10). Love lasts even beyond the day of judgment (4:17-18). Love is exclusive of all other commitments (2:15f.). It challenges response to the great Lover (4:19-20) and to one and all who are objects of his love (3:16ff.). And it goes without saying that love is not just a matter of talk; it involves costly, sacrificial self-giving (3:16-18). No wonder a marvelous story is told of John, when he was an old man — for he had deeply understood his Master's teaching on love. St. Jerome tells us that St. John was carried into the Christian assembly at an advanced age and was asked to give a message. "Little children, love one another," he said. When they asked for more, he repeated, "Little children, love one another." They then asked him why he gave no variation on this theme, and he replied, "Because it is the commandment of the Lord, and if it is done, it suffices."[1] There we see a man who had been permeated by the love of God: so much so that in extreme old age it was just love that shone through.

Love in 1 Peter

If we look at Peter's writings, love is no less central. He bids brothers and sisters in the Christian family to greet one another with the kiss of love (1 Peter 5:14). He urges them to extend deep love to one another, for love covers a multitude of failings (1 Peter 4:8). Indeed, it is the crown of all the virtues, as 2 Peter 1:7 makes very clear. There is something tremendously attractive and genuine in such love for the brethren (1 Peter 1:22; 2:17). And it all springs from loving the Jesus we cannot see, the Jesus who first loved us (1 Peter 1:8).

Love in James

James takes on the tension between law and love. He calls the injunction "You shall love your neighbor as yourself" the royal law, the law of the kingdom of God (2:8). In point of fact, law and love are friends, not ene-

---

1. Jerome, *Commentary on Galatians*, 3.6.10.

mies. They come from the same source, the same God who is love, and who created a law-governed world for law-abiding citizens. Law without love becomes legalism, and Jesus came to deliver men from that. But love without law becomes soft and sentimental (if it does not degenerate into license). And Jesus came to deliver us from that, too. But more: love itself *is* a law. "This I *command* you, to love one another" (John 15:17, italics mine). Again, "If you keep my commandments, you will abide in my love" (John 15:10), or "If you love me, you will keep my commandments" (John 14:15). The Jews had 613 commandments that they tried to keep. Jesus gave only one. "A new commandment I give to you, that you love one another; even as I have loved you, that you also love one another. By this all men will know that you are my disciples, if you have love for one another" (John 13:34-35). If only we fulfilled that one commandment, most of the subsidiary rules and regulations imposed by churches would be utterly unnecessary.

Love in Hebrews

Hebrews has a lot to say about love, especially chapter 13. It seems that the author wants to concentrate, at the end of his letter, on the three great Christian virtues of faith (chapter 11), hope (chapter 12), and love (chapter 13). This love is very challenging. For it is a love specifically directed towards the Christian brotherhood (often not the easiest people in the world!). It is a love that takes in strangers and offers them hospitality. It is a love that profoundly marks the marriage of Christians; it is warm and pure. It is a love that shares possessions, and is content with what it has (13:1-5). There is far more in the chapter that springs from Christian love — obedience to church leaders, the exchange of news and prayers, and so forth. But enough has been said to show how love runs through the spirituality of the first Christians like silver thread in a tapestry.

Love in Paul

Nobody in the early church is clearer on the centrality and the power of love than St. Paul. It has a dominant place in nearly all his letters.

Take, for example, his letters to the Thessalonians. He rejoices to recall the hard work that emerged from their love (1 Thess. 1:3). He rejoices to hear that their faith and love are making an impact (3:6). He wants them to overflow in love towards one another (3:12). This will mean daily putting it on like a breastplate (5:8, for it does not form a natural part of our endowment, this supernatural *agape*). And that love is meant to reach and encourage their Christian leaders. Clearly love was an outstanding feature of this basically rather quarrelsome Greek city, once they had surrendered their lives to the Lord who loved them so much. Naturally, then, Paul confidently expects to see "the love of every one of you for one another increasing" (2 Thess. 1:3).

If we find such emphasis on love at the beginning of Paul's correspondence, it is even more apparent in his later writings. Take Ephesians, for example. He astounds them by informing them that God *chose* them to be blameless before him in love — chose them before the foundation of the world (1:4). He rejoices to have heard good news of their faith and love (1:15). He is overwhelmed at the great love God has poured out upon us, selfish rebels though we be, in giving us new life through Jesus (2:4-5). In his prayers he beseeches God that they may be "rooted and grounded in love," as Christ is "made at home" in their hearts (3:17). He wants them to experience the love of Christ that defies description (3:19). The Christian life is not easy: human hassles occur as much among us as among anyone else, and so he encourages them to put up with one another in love (4:2) and, later in that chapter, to tell the truth in love (or the Greek word may be translated "act honestly" in love). Without that, the Christian community cannot hold together. And he longs for its coherence and growth into the very body of Christ that the Lord intends it to be, as it "makes bodily growth and upbuilds itself in love" (4:16). Finally, he asks them to deliberately "imitate God, whose children they are," and live their daily lives in love, "as Christ loved us and gave himself up for us" (5:2). They can never manage this by themselves, and the letter ends with clear awareness of the fact, and points to the source from which their love can be replenished: "Peace be to the brethren, and love with faith, from God the Father and the Lord Jesus Christ. Grace be with all who love our Lord Jesus Christ with love undying" (6:23-24).

It is very evident that this humanly irascible, arrogant, activist man Paul has been suffused with the love of God, and longs to see it as the hallmark of all Christians. This is a major theme in all his letters, as we have seen in these two Epistles, the one drawn from his early writings and the other from his latest. But nowhere does he delve more deeply into it than in the famous hymn of love, 1 Corinthians 13.

The Hymn of Love (1 Corinthians 13)

Any comment on this marvelous chapter runs the risk of spoiling it, but let us at least try to break through our familiarity with it by asking some pertinent questions.

What Is the Indication of God's Presence?

That was a live issue in Paul's day, as it is in our own. Hebrews and Greeks both spoke with a divided voice.

On the one hand there were plenty who maintained that God showed his hand in the non-rational. That is where we should look if we want to see the Spirit at work. In the Old Testament you might think of Saul dancing like a dervish, or Samson smashing the Philistines. Among the Greeks, even so rational a thinker as Plato could maintain, "It is by *mania* [ecstasy due to inspiration] that the greatest blessings have come to us,"[2] and the prophetess at Delphi worked herself up into a frenzy of possession by the god before uttering the oracles that had such an impact on ancient society. The Dionysius cult, the Cybele cult, and many others sought divine inspiration in the non-rational.

On the other hand there were plenty to urge that rationality was the supreme mark of the divine in man. Socrates was the outstanding example of this in the Greek world, and in the Old Testament there was a strong emphasis on God revealing himself in a way that was intelligible, not incoherent.

But if we ask Paul how he discerned the presence of his Lord, he would have to tell us that it is neither in the rational, like the philosophers for whom the Corinthians sometimes mistook him; nor in the non-rational, like the Corinthians who were clear that God manifested

2. Plato, *Phaedrus*, 24c.

himself supremely in charismatic gifts. It was in love that God was most clearly seen. Love takes us to his heart.

How Important Is Love?

Love is the one indispensable ingredient in the use of the spiritual gifts that Paul is dealing with in chapters 12–14 of 1 Corinthians.

The tongue speaker cannot do without it (13:1). At Corinth tongues were prevalent, and it seems that some people were using this gift to make others feel small and to display their own supposed spirituality. Parading a spiritual gift in this way is horrible. It makes it sound less like the language of heaven and more like the clanging of an empty gong or the frenzied clashing of cymbals such as you might encounter in the Cybele cult. Tongues without love is disastrous. It concentrates on the non-personal and the non-ethical. It encourages pride. It is divisive. Unloving insistence on it has split many a church, just as dogmatic rejection of it has.

The man of knowledge cannot do without love either (13:2). Whether it is spiritual knowledge, depth of psychological insight, or sheer learning — all branches of knowledge are disastrous without love. They give the misguided impression that God is interested in how much we know, not in how much we love.

The man of faith cannot do without love either (13:2). Great heroes of faith are a tremendous challenge and inspiration to us. We love to read their stories. But what the biographers often omit to tell us is where there has been disaster in their family life: wives have felt neglected, and children deserted, because their dad has always been away on some hare-brained adventure of faith. Usually you find that such children rebel against Christianity when they grow up. That is because even faith without love is worth nothing.

The public benefactor cannot do without it (13:3). The millionaire may endow a research chair at the university, or a home for dispossessed cats. But without love, what is achieved in the long run? Our possessions, be they great or small, will all be left behind us one day, when we come to die. We shall only have our characters to take with us. And they are molded by love.

The martyr cannot do without love (13:3). He may make the supreme sacrifice — perhaps (if the reading *kauthesomai* is right) by one of the most painful ways, being burnt. If *kauchesomai* is the right reading, it would mean that he does it in order to have something to be proud of. In either case, unless sacrifice is accompanied by love, it is a cold, stoical thing. Without love, we gain nothing.

It is not what we know that matters; not how gifted we are; not how much we believe; not even what we do. It is what we *are* that is crucial. And that is valid in God's currency precisely insofar as it reflects his love.

How Does It Show?

It shows as the life of Jesus in us. In 1 Corinthians 13:4-7 Paul allusively sets the love of Jesus over against the failings that were so evident in the Corinthian church. They claimed to be following the "higher" way of spiritual knowledge and experience. But Jesus beckoned them to the "lower" way, the way of the Servant, the way of love.

Love is patient (13:4). The Corinthians were not. They were impatient for their rights in lawsuits, for their satisfaction in sex, for their chosen spiritual gifts.

Love is kind (13:4). The word means generous. The Corinthians were not like that. The rich ate all the supper at the love feast before the Holy Communion, so the poor slaves, who arrived late after work, had none.

Love is not jealous (13:4). Many at Corinth were jealous of their more talented friends.

Love does not make a parade of itself (13:4). Unlike many at Corinth, it is shy and self-effacing.

Love does not grow puffed-up with self-esteem (13:4). Many of the Corinthian Christians seem to have been behaving like that, as they dined out on their spiritual experiences and achievements.

Love does not go fishing in the pool of shame[3] (13:5). It sets out to cover sins over, not to rake them up: unlike the Corinthians.

Love is unselfish (13:5). Jesus was supremely unselfish, but that was not mirrored in the lives of his disciples at Corinth.

3. This is the probable meaning of *aschemonei.*

Love is not irritable (13:5). The short-tempered, irritable, divisive Corinthians had a lot to learn from Jesus in this respect. Love foregoes the sharp retort and the snide comment.

Love is not moody (13:5). It does not brood over wrongs, real or imagined. There must have been a lot of that going on at Corinth in between the lawsuits and the adulteries.

Love does not revel in what is evil, but delights in what is true (13:6). That was the very opposite of the scurrilous gossip and the church divisions that prevailed at Corinth.

Love can put up with everything (13:7): loneliness, misrepresentation, pain, neglect, opposition. But the spiritual showmen at Corinth could not. Love believes the best about people, not the worst (13:7) — unlike the Corinthians, so ready to credit malicious rumors.

Love is experienced in the here and now: it is the sure platform for hope in what we cannot see (13:7). But there was little sign of that at Corinth. They were weak on future hope (ch. 15) because they were so weak on present love (ch. 13).

Love endures whatever comes, without degenerating into cynicism (13:7). There was little of that stickability in volatile Corinth.

Finally, love never gives up (13:8), like the love of Jesus on the cross. It lasts into the life of heaven itself. Love at Corinth had clearly collapsed.

The contrast Paul is seeking to highlight is seen very clearly from the following simple exercise: try substituting "I" for "love," and see what it looks like.

> I am patient and kind. I am never jealous, give myself no airs. I am not puffed up with pride, and I do not dig in bins of other people's shame. I am unselfish, never irritable or moody. I turn my back on evil and revel in what is true. I put up with everything, believe the best about people, am full of hope, can keep on enduring whatever comes, and I never give up.

It sounds ridiculous, does it not? Pompous and totally untrue. But try it for size if you substitute Jesus instead of "love."

> Jesus is patient and kind. Jesus is never jealous, gives himself no airs. He is not proud, and does not dig in the bins of other people's

shame. He is unselfish, and never irritable or moody. He turns his back on evil and revels in what is true. He can put up with everything, believe the best about people, remain full of hope, and he keeps on enduring whatever comes. Jesus never gives up.

That does not sound ridiculous or pompous, does it? It is the simple, unvarnished truth. Paul's whole picture of love in 1 Corinthians 13 is really a portrait of Jesus, and his longing is that it should be painted into the characters of his readers.

How Does Love Wear?

Wonderfully well. Loving self-giving is the way of Jesus. When the days of all our earthly gifts and talents are over, when all prophecy has been fulfilled, when tongues are taken up into the song of heaven, when we know as we are known, when faith is swallowed up in sight and hope is fulfilled in complete possession by the Beloved — then love remains. The redeemed will still be united in that glad self-offering to God and to the brethren that imperfectly marked their earthly pilgrimage. Love is the language of eternity.

John Wesley has a marvelous passage about the ultimacy of love, in his *Plain Account of Christian Perfection:*

> It were well that you should be thoroughly sensible of this — the heaven of heaven is love. There is nothing higher in religion — there is, in effect, nothing else; if you look for anything but more love, you are looking wide of the mark, you are getting out of the royal way. And when you are asking others, "Have you received this or that blessing?," if you mean anything but more love, you mean wrong; you are leading them out of the way, and putting them on a false scent. Settle it in your hearts that . . . you are to aim at nothing more, but more of that love described in the thirteenth Corinthians. You can go no higher than this until you are carried into Abraham's bosom.[4]

4. John Wesley, "A Plain Account of Christian Perfection," *Works* 11.374 (London: Epworth Press, 1968).

Did It Continue?

The first Christians were very clear that this teaching on the supremacy of love was to be taken with the utmost seriousness. The earliest Christian book that has come down to us after the New Testament period is *1 Clement,* from the 90s of the first century. And there Clement, bishop of Rome, writes to rebuke the Corinthians for falling short of the love to which Christ called them, and of which Paul had written to them. They were schismatic and had deposed their leaders. Clement writes to tell them to practice what they preached:

> Let him who has love in Christ keep the commandments of Christ. Who is able to describe the bond of the love of God? Who is sufficient to tell the greatness of its beauty? The height to which love lifts us is inexpressible. Love unites us to God. Love covers a multitude of sins. Love bears all things, is long-suffering in all things. There is nothing base, nothing haughty in love. Love admits no schism, love makes no sedition, love does all things in harmony. By love have all the elect been made perfect: without love nothing is well-pleasing to God. In love the Lord has taken us to himself. On account of the love he bore us, Jesus Christ our Lord gave his blood for us by the will of God; his flesh for our flesh, and his soul for our souls. . . .
>
> Let us pray therefore and implore of his mercy that we may lead blameless lives in love, free from all human partisanship, free from blame.[5]

And he goes on to challenge them to repent and to put right the divisions among them.

Ignatius, his contemporary, shows that he has learnt this lesson equally well. "The beginning of life is faith, and the end of life is love. When the two are joined together, it is God at work; all other requisites for a good life follow on from them."[6] Significantly he quotes Jesus' words, "The tree is known by its fruits" and concludes, "so those who profess to belong to Christ will be seen by their deeds."[7] And they were. Tertullian the Christian and Lucian the pagan corroborate one another

5. *1 Clement,* 49-50.
6. Ignatius, *Ephesians,* 14.
7. Ignatius, *Ephesians,* 14.

on this point. Both had often heard on pagan lips the remark, "Look how these Christians love one another." It showed in so many ways. Tertullian describes some of them. "Our giving is expended upon no banquets or drinking bouts or thankless eating-houses, but on feeding and burying poor people, on behalf of boys and girls who have neither parents nor money, in support of old people unable now to get about, as well as for people who are shipwrecked, or who may be in the mines, or exile, or in prison."[8]

There is an enormous amount of evidence in the writings of the second and third century to show the phenomenal impact of the Christian cause: and love was the secret of their spirituality. A love that treated slaves as brethren, a love that supported widows and orphans, a love that formed trade unions to support the powerless, a love that cared for prisoners and those languishing in the mines, a love that poured itself out on those who were hit by natural disasters. A good example of this is recorded by the historian Eusebius. A terrible plague had occurred:

> Then the Christians showed themselves to the heathen in the clearest light. They were the only people who amid such terrible ills showed their fellow feeling and humanity by their actions. Day by day some would busy themselves by attending to the dead and burying them (for there were many to whom nobody else paid heed). Others gathered in one spot all who were afflicted by hunger throughout the whole city, and gave bread to them all. When this became known, people glorified the Christians' God, and, convinced by the deeds in front of their eyes, confessed that the Christians alone were truly pious.[9]

We could go on. But the point is clear. The early Christians knew that the yardstick of their spirituality was love, love that derived from God, and love that therefore had to be reflected indiscriminately to all in need. Love was the badge they wore, and they were content to be judged by their display of it. All of which prompts, at the end of this book, a final question, drawing out the implications of Paul's hymn to love.

8. Tertullian, *Apology*, 39.
9. Eusebius, *History of the Church*, 9.8.

How Do We Stand?

We Christians shall not be judged by our gifts or by our learning, but by our love. How shall we fare?

How shall we fare when *our churches* are judged in this light? Much that we do in our churches is totally irrelevant to the call of love, the needs of people around us, and the work of the kingdom of God. We are preoccupied with our petty internal concerns, our constitutions and our synods. We must look like an irrelevant Sunday School for the pious, instead of the commando forces of the king of love. Our churchy language and our introversion make it hard for others to join us. Our ineffectiveness and lack of cutting edge alienates the young. Our divisions and quarrels disgust the onlookers. Can our badge be said to be love? Yet without it we are nothing.

How shall we fare when *as individuals* we are judged by this standard of love? Our attitudes at work, in the family, to our partner maybe. Our response to crying needs all around us, to personal disappointments, to being let down. How much do we really love the Lord? A difficult question to answer, as St. John realized. So he gave us a helpful barometer: "He who does not love his brother whom he has seen, cannot love God whom he has not seen" (1 John 4:20).

How shall we fare when *our suffering* is judged in this light? We have all met sufferers who positively shine with the love of God. It is a blessing to go and visit them. They treat their sufferings like medals to be worn proudly on their chest. How do we react in suffering, or towards those who make life hard for us in the family or in the office? Love is the standard God looks for.

How shall we fare when *our giving* is judged in the light of love? The waste we contribute to, the opulence we enjoy while others starve, will rise up in testimony against us. So will the poverty of our actual giving to God's work.

How shall we fare when *our caring* is judged in this light? Not many churches, at least in the West, are noted for their involvement with the hungry, the prostitutes, the AIDS victims, the alcoholics. We prefer to pass by on the other side of the road, rather than display the love of the Good Samaritan. God will surely judge us for this.

How shall we fare when *our evangelism* is judged on the same principle? The total lack of evangelism in churches that give the impression they are not particularly anxious to introduce others to the Savior they profess to love. The hard, unloving evangelism in other churches where there is some attempt at outreach but where the attempt is so strident, so complacent, so alien from the situation of those addressed that it savors more of marketing than good news. On the whole we do not tell people the gospel because we do not love them enough to bother. Or else we do it in a way they find hard to accept — because we do not love enough to learn a better way. We are driven back to St. Paul's conclusion, "Without love, I gain nothing."

And how shall we fare when *we come to die,* and when the question is not how much we have now, or how much we have given, or how much we have done. The one question we shall be bound to answer is this: "How much have you loved?" That is the core, the heartbeat of New Testament spirituality. How shall we fare then?

Index of Subjects and Names

Index of Scripture References

Made in the USA
San Bernardino, CA
08 March 2014